CHANGING MY MIND

Changing My Mind

MARGARET TRUDEAU

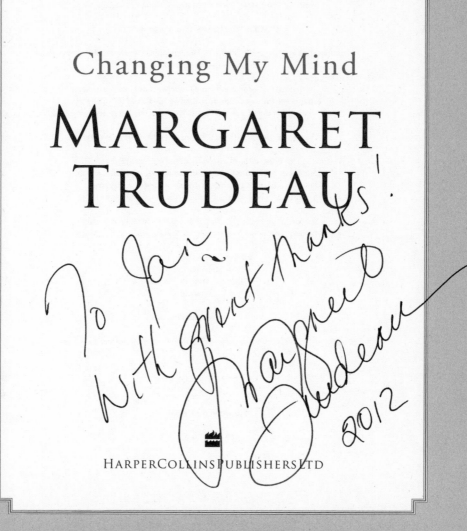

To Jan!
With great thanks!
Margaret Trudeau
2012

HARPERCOLLINSPUBLISHERSLTD

HarperCollins Publishers Ltd
2 Bloor Street East, 20th Floor
Toronto, Ontario, Canada
M4W 1A8

www.harpercollins.ca

Library and Archives Canada Cataloguing in Publication information is available

ISBN 978-1-55468-539-4

Printed in the United States

RRD 9 8 7 6 5 4 3 2 1

To my brave daughter, Alicia Mary Rose Kemper, and all the daughters of mothers who struggle with a mental illness

CONTENTS

"There's something different about Margie," my parents would sometimes say to others as they tried to fathom my behaviour as a child. My father and mother couldn't put their fingers on it, had no name for it, but whatever it was set me apart from my four sisters. My siblings accepted things, and I didn't.

There was a ferocity in young Margaret Joan Sinclair. Growing up in Vancouver in the 1950s, I was often capricious and temperamental, quick to laugh, even quicker to feel despair; prone to flailing my arms, pouting and crying when things didn't go my way or I thought something was unfair or I was bullied by my sisters. I often felt raw and thin skinned—absurdly so. And I couldn't bear to think of people in pain. My mother would say, "Margaret, how are you going to get through life if you take things so badly?"

To put it mildly, I was a drama queen—but that phrase falls far short of capturing what assailed me then. I was a quicksilver girl who saw every leaf on every tree. For me, there was no middle ground between sinking and flying, and once I was into my early adult years, my roller coaster got wilder and faster: I seemed to rise and fall with the same reckless velocity. I wince at some of the things I did as the young wife of Canada's fifteenth prime minister, Pierre Elliott Trudeau. Looking back as a mature woman, I finally forgive that twenty-something version of myself and her youthful follies—and I totally admire her spirit and how she lived on the edge.

What "Maggie" (as the press called me) did not know is that her brain chemistry was abnormal: I suffered from manic depression, or bipolar disorder, as we more commonly call it today. Only when I was pregnant was I truly happy, and only because maternal hormones—the great biological imperative to the rescue—had given me respite from my "madness." But even had I been properly diagnosed forty years ago, treatment options were limited.

So much has changed, and one of my hopes for this book is that by telling my own story, that message can be delivered. If I can't be a role model, maybe I can be a dire warning. At any given time, three million Canadians suffer serious depression and at least 1 per cent of the population—more than 330,000 males and females—suffers from bipolar disorder, a form of mental illness that inflicts a $15 billion economic burden on the nation every year. American authorities believe that the figure for bipolar sufferers in that country is at least 2 per cent. Only cardiac disease does more damage and draws more dollars from the health care budget than mental illness. Those afflicted men and women, some of them very young, should know that there is light at the end of the tunnel, that their lost lives can be regained.

Another one of my hopes for this book is that friends and

family of those suffering mental illness will learn the markers of depression and gain the confidence to intervene and help.

The journey to get where I am today has been a long and perilous one (never mind a very public one), but that's partly because I was in the dark about my condition for so many years, as were those trying to help me. Today I am as happy as I have ever been in my life. Only my time as a young mother comes close to matching my level of satisfaction. I am sixty-one years old as I write these words, and people laugh when I tell them that I was a teenager until quite recently.

I now live in my lovely, bright and airy condominium—"Grandma's house," as my four grandchildren call it—in a grand old building near the mountain in Montreal. My contentment, you should know, is not solely drug induced. I take a mild dose of a mood stabilizer, and likely will for the rest of my days. Family, friends, meaningful work, exercise, diet, meditation, yoga, nature, gardening, lessons, cooking, music and art all play a role these days in keeping my demons at bay.

The bipolar cross is a heavy one to bear, and I have carried it pretty well all my life, and will go on carrying it until my last breath. The really exciting news from research in the field is that early treatment of bipolar disorder actually reprograms the brain and promotes healing. There are so many breakthroughs—such as transcranial magnetic stimulation that can rewire the brain—and so much reason for hope. Later in the book, three medical experts will describe some of the latest thinking on bipolar disorder. I'm really pleased that that resource and the practical insight it gives form a part of this book.

When I was fifty and still in the throes of bipolar disorder, I considered the fact that many of the women in my family lived to be one hundred years old. And I thought, "Oh no, fifty more years of *this*?" Now I'm thinking, "Only thirty-nine more years? What a shame."

For those who suffer from any form of mental illness, mine is a cautionary tale. Hippocrates and centuries of doctors who followed in his wake would brand my particular form of illness "melancholia," but they had no clue how to treat or manage it and no idea what caused it. Victims, their families and their friends all suffered horribly and unimaginably. If the suffering continues today, that's only because many of those who are "different" have no name for their paralyzing sadness, no sense that they can be helped or no courage to admit they need help. When you're severely depressed, you can hardly speak. My great desire is that this book gives words to people who cannot articulate their pain and despair and who have no understanding of its source.

This reflection on my life has one recurring theme: Margaret Trudeau was able to come out the other side. So can you.

CHAPTER 1

THE BRAWLING SINCLAIRS

My grandmother once told me when I was very young,
"Margaret, you're one of the more delicate flowers in the garden. But you're also
a perennial." Only later did I understand that she was remarking
on how fragile I was and yet how durable. A perennial is an
eternal flower, one that keeps coming back year after year.

ROBERTS CREEK, BRITISH COLUMBIA, AUGUST 1958

Fish, salmon in particular, brought the Sinclairs from Scotland to
Canada in 1911.

My paternal grandfather, James Sinclair, was born in Wick,
in the high north of Scotland, and grew up farther south in Banff-
shire, historically a major supplier of salmon to Europe. The
nearby River Deveron is still well known among fly fishers for its
sizeable catches of salmon, sea trout and brown trout.

My grandfather had been caught poaching salmon from
that same river, which was then known as the "laird's river." The

game warden happened to be a friend, and he was understanding but firm.

"Jimmy," he warned, "if I catch you again, you'll have to go to jail."

"If I canna fish," James Sinclair replied famously in family lore, "I canna live."

He was a schoolteacher in the town of Grange, but he had struggled to feed his family on his meagre wages, and so he went home, pulled out all his maps and decided to seek his fortune (and new fishing grounds) in the British colonies. British Columbia, with all its spawning rivers, its many lakes and long ocean coast, and some of the biggest salmon in the world, beckoned. He never regretted the move.

My grandfather prospered in Vancouver, where he enjoyed a stellar and path-breaking career helping to establish the area's first vocational school, which still exists—Vancouver Technical Secondary School. He remained a passionate fisherman. He saved up enough money to buy a cottage on the Sechelt Peninsula, and he would spend hours on the porch of his boathouse making spoons and lures for the salmon he planned to catch. Some of my Scottish relatives were a little on the dour side, but not my grandfather. He was fun. I remember him playing the Pied Piper in his rambling old house during parties and at Christmas, leading the shrieking grandkids up and down the stairs as he played the harmonica.

My paternal grandmother was Betsy Ross, another northern Scot, who was as tough as she was sweet. She ran a tight ship. They had a beautiful plum tree in the garden, and Grandma made plum jam from the fruit. She wasn't the gardener that my other grandmother was, but she did grow some things, as any sensible Scot would.

James George Sinclair, the son of James and Betsy, was just two when the family left Scotland. Dad inherited his father's burr and retained it all his life; the accent especially came out when he was telling stories. And he loved to tell stories. He was also a very good mimic.

He was a smart man, my father. He studied engineering at the University of British Columbia and was awarded a Rhodes Scholarship to study mathematics at Oxford University. He sent home wonderful letters describing how, as a Rhodes Scholar, he had been invited to Lady Astor's for lunch on a Sunday. A classically prudent Scot, he knew it would tax the family budget, but it seemed important to him to own a well-cut, well-made suit—a navy-blue blazer with gold buttons.

Later, my father studied mathematical physics at Princeton and took up his father's profession—teaching, in his case at a Vancouver high school. One of his brightest students was Kathleen Bernard, and in 1940, when he was thirty-one and she was just nineteen, they got married. Looking back at this May–December marriage, I wonder if it paved the way for my own wedding to a man who was two years older than my mother.

My father was a big, imposing fellow, six feet two inches tall. Jimmy Sinclair was gruff on the outside but he was also a good man, fair and sweet, and he was stern with my sisters and me only when we dared cross our mother or disrespected her. Then came the wrath of God. He doted on my mother and loved her so much. I never heard a cross word between them. Such total harmony was little use as a role model for my own marriage. I never heard my parents fight and did not know that it was possible for a wife to quarrel or argue with her husband. Suppression of anger, I believed, was how to cope.

My father, for all his intelligence, was also a simple man with simple tastes. He would come down to breakfast wearing a green business suit, a blue tie, and one sock coloured navy, the other brown.

"Oh, Dad-dy! Look at you!" we sisters would all yell, imploring him to wear clothes that matched. He didn't care. He always said, "I dress to keep warm and I eat to fuel my body." Years later, he dined one Christmas with Pierre and me at 24 Sussex Drive, where staff had opened a Château Latour from the 1940s—an extraordinary bottle of wine—to honour his presence. "Don't waste the good stuff on me," he told them, and asked for some cooking wine from the kitchen.

In his political thinking, he was a left-leaning Liberal. He was born into the Presbyterian Church but never attended services. "Too harsh," he said of that brand of Protestantism.

My mother was outstandingly beautiful. Tall, with hazel eyes and raven hair, Kathleen had the finest, most beautiful skin, which turned bronze in the sun thanks to the Malaysian blood that coursed through her.

Her great-great-great-great-grandfather William Farquhar was a Scottish-born British officer in the East India Company who played a pivotal role in the founding of Singapore in the early nineteenth century. After the British lost both Java and the tiny

Malaysian sultanate of Malacca to the Dutch, General Farquhar set out to find a new port and, together with Sir Stamford Raffles (lieutenant-governor of Java), founded Singapore. But the two men had a falling out over the way Singapore was to be settled.

Sir Stamford abhorred gambling, cockfighting and the notion of indentured servants, and he wanted the waterfront preserved for government buildings and residences. The more easy-going Farquhar, who spoke Malaccan and who had great respect for the Malaysian culture, knew that local people weren't about to abandon all their bad habits overnight, and he reserved the waterfront for the merchants.

When Raffles returned after several years away and saw that his orders had been ignored, he dismissed Farquhar. On the day William left, in 1823, the roads were so densely packed with people wanting to say goodbye that it took him three hours to reach his boat. He left behind Antoinette Clement, his companion for some twenty-five years, and their five children, settled on a rubber plantation. There was no thought of her joining him; she would have found the Scottish climate and the imperialist thinking of the day equally unwelcoming. Once back in Scotland, William Farquhar married a new wife.

While still in Singapore, between 1819 and 1823, my ancestor commissioned various Chinese artists to illustrate local plants, mammals, birds, fish and insects found in Malacca and Singapore. Some 477 watercolours were completed, and several copies of the original paintings now hang on the walls of my Montreal condominium.

My mother, then, could trace her line back to "a country wife," since Antoinette was the daughter of a French officer and a Malaysian woman. In colonies all over the world, men of various empires took up with local women, in the way that soldiers, explorers and fur trade managers in Canada took First Nations women as wives ("a bit of brown," they were sometimes called). Several years ago, the CBC-TV genealogy series *Who Do You Think You Are?* followed me to Singapore, where I probed my own roots.

It turns out that William Farquhar and Antoinette Clement's eldest daughter, Esther, married a British officer named Francis James Bernard. But Francis did exactly what his father had done: in 1827, he left Singapore on a trading ship, leaving behind Esther and their five children. She died there, destitute, at the age of forty-one. No point in decrying such behaviour; blame the times.

Esther's descendants found their way to Australia, from there to Manitoba, then to Penticton in the British Columbia interior and finally to the west coast.

My mother was such an elegant and well-mannered person, with a deep well of tolerance and compassion. In hindsight, I think my mother's strengths and values helped me as a mother. Mom is ninety years old as I write these words, and she can look back on a hard life—though I doubt she would say that.

Firm but kind by nature, she was a quiet, long-suffering soul, and mostly content with her lot. She had emerged from a solid working-class family, found a good and loving husband, raised five daughters—nothing to complain about, and no use in any case. Still, she did suffer at times from depression and she never got the treatment she needed. There is some evidence that genetics plays a role in bipolar disorder, but I'll never know what role that played in my own illness. I know only that my mother was alone much of the time and worried much of the time.

When my father went overseas for the war in 1940 (he served in the Royal Canadian Air Force in North Africa, Malta and Sicily until 1945), he left behind a pregnant wife. While her husband was off overseas, my mother and her sister, whose husband was likewise off fighting, moved in with their mother. Before leaving, my father was elected as the Liberal member of parliament for North Vancouver—a position he held until 1957, including a seven-year stint as minister of fisheries in Prime Minister Louis St. Laurent's government, one that finally fell to John Diefenbaker's Tory wave in 1958. (Imagine the pride of James Sr. when James Jr. was put in charge of *fish*.)

All through the 1950s, my father travelled widely—to Europe, Ceylon, the USSR and China—on political matters. Even when he was home, he worked most evenings studying briefs or engaged in riding business. My mother was very much a single mother, often alone with her daughters on the coast while her husband worked in Ottawa, or shuffling the family between homes in Ontario and British Columbia. When they were apart, reconnecting involved either a five-day train trip or thirteen hours on a Vickers Viscount prop plane.

In those days, the wives of politicians would travel mostly by train from Ottawa back to their homes in their husbands' constituencies. My mother would keep company with John Diefenbaker's first wife, Edna, and they became great friends. Edna and John lived in Prince Albert, Saskatchewan, so Mom had Edna's companionship that far and continued on to the coast. My father was a member of parliament for eighteen years in total, and only in 1952, when he became a cabinet minister, did we actually live in Ottawa.

Because she married and had children so early in life, my mother's own education was limited. She did become a nurse, and my father used to joke that by marrying her he had "saved her from washing loggers' backs." Later, when her daughters went off to university and brought home interesting books, she joined a "living-room learning class"—what we would now call a book club. Bridge and the company of good friends were two of my mother's passions.

Mine was a happy childhood, but there was not a lot of touching in my family. That's simply how it was in those days among WASPs (white Anglo-Saxon Protestants). If I was hurt as a child, I could crawl into my mother's arms and be comforted. Sometimes I'd fake being hurt to get that comfort. Physical hurt was one thing; psychological hurt quite another. "Let's have a pot of tea" was sometimes my mother's response. Her own mother had cautioned against any excess of emotion; our joys and sorrows were always to be measured.

I was the fourth of the five Sinclair girls, "the Brawling Sinclairs" as my father used to call us. Each of us competed for my father's love and attention, and all of us adored our mother. There were all the jealousies you would expect to find among so many sisters. We did everything as a family. My father took pride in the racket and the standing of such a respectably large group—even if we were all girls.

My eldest sister, Heather, who was seven years older than me, mothered me, as is often the case in large families. Jan was next, and the eldest of the middle three sisters, who were each just fifteen months apart in age—making for a lot of sibling rivalry and conflict. Jan had a lively wit and a wicked tongue, and she was always interested in social issues. At first, she was a red-haired, freckled, wild-tempered tomboy, but later she became a great beauty. Jan and I have always been especially close, and we have remained so, through thick and thin. Lin would become a beauty queen (Miss Simon Fraser), but more often than not had her nose buried in a book. Betsy, the youngest by four years, was my father's favourite, with her blond hair and features so like my mother's. My father used to joke that when Betsy grew up, he was going to turn my mother in and marry Betsy. She was the baby we all loved.

All of these strong women, along with my strong mother and father, were my net, my underpinnings. In some ways, I'm closer to my friends than I am to my family. I choose friends, after all. But my family was and is critically important to me.

As for young Margaret, well, I was not an easy child. I remember an incident that occurred when I was six years old. I was terribly stressed because I was thinking, for the first time in my life, about infinity and mortality. I couldn't sleep; my mind was on fire.

"What's wrong?" my mother asked. "Why are you so agitated?"

I blamed Daddy. This was a school night, and my mother had gone out to play bridge with friends. My father—on baby-sitting duty—had let us watch television, then available only in black and white. He never much liked TV, didn't understand it, and normally it stayed off on weeknights. On weekends, we would watch Lawrence Welk, Perry Como, *The Ed Sullivan Show* and a drama set in Quebec called *The Plouffe Family.* The paucity of television never bothered us because we were a family of readers, voracious readers.

But this evening he had let us watch *The Hound of the Baskervilles,* and the dogs really, really scared me. I had also seen coverage of a plane crash earlier and I knew that my father was heading off shortly to Russia on a diplomatic mission. What if Daddy crashed? What if he died? What if? My mind was on fire with these thoughts.

My father had always longed for a boy, and I was as close to a son as he got. My sisters were all going to succeed in their own particular ways, but I was the one he singled out, the one with the extra spark, the child most like him. My mother considered me the most selfish of the family—and she was probably right.

My father treated us all much like boys on the Saturdays he was at home, when our tasks might include helping him lay a new patio for the house or planting roses in the garden during one of his spring work bees. Especially after he left politics in 1958, his do-it-yourself projects grew more ambitious—the former minister of fisheries, for example, painted a magnificent mural of fish on the swimming pool's retainer wall.

Mine was a healthy, loving childhood for the most part. But when my moods grew too agitated and I was overexcited, I was sent to my room and told to stay there until I had a "better atti-tude." I wonder now what there was in a little girl's room that could have helped me deal with these raging emotions.

I was always showing off and asking questions. To please my mother, I learned a lesson that would, paradoxically, only make my later life much worse: I understood that I would be loved only if I learned to suppress my emotions and become a pleasing lit-tle girl. I was not to mention to anyone these wild and terrifying thoughts that constantly raced through my mind. Instilled in me was the need to please and be approved of. I felt loved, but I also felt different, different from my sisters, and often very lonely. My rebelliousness began to simmer.

Even as a small child, my thoughts would race ahead and I would say things without thinking them through and then find myself miserable and embarrassed. One day, when I was about seven, my teacher decided to teach us the musical notes by get-ting us to sing out phrases to match their rhythm. She chanted out a sequence and one little girl put up her hand: "I love you." The teacher beamed. Then came a second, somewhat longer, sequence. I put up my own hand: "I do not love you." I was made to stand in the corner, feeling humiliated. I had meant no harm; the words had just leapt out.

Dad was keen to turn us into healthy, vigorous children, and more than happy to leave culture to later days. The result was a curiously barren childhood in one way—no ballet lessons, no ser-ious music, no art. The only music he enjoyed was the bagpipes.

The dinner table was where we were expected to learn about life and what it meant to be a family, but the noise was overpowering as everyone tried to compete for Daddy's attention. Only my mother stayed silent. As I grew older, I found the racket nearly intolerable. As a treat, my father would take us all out to a nearby restaurant, where we were so unbelievably loud that I would cringe with embarrassment. At these dinners I developed my hatred for labels.

"And this," he would declare to anyone listening, pointing at me, "is number four."

"No," I wanted to yell back. "I'm not number four. I'm Margaret!"

We may have lacked a grounding in the arts and culture, but exposure to nature we got in spades. When John Diefenbaker brought the Conservatives back into power in 1958, my father left politics. He bought a plot of land in North Vancouver and built his dream house at the end of a dead-end street on the edge of a ravine with a view down the creek. Our first summer was spent damming the creek and building a path to the artificial pool. What a fiasco—after we all fell ill, it was discovered that "the creek" was actually one of North Vancouver's hidden sewers.

But the creek got cleaned up and the dream house felt like a dream house once more. Ours was a ranch-style frame house, split-level, with a pool and a patio, a bedroom for each of the girls, a fancy kitchen and a splendid view of the harbour.

Soon after, my father bought a second house, an old cabin up on Hollyburn Mountain, Vancouver's northernmost mountain, with spectacular views of the Georgia Strait, the Gulf Islands and Grouse Mountain. The cabin had no running water or electricity and was set deep in the forest, surrounded by fir trees, pines and blueberry bushes. There were mountain lakes all around and, in winter, deep snow, which we gathered in buckets and melted down for water. We named the cabin High Hopes, after a song sung by Frank Sinatra in the 1959 film *A Hole in the Head*. The song, in part about an ambitious and hardworking ant achieving the impossible ("Oops, there goes another rubber tree plant" is the refrain), perfectly described the spirit and location of our old round-log cabin.

My father and mother had spent time in their youth at ski clubs. Hollyburn was their mountain, the scene of their romance, and what was sacred to them would become sacred to their daughters. Every weekend we either took the chair lift up the mountain or hiked with our provisions on our backs. The log cabin offered the dream life for my father. He loved chopping wood and laughing with his girls. We liked the simple and the real. During the day, we hiked, cross-country skied and tobogganed. At night, we played games—hearts, whist, crazy eights, cribbage and Monopoly. My father loved Scrabble; the game gave us all a taste for words.

My father's virtual son, I became a tomboy, building forts in the woods and having adventures on the lakes. These were happy times. The five girls slept in a dormitory in the cabin's attic, and on the wood stove there was always a pot of soup simmering for when we came in cold from the woods. "Mountain soup," as we called it, was a blend of tomato soup, Lipton's onion soup and beef consommé, eaten with bread. (With some adjustments—I lose the Lipton's and substitute natural ingredients—I still make that soup.) The cabin on the mountain was the best gift my father ever gave our family. I'm sure he thought the cabin was a way of keeping the family all together, and of keeping an eye on his daughters.

We all felt safe there, and we were—most of the time. On one occasion, a black bear wandered onto the front porch and got into some of Dad's preserves. Some tins contained peaches, some oil, and the bear loved the peaches and loathed the oil. The latter made him furious, and he began to wreck things on the porch and toss the tins of oil as far as he could (which was far) into the bush.

I look back on all the fun we had at the cabin and I'm reminded of the folly of thinking we have our children for a long time. We parents should make the most of our brief time with our children. I love families that are strong and interactive and almost exclusive, because their priorities are right. By the age of seven, we've already lost our children to their peers. My father and mother were so right to give us a connection with nature through that cabin. I've never lost that attraction. When I go on speaking tours, I'll look for places to run or walk—the river and park in Moose Jaw, Saskatchewan, or the dikes at Wolfville, Nova Scotia. I continue to feel this need to get in touch with nature.

As I grew older and became more self-aware, I discovered in myself a great fear of hostility and confrontation, which would leave me cowed and subdued. I remember much laughter and many tears as I engaged in sibling rivalry. My cousins were mainly other girls, and growing up in this exclusively female atmosphere only intensified my desire to make something of my life. Equality of the sexes and the importance of education were a given in our household. There was no question: I would go to university and find a career. The Sinclair sisters were not going to learn to type, for my father maintained that typing would invariably lead to our finding jobs as secretaries, a thought he deplored. He did, however, approve of my learning to cook and sew in home economics class.

When I was sixteen, I was chosen by my high school, Delbrook Senior Secondary, to represent it on the teen fashion council of the Hudson's Bay Company. One girl from every school in the city spent Saturday mornings listening to a model talk about grooming and poise and charm; afternoons were devoted to helping out in the different departments of the store. I wore a neat little uniform and prided myself on my weekly paycheque and the charm with which I handled the customers. When someone on staff suggested that I think of a post as a trainee store manager, I reacted strongly: I did indeed have a working life ahead of me, but not in a department store.

I had something far more glamorous in mind—writing stories as a foreign correspondent, perhaps, or travelling the world as an ambassador. I had seen for myself the interesting life women with their own careers led, and I resolved that whatever else might happen to me, I would have a serious working life of my own.

A good friend once described me as "every guy's great date." He meant to flatter me, but the fact is I never much enjoyed dating.

My parents wouldn't let us start until we reached grade ten, and then, like my sisters and their friends before me, I commenced the round of chaperoned Saturday-night parties, hand holding after school, long, intense telephone conversations and the wearing of special signs and tokens that meant a girl was going steady with a boy. But from the start, I always seemed to get something wrong. Perhaps because I had no brothers, I could never see boys as friends.

With my intense desire to please, I never wanted to offend anyone, so rather than fight to keep my clothes on in the back of someone's car, I preferred to skip casual dates and link myself to one boy for as long as possible. But it didn't stop me from being a terrible flirt. I look back and I see that I was a highly sexualized teenager.

With my father's encouragement—he promised Lin and me a car if we went there—I applied to the newly opened Simon Fraser University and we duly took possession of a beige 1966 Volkswagen Beetle. Simon Fraser had been built on the top of a mountain overlooking Vancouver, and the long, winding road that led up to it added to a sense of remoteness and isolation. The campus was all concrete and glass, and because Vancouver is a rainy city, it was grey, always grey. My first year was merely a continuation of my school days. I was a good student, I dated a football player and I won a first-class scholarship, which delighted my father. All through our childhood I can remember him repeating, again and again, that with good education and good manners there would be no doors that would not be open to us.

My second year at university, 1966, everything changed. I was studying political science, anthropology and sociology (mostly the latter) and was soon deep in the political dramas and tensions of the time, outraged by the spectacle of American soldiers in Vietnam and eager to seek out gurus in mysticism and freedom. Only later would I learn that sleeping well, eating well and working hard were important to balance my polarized emotions. My moods had more or less been kept in balance by the sense of discipline and order in our house.

My emotions began to slip out of control, distorted further by lack of sleep and the wrong kind of food—steamed cafeteria food, hamburgers, junk. What I now understand is that there was almost no margin of error in my brain chemistry balance. Bad food was one factor that helped derail me. There were others.

Caught up in the student movement of the late 1960s, I railed against poverty and injustice, watched the news coverage of Vietnamese children fleeing the napalm and fantasized constantly about changing the world. Sad spectacles plunged me into excessive misery; excitement fired me to great heights.

My first real love around this time was Phil Stanworth, a graduate student in sociology and a teaching assistant. His long hair and English accent irritated my father, who thought of him as a "limey outside agitator." My father's disapproval did not upset me too much as he was always gruff with our boyfriends and protective of his girls. Phil taught me how to study, how to question, how to think.

My education was now taking place continuously both inside and outside the classroom. On the faculty, there were Marxists and Maoists, Liberals and Trotskyites—many of them misfits and miscreants who had been kicked out of Berkeley and Columbia—and we talked and talked and talked. Stuck away on that grey and windswept mountain arguing through the night with brilliant people was a wonderful way to spend a year growing up. That year changed me. But I never quite got away from being more spectator than participant. Just as at school I had always refused to become a cheerleader, so now I didn't join the other students in their sit-ins. I didn't want to be a sheep among leftists, any more than I wanted to be one among conformists. I began to question things in a way I never had before.

And, like many of us who grew up in the 1960s, I was drawn to the drug and rock-and-roll culture all around me. The Beatles had come to Vancouver when I was sixteen, and I had found their songs and lyrics overwhelmingly exciting. Smoking marijuana was something we students were beginning to do, and we thought there was nothing wrong with it. One day I went with friends to a cottage near the sea, where the gulls screeched at us over our heads. We sat on the beach for hour after hour, listening to "Penny Lane" and "Strawberry Fields Forever," and when it rained we retreated inside and watched the spray hitting the window panes.

Because I was the newest arrival, I cooked the meals. Getting marijuana was easy; some grew dope in their gardens. But at the cottage I tried a hard drug, mescaline. I watched the veins in my hands stand out, saw visions of blood flowing and wonderful colours, and for a while I sat in a tree and wished that I was a bird. I really thought that I was opening the doors of perception, the ones that William Blake and Aldous Huxley had written about, and that I would find the secret to love, peace and compassion. This was exciting, as everything was exciting in those days, but I did not particularly want to try that drug again. I did go on smoking marijuana, though, and I must have left a few marijuana seeds in a shoebox in my cupboard. My mother chanced across them and asked me why I was keeping a stash of dried old mistletoe seeds.

In my last years at university I would study the English Romantic poets—Blake, Coleridge, Keats, Wordsworth. I realized then I should have been studying them all along. I was trying to expand my consciousness, and these brilliant poets with their mythic imaginations were helping me on my way. The poetry and letters of Keats just sang to me, and forty-three years later I still have his work by my bed. Keats believed that we should embrace the world, even its contradictions, and that mysteries abound beyond our ken.

In this confused, excited, cheerful state of mind, full of hope for the future but deeply unsure of what that might be, I set off for what my father suspected would be our last holiday together as a family. Our destination that Christmas of 1967 was Club Med on the island of Moorea in Tahiti. There I met and began dating a good-looking Frenchman called Yves Lewis, whose grandfather was one of the founders of the Club Med empire and who was on Moorea to teach water-skiing (he was the French national champion) during a year away from school. At sunset, the guests would have their happy hour and Yves would put on a demonstration of all he could do on skis out on the bay, including barefoot skiing. Yves could do it all, and he was the best in every skiing category.

He was twenty-one and dazzling in so many ways, with his green eyes, silvery blond hair, bronzed body and degree in sociology from the Sorbonne. Yves was also a gifted flautist and danced the traditional Tahitian dance, the tamure, so skilfully that even the Tahitians stopped to admire his form. He was quite mesmerizing, though modest and aloof at the same time.

One very hot afternoon after I had been water-skiing, I stayed out on a raft, resting and looking out at the white beach and the green palm trees. I observed a man slalom-skiing in the bay, and I followed his progress idly, impressed by his grace and skill and the huge walls of water he was casting up as he cut back and forth across the wake of the boat. Later, he joined me on the raft and we started to talk.

My first thought was that he was old, with old skin and old toes, and that I infinitely preferred the good-looking young Yves. This man, though, did have nice legs—they were perfectly toned and muscled. He was clearly an athlete who took care of himself. My mother, who had been watching us on the raft, asked me if I realized who I had been talking to.

"Oh, Pierre someone or other," I told her.

She laughed. "That's Pierre Trudeau, the justice minister, the black sheep of the Liberal Party."

The title didn't mean much to me. In any case, he was old—and "square," to use a word then commonly used to describe anyone who was conventional. This blue-eyed man on the raft was forty-eight years old, born in 1919. The *Titanic* had sunk only seven years before he was born, and the First World War was barely over when he came into the world and let out his first cry. I was nineteen, born in 1948—three years after the Second World War ended. The man on the raft was old enough to be my father, and almost old enough to be my grandfather.

But I was a born flirt, and we were soon talking—or rather, I talked, and Pierre asked me question after question, drawing me out in Socratic fashion. We talked about Plato and that age-old question of whether life was real or an illusion. He talked about the book he was then reading—Edward Gibbon's *History of the Decline and Fall of the Roman Empire,* a classic of the eighteenth century. Pierre was a good listener and easy to talk to. Soon we were going snorkelling together, though in my hippie, youthful fashion, full of the prejudices of the young, I went on finding his shorts and striped T-shirts staid and old-fashioned.

Pierre, who had been schooled by the Jesuits, was possessed of a rational, well-disciplined mind. Feeling out of touch with young Canadians, he was keen to pick my brains about the student rebellions at Simon Fraser University, and about the drug culture on campus and elsewhere. This holiday was meant as time for him to ponder a critical decision—whether to run for the leadership of the Liberal Party. Lester B. Pearson was still the prime minister, but he was stepping down and a leadership convention was planned for the following April. The winner of that contest would become the next prime minister.

Over breakfast one morning at the resort in Tahiti, while Pierre was sitting with friends at the far end of our shared long table, he had apparently said to them, looking discreetly at me, "If I ever marry, she's the one."

CHAPTER 2

FROM PEASANT DRESS
TO WEDDING DRESS

"You can either marry her, or adopt her."

JOHN DIEFENBAKER ON HEARING THE AGE OF THE PM'S NEW BRIDE, MARCH 1971

For an entire generation of youth in the late 1960s and '70s, the travel destination of choice was Morocco—the food was cheap, the dope plentiful and the culture exotic, and the beaches and warm sun beckoned.

Perversity and a desire to irk my father (who was appalled at the idea) simply made Morocco that much more appealing.

All my father could talk about were the perils of white slavery, poverty and pestilence; he had served in North Africa during the Second World War. All I could think about was the idea of freedom. One of my sisters had gone to Europe and travelled around on a Eurail pass; that didn't interest me. I have always lived spontaneously, and I was bent on becoming a new person, on reinventing myself. In Morocco, I thought to myself, I will go with the flow.

My last months at Simon Fraser had been something of an anticlimax. I had taken a semester off to make money, and now my friends were all ahead of me and I felt out of tune with my surroundings. I indulged my new-found passion for the Romantic poets and moved into a dark basement apartment in Burnaby, a Vancouver suburb.

This was a lonely and frustrating time. I went home every weekend for Sunday dinner but increasingly felt distant from my family. I did graduate, with a decent degree, and like many Canadian middle-class students, I decided to have a holiday after graduation, paying for it by cashing in some shares from a legacy that my grandmother Sinclair had left me.

I flew to Geneva after Christmas in 1968 and met up with Ross, a friend from school days. We drove his shiny new Ford Cortina through France and Spain and down into Morocco, finally stopping at the coastal city of Agadir. We had found sun and sea and an agreeable hippie commune of sorts, one that shared showers with a tourist camp nearby.

With the money I had been given, I was one rich hippie and I set myself up grandly—in a little bamboo "house" I built on the beach, complete with charcoal burner, cooking pot, sleeping mat and a tarp to keep out the rain (but it never did rain). Every night, there were campfires on the beach with fellow pilgrims from all over the world, some of whom had brought their guitars. The lucky ones came in VW vans, outfitted with galley kitchens and curtains. At night, we would walk along the beach under the stars, and because there was phosphorus in the sea water, every time we made a footprint in the soft sand it would fill in with water and it, too, would sparkle like stars, as if the stars themselves had dropped from the night sky. It was magical.

When Ross left a few weeks later, I threw in my lot with the hippies, learned to eat what food there was (clementines and fresh round loaves of bread were fantastically cheap) and abandoned my conventional notions of sexual morality. For the first time in my life, I had a real sense of peace, freedom and tranquility. I was not lonely, at all. And I revelled in the knowledge that no one from my past life had the faintest idea where I was.

After that I wandered from one hippie commune to another, experimenting and growing up—or so I imagined. I smoked kif, a strong mixture of black tobacco and hashish (the word *kif* comes from the Arab word for "pleasure"), and ate so little that I became malnourished. But then, so did many of us on the hippie trail. I lost pounds and even my possessions. A series of thefts left me with only a small leather suitcase containing some jeans and shirts, and a Liberty cotton cosmetic bag containing face cream and soap.

I also carried with me a record player—a cheap, battery-powered model I bought in a souk in Tangier—and eight prized albums, including the Beatles' White Album and the Rolling Stones' *Let It Bleed*. This made me very popular, since listening to rock music seemed to be our favourite pastime. I spent a while in Essaouira, a small town farther up the coast, where I joined Moroccan women in their hammams—the Middle Eastern version of the steam bath, one that features lots of scrubbing, vigorous massage and splashing on of bowls of hot and cold water. I remember those cleansings as a wonderful cultural experience.

I found Moroccans kind and generous with their hospitality. I remember hitchhiking near El Jadida, an old fortified town on the coast south of Casablanca. We were approached by a charming young man on a motorcycle who invited us to stay with his family at their farm. This boy had been studying in the United States and knew English, so he was the proud translator for his family. I remember sitting on mats and watching a chicken get decapitated in preparation for the meal. We laughed and told stories and were made to feel welcome. The generosity was so spontaneous, so unorganized—and that was a first for me.

And in the morning, there was warm bread with fresh butter and yogurt and honey. I learned that Muslim tradition has it that when a stranger comes to your door, you invite him in and offer him hospitality for three days, for this stranger could be the prophet in disguise. However, should the guest behave badly during that time, the host has every right to eject the visitor, so the custom encourages civility all around. I encountered such hospitality in Morocco and never once did I feel threatened.

Later, in Marrakech, I stayed with another family, and I remember going up on the roof to admire the stars. Up there was this doleful, rather smelly sheep that would be slaughtered next day during the feast of Ramadan. The streets in Marrakech were hard-packed, with little gutters on the side, and they literally ran red with sheep's blood that day. A minor earthquake added to the drama. I was offered a sheep's eyeball to eat, and I did eat it, though I wondered if I was being tricked—but no, the custom is meant to honour elders or special guests.

In Morocco, there were no taboos. Away from the strictures and machismo of North America, I finally learned to treat men as friends while enjoying making love. I was now living a life my puritan upbringing had never allowed me to imagine possible. After a month in Essaouira, I crossed the mountains and headed inland to Marrakech in an ancient bus, sitting next to a sheep trussed up by its four legs.

Every word of William Blake seemed to me then the embodiment of perfect wisdom. A mystic and a visionary heavily influenced by the American and French revolutions, a man of extraordinary imagination who said that he both saw and conversed with angels, Blake created his own incredibly complex and elaborate personal mythology. He was the perfect poet for the counterculture revolution. Bob Dylan was influenced by him, as was the poet Allen Ginsberg. I still admire Blake; I have books of his art and have been to the Tate Gallery in London many times to see his engravings. One might argue that the title of one of his epic poems, *The Marriage of Heaven and Hell,* neatly sums up a good portion of my life.

So Blake was my poet, and Morocco my sacred and magical place. For a while I even thought of buying an apartment in Tangier and staying on indefinitely in Morocco, but my father, in a letter to me, firmly talked me out of it. As for the marijuana, it did something that nothing else had ever done in my life: the drug (a milder version of the stuff now available) stopped my mind racing so fast, it gave me ballast and it allowed me to enjoy what I saw, heard and smelled around me, rather than having my thoughts scattering away in bursts of energy and tension.

While in Morocco, I met two people who were to have a profound effect on me. They were both artists, one a singer and poet, the other a painter. Both were in their thirties and had seen and read and experienced things that I had never even contemplated.

The first was Leonard Cohen, whom I met in Essaouira, where he was staying with a French girlfriend named Claire. He was a good-looking man of medium build, with thick, dark hair and a very sonorous, low voice. His second novel, *Beautiful Losers,* had come out a few years earlier, in 1966.

Leonard suggested that I visit them in Casablanca, and we spent a few days together in a hotel there, talking, joking, serious one minute, laughing the next. Leonard would take the time to think before he spoke, something I would have done well to emulate. He was poetic and spiritual in a way I found very attractive, and in the gardens of the hotel we talked about everything under the sun while tucking into huge pots of tagine—a delicious, slow-cooked Moroccan stew made with vegetables and fruits and spiced with saffron, ginger, cumin and paprika. We would talk through the night, going down roads of spirituality that I hadn't imagined existed. At university I had spent hours listening to his music, reading his novels and poetry, and I felt extraordinarily honoured to spend time with him.

I went on to Tangier, where I rented an apartment in the European quarter and planned to work with a fashion-designer friend for a few months. One morning I felt a stab of pain in my left hand. A young French doctor diagnosed a break in a small bone and put my hand into plaster. Instead of getting better, the pain got worse; throbbing, agonizing pain drove me back to the doctor a few days later. He was not sympathetic, told me to stop fussing and gave me a tranquilizer.

That night my whole arm grew numb and I wandered out into the streets screaming, almost frantic with pain. A kind Moroccan woman, seeing me, asked me what was wrong. I showed her my arm. Within minutes I was in her car on the way to the hospital, where a surgeon removed the cast and discovered that far from a broken bone, I had developed osteomyelitis—an inflammation of the bone marrow caused by infection. My hand was blue-grey in colour and already looked shrunken. I was put onto morphine and for a few days the surgeon worried that he might have to amputate. I stayed in the hospital for two weeks, slowly getting better, and tended to by extremely gentle Catholic nuns, true sisters of mercy.

My second new friend was an artist named Ahmed Yacoubi who had a studio in Tangier and was already making a name for himself in New York art galleries. He would later exhibit all over the world; writers such as Paul Bowles befriended him, and William S. Burroughs wrote about him. Bowles and his wife, the playwright Jane Bowles, met Ahmed when he offered his services as a translator. He would draw pictures to explain the meanings of Arabic words, and both writers immediately recognized his pure talent as a painter and helped launch his international career.

Ahmed's studio was a wonderful place, full of carpets and cushions, low tables and priceless pieces of Moroccan art. He was a man who loved to cook. Then in his late thirties, Ahmed was gentle and adult, the first man from another culture I really got to know, and I sat for hours listening to him talk—he was also a storyteller and would later be published. I would watch him paint, and I was with him when he did a portrait of me. Ahmed wanted me to stay with him. Instinctively I knew that it couldn't work, so I moved on again, but I had begun to see the possibility of other ways of thinking and living.

By this time, I had been in Morocco nearly five months. For a little girl from North Vancouver, Morocco had been a revelation of another world of freedom and choice. But I was growing restless. I was getting sick of the hippie world, and I was beginning to feel buffeted by the amount of drugs that were pressed onto me and by the reliance on them that so many of my new friends seemed to feel. An unpleasant episode with a dealer in cocaine and hash (he was trying to recruit me as a mule to transport drugs across borders) convinced me that it was time to go home. I realized how lucky I was that nothing terrible had happened to me, and I felt that I had grown up. But whatever I was writing in my letters home must have alarmed my mother: she burned them without showing them to anyone.

What was more, I was longing to see Yves Lewis again. At our last meeting, he had told me to go away, learn about life, become an adult, and that we should then meet again and see where we stood. I now felt worthy of him. But I was in for a nasty shock. I had gone too far in the wrong direction. He wanted me freer; he got me back too free.

I sought him out in Berkeley, California, where he was teaching. This was July 20, 1969, the time of *Apollo 11,* the first manned spaceship to land on the moon. Yves and I went to a backyard party at a friend's house in San Francisco near the campus. We were to a bring a bottle of wine and a poem or song about the moon, and we sang to the moon that magical night.

The reunion did not go as planned. Yves, who was a hot-headed political animal yet possessed of an almost Zen calm, was contemptuous of my frizzy hair and my granny glasses and the faraway look in my eyes.

"You used to be such a chick," he told me. "You've become a fat brooding hen"—I was talking about marriage and children. "Come back," Yves said, "when you've learned something real about life." Crestfallen, confused and totally without a plan for the future, I went back home. But home was definitely not where the heart was.

I had been welcomed back from Morocco with a splendid prime-rib dinner, one that my mother had gone to great pains to make. I was aghast.

"You're not still eating flesh, are you?" was my response. I had become a vegetarian and had turned to brown rice and a macrobiotic diet. As for my father, he held top-dog positions between 1960 and 1973 at Lafarge, a multinational cement company. I held him partially responsible for all the heritage build-ings being torn down in Vancouver to make way for concrete towers. You can imagine the pitched battles between the flower child and the cement baron. We fought about politics, values, money, music, greed, plastic, sugar as poison and Coca-Cola as the enemy—everything and anything. I was a hippie who thought hippie thoughts: I had flowers in my hair from an early age.

I was still in Morocco when my father wrote a letter to Doug Abbott, my godfather and a former finance minister in the same cabinet my father served in, that of Prime Minister Louis St. Laurent. My father allowed that of the five Sinclair sisters, I was "the best scholar of the lot" (though he added that I was "very leftish"). I'm not sure I agree about the "best scholar" part. My intelligence is enviable in a way, but it's flash intelligence. I pick up things quickly (I skipped grade four) and I have a photographic memory, but I can't or won't do the grunt work, and the logic wasn't always there, or the discipline. My sisters would lock themselves away and study; I wouldn't.

Even before going to Morocco, I was a pain: I was a perfectionist and a meticulous Virgo who was convinced I knew best—how to make a salad, tell a story, polish a floor. The trip to Morocco had only filled my head with disdain for the world I had left behind. My sisters had all embarked on their career paths, and they laughed at me.

When I returned from Morocco, there was no place in the house for me, no place in every sense. My father built a lean-to— a bizarre and makeshift addition to this otherwise lovely house. The lean-to's roof was wavy fibreglass that let in the light but kept out the rain, the kind of roof then fashionable on garden sheds. He hauled in a bed, and this was where I slept for about a month. Finally, wearied by all my challenges, my parents banished me to my grandmother's house.

So, one day in August of 1969, I went to see my grandmother on the Sechelt Peninsula, thinking that I would take refuge in her cottage perched on a cliff above the sea overlooking Howe

Sound. Hers was indeed a magical place. I had always regarded her little house—with its tarpaper roof and robin's-egg-blue window frames, its garden of rose bushes, fruit trees and vegetables, and the great forest stretching for miles around—as a safe haven. The place offered a profusion of lilies, nasturtiums and pansies, many grown up from the cuttings she scattered when working on her garden.

My sisters and I had spent many happy summers there. The nearest store was a mile away down a dirt road, so my grandmother's garden was very much an edible garden. When the weather was nice, we'd walk to the store along the beach. I remember playing baseball on the road with the neighbours' kids and listening to an elderly Irishman who lived next door, a kind fellow who always had a bowl of candy and stories to tell.

My grandmother, Rose Edith Bernard, was the strongest woman I had ever encountered. A plain prairie woman then in her late sixties, strong and proud and self-sufficient, Rose, as eldest child, had helped raise her siblings when her mother died, and later taught school for many years. Rose's husband, Tom Bernard—a modest, Malaysian-born man who had worked for the railway in Penticton—died the year I was born. Every day of her married life, Rose would make a pot of rice and have it at the back of the stove for him, because that's what he was used to back home.

I remember the blue rinse my grandmother put in her hair, and the little rituals she had, like listening to classical music on an old radio at the same time every day. She would sit in her chair, put her feet up on a footstool and close her eyes. Her days were ordered and efficient, and she was always busy in the garden or making her own clothes, her own blackberry wine.

Rose Bernard believed that idleness was the work of the devil, so there was time set aside for the Sinclair sisters to play, and time to do chores—weeding, painting, sewing, mending and, one time, constructing a bird bath out of brick, chicken wire and cement. Looking back on those times, I have to agree with my grandmother: work truly is the cure for a lot of ills.

But on that day in 1969, just weeks from my twenty-first birthday, I sat on a log on the pebble beach below the cottage at Roberts Creek—dreaming, waiting for the tide to come in, listening to the cries of the seagulls and the soothing roar of the waves on the shore.

There I slowly returned to some kind of normality. The days passed, and I brooded, walking up and down the shore, watching the seals and the sea lions. When I grew bored, I poked among the rocks for starfish and crabs. I wallowed in memories and tried to avoid thinking about the future, certain only that an ordinary life of convention and respectability, of bridge clubs and nine-to-five jobs, was not for me. Then came a phone call that changed my life.

My grandmother was on a party line; in those days, rural telephone users sometimes shared the same line, and a distinctive cadence told the homeowner when the call was for her. My grandmother, who didn't get a lot of calls, picked up the phone after hearing three long rings and one short ring. On the other end was my mother, doubtless with some trivial and prosaic question, asking for me. I sauntered ungraciously to the telephone.

"Margaret," she said, trying and failing to sound casual, "an old friend has just called, someone you once met on holiday, and he wants to take you out on a date."

I was outraged. A date? I informed her curtly that I didn't date. She was crestfallen. She knew that I was in a low period; that was partly why I had been dispatched to Grandma's house. My mother thought that an evening out might cheer me up.

"Don't you even want to know who it is?" she asked. I was curious but tried not to show it.

"Well," I said finally, with all the truculence of a bad-tempered teenager, "who is it?"

"Pierre Trudeau," said my mother, flattered that he had taken an interest in her daughter and adding that he was coming to Vancouver for a meeting. In April 1968, following victory at the Liberal Party convention in Ottawa, Trudeau had been named the prime minister of Canada. As was our custom, my sisters and I had all attended the Liberal convention. My father was backing John Turner as candidate. Like me, my sisters—who had all met Pierre in Tahiti—were backing him, of course.

I was intrigued enough to agree to return to Vancouver. Pierre, as I soon discovered, was already dominating the Canadian political scene as no other prime minister ever had, and was at work on sweeping changes to social policy and talking of a place for francophones in the Canadian mainstream.

To prepare for the occasion, my mother insisted that I put away my trailing skirts with the twinkling mirrors and the sequins, the sandals and the beads, and that I wear something formal. The products of our day's shopping—an elegant, short white dress, and a visit to the hairdresser to iron out my frizzy hair—succeeded only in turning me into a Barbie doll, complete with a diamond brooch and shaved legs.

For my part, I had two distinct and slightly contradictory images of Pierre. On the one hand, there was a nice-looking middle-aged man who wore old-fashioned shorts and striped T-shirts; on the other, there was the charismatic leader whose ascent to power I had witnessed at the Liberal convention in Ottawa, when Trudeaumania swept the floor.

When he came through the door of my parents' house in North Van, I liked the look of him immediately. This was late summer, and he was tanned, which looked good against his white shirt, blue blazer and coloured ascot. He wore dark glasses and a flower in his buttonhole. I liked his charm, his boyish manner, and I couldn't stop myself sneaking a quick look at his tight butt. He was confident, flying high, a good first year as prime minister behind him and the country at his feet, and he had about him such an air of fun, such a charming, teasing expression, that he made me laugh at once. Poor Pierre, on the other hand, remembering a simple young girl, without artifice, in a bikini on a beach, was clearly taken aback by my over-groomed, stilted appearance.

Still, our evening was wonderful. I got him out of the house as soon as I could, unable to stand the nervous giggling of my sisters or the feigned relaxation of my mother. A blue Pontiac sat in the driveway with two plain-clothed officers in the front seat, both with the unmistakable muscles and air of security of policemen. We set off to catch the gondola to the Grouse Nest, a restaurant at the top of Grouse Mountain. For a moment, it occurred to me that I should perhaps be wary of this man, but then that notion passed. We quickly resumed the long conversations we had begun in Tahiti and I soon forgot who he was and saw only the man sitting across from me: the most charming, easiest, most interesting man I had ever met.

Within minutes, I had blown my cover. The little French dress was a sham, and we talked about student revolution and Berkeley and Morocco. Pierre was so obviously relieved that there was a real human being inside the Barbie doll that he gave me every encouragement, and I was hugely flattered by his attentiveness and charm. I was also embarrassed at the thought of asking him questions about his own life. How could I really say, "Tell me, what's it like to be prime minister?" We danced, we poked fun at the touristy restaurant and we laughed.

Later that night, as he dropped me off at home with a brotherly kiss goodbye, he asked me whether I had ever considered a job in government. I hadn't, but I did now. I was already infatuated—by his manners and courtesy, his air of experience and a strange quality he had of making everyone about him want to be as pleasing as possible. In my imagination, I was already seeing myself at his side. For all my rebelliousness, I was my mother's daughter at heart and could envisage no future without a husband and children.

Within a month, I had moved to Ottawa and found a job in the Department of Manpower and Immigration as a sociologist. My parents were overcome by my sudden transformation. Overnight, I began eating properly again. I sewed myself neat, tailored suits, appropriate to the city life I imagined.

Two weeks transpired before I mustered the courage to call Pierre, and when I did he was clearly extremely surprised; he had not expected me to take his words so literally. But his voice was warm and faintly amused, and he asked me round at once for dinner at the prime minister's residence at 24 Sussex Drive. This was October, a warm, early-autumn evening, and the lawns surrounding the large stone mansion were scattered with falling leaves. I approached the door with some trepidation.

I had turned twenty-one years old on September 10, and here I was knocking on the door of the prime minister's house for a dinner date.

The door was opened by a cheerful woman who led me into the library, a room I found soulless and bleak, home to shelf upon shelf of art books and volumes of philosophy, political treatises and leather-bound theology. What I had seen of the hall, with all its paintings of heavy Canadian landscapes, only added to an impression of austere and grey formality.

Over a dinner of spaghetti (overcooked) with a little oil drizzled over top and chocolate chip cookies for dessert, I looked around me and saw a barren, cheerless decor. Still, the evening was charming, delightful, grown-up and very easy. I felt as if Pierre and I had known each other for a long time. Our romance began.

The more I saw of Pierre, the more I liked him. Bit by bit, I managed to get him to reveal something of his own past. I discovered that his father had made his fortune by buying service stations during and immediately after the Depression, that he had been a funny, boisterous father even if highly ambitious for his elder son and that Pierre had been brought up in luxury, transported by chauffeur to the prestigious Collège Jean-de-Brébeuf in Montreal every day. I learned that he had overcome his excessively shy nature by taking boxing lessons and that he had grown up speaking both French and English at home, so that he was fully bilingual.

I heard how he had taken a first degree in law and then a master's in political economy at Harvard before getting caught up in Québécois politics, losing his job and spending many months travelling the world. And that he had become a teacher of constitutional law at the Université de Montréal before becoming the member of parliament for the west Montreal riding of Mount Royal and then minister of justice in the Lester Pearson government. He made a name for himself with sweeping reforms of the legal system, championing human rights and fair play and becoming the much-loved rogue of the Liberal Party.

However, our romance was not all easy. Pierre was a very private man, and I was a far cry from the kind of woman whom Canadians would consider a suitable wife for their prime minister. What was more, he was widely regarded as a reserved and cautious bachelor and had lived for many years with his mother, taking out few women, until he had suddenly been catapulted into the leadership of the Liberal Party and the public eye. For years, magazines had been running articles asking "Whom should Trudeau marry?" and his name had been linked to the singer Barbra Streisand (who once described him as a "tantalizing blend of Marlon Brando and Napoleon") and to Madeleine Gobeil, who taught French literature at Carleton University in Ottawa and who would go on to become director of arts for UNESCO.

I was beginning to discover that behind the silky, charming manner and the absolute confidence that had given Pierre Trudeau something of a reputation for arrogance lay a curiously solitary figure. I hated the way that people would stop talking whenever he approached them, and the way that everyone stared at him—and us—with awe and admiration. So he and I stopped going out in public together and instead spent our evenings alone at 24 Sussex and, best of all, at the prime minister's country house on Harrington Lake.

Located several kilometres north of Ottawa in the Gatineau Hills, the Harrington Lake estate comprises thirteen acres in Gatineau Park. The place was born when supporters suggested to then prime minister John Diefenbaker that he needed a country retreat, a quiet and tranquil place where a busy leader might have time to, say, go fishing. One story has it that when Diefenbaker was touring the property he was dubious at first, but the caretaker taking him around had been instructed to make sure the PM caught a trout, which he did. In 1959, then, Harrington Lake became the official country house of the prime minister of Canada.

Unlike 24 Sussex, which is an old lumber baron's mansion, stately and heavy, Harrington is a simple white clapboard house with a screened-in sun porch along one side and magnificent views over the lake to the forests beyond. Accented by green shutters, the house is plain but sprawling—sixteen rooms and more than eight thousand square feet. The widow's walk over the sun porch allows for a splendid, lofty view of the lake, which the English called

Harrington and the French called Mousseau. Families with those or similar names settled the area in the early nineteenth century, as did the Meech family. Meech Lake, site of that famous accord signed in 1987, is close by.

The house at Harrington Lake—the one place Pierre truly loved and scene of the happiest days of my marriage—has wooden floors and white-painted panelling, with two vast stone fireplaces at opposite ends of the house, in the sitting room and dining room, where we burned great logs of wood. On Saturdays and Sundays, whatever the weather, Pierre insisted that we spend at least four hours outside—hiking, canoeing and swimming in summer, cross-country and downhill skiing and skating in winter. Pierre had a raft built, and we anchored it some distance from shore; we would sunbathe there for hours in total privacy. He loved the place for its solitude and simplicity.

What I found so wonderful about this time was that Pierre totally allowed me to be myself, and that he seemed to love everything about me. The twenty-nine-year difference in our ages bothered neither of us. We never thought about it, though, looking back, we should have.

By Christmas, we had settled into a routine. We met for dinner once or twice a week, when Pierre's chauffeur collected me at 7:00 p.m., and Pierre walked me home around 10:30 p.m., when he had to get back to work. Occasionally we went to a restaurant in the more unfashionable places, and photographers who did catch us simply assumed that I was one of the prime minister's many occasional dates.

At Harrington Lake, I had my own room and we were very discreet. But we felt private and absolutely free. Best of all, perhaps, were our trips to Pierre's remote, simple cabin at Morin-Heights in the Laurentians. On these occasions, I came to love and admire Pierre's self-sufficiency, his conscientiousness, his disregard for social conventions and his seriousness.

But we also laughed a lot. These were idyllic days, and the contrast between them and the rest of my life made me feel that I was split in two. I had told only two people, my sister Lin and a friend in Toronto, about the seriousness of my relationship with Pierre. There is definitely something devious about me: I took perverse pleasure in my double life, leading my friends on to think I was doing one thing while in fact I was doing quite another. I even played a game with myself, tricking my friends into talking about Pierre, the prime minister of Canada, while I laughed silently to myself.

One of my favourite photos of all my time with Pierre was taken in the summer of 1970. We're on the ferry from Horseshoe Bay in West Vancouver, heading to Gibsons on the Sechelt Peninsula and a rendezvous with my grandmother Rose Bernard. In a very real way, I was seeking her approval of the man I was to marry.

I wanted the blessing of a woman I very much admired. My grandmother once told me when I was very young, "Margaret, you're one of the more delicate flowers in the garden. But you're also a perennial." Only later did I understand that she was remarking on how fragile I was and yet how durable. A perennial is an eternal flower, one that keeps coming back year after year.

The light that day was dazzling and the photo shows us both in sunglasses, sitting on the deck, leaning against a wall and basking in the sun. Pierre is barefoot and his elbows are resting on his knees. He is the picture of a very relaxed man. My hands are hugging my ankles and I'm smiling.

I look back on that moment as one of sweetness and innocence. Canadians on board recognized Pierre, of course, but they were so warm and polite, wanting to shake his hand. Among the well-wishers was a group of Brownies in their uniforms and badges, which seemed so familiar to me. I had worn that uniform as a child. These girls were eleven and twelve years old and they were charmed and delighted when Pierre teased them.

Then some German tourists approached and in heavily accented English asked, "Why are these children and old people coming to your feet? We are curious."

Pierre explained to them that he was their Willy Brandt—then chancellor of West Germany.

"Ah," they exclaimed. "Nice to meet you, Mr. Prime Minister."

We pressed on to my grandmother's house, where Rose Bernard—ever the straight-talking Tory—lit into Pierre for allowing French on cereal boxes. She liked to read the boxes as she ate her cereal in the morning, and she argued that the French was cutting into the English. And besides, she said, there wasn't one francophone in her community. Later Pierre would say, rather famously, "Well, turn it around," to the anglophone complaint of French on cereal boxes. But my grandmother may have been the first to voice the lament to him.

Before our wedding, Pierre teased her, asking her what an Anglican thought she was doing in a Catholic church. Pierre's beloved mother, Grace Elliott Trudeau, was of Scottish ancestry, so naturally Rose and Pierre hit it off. She flirted with him.

Given what soon followed, you will understand why I cherished that moment on the ferry. What I had to get used to was that everywhere Pierre went, he was accompanied by RCMP officers who were trained to guard him, though they kept their distance— as they did that day on the ferry. I found the constant tailing irksome, but we could, and did, joke about it.

Then all joking ceased. On October 5 of that same year, 1970, the British trade commissioner, James Cross, was kidnapped in Montreal. Five days later, Pierre Laporte, Quebec's vice-premier and minister of labour, was also captured by the Front de libération du Québec, while he was playing football at dusk on a field near his home. The FLQ cell that held him hostage demanded the release of a number of political prisoners.

Pierre invoked the War Measures Act and ordered mass raids and arrests but said that he would not deal with terrorists. On the sixteenth of October, 497 people were rounded up and arrested. I was with Pierre next the night when the red emergency phone— kept in the closet at Harrington Lake above his sweaters—rang ominously. The news was that Pierre Laporte had been found dead, strangled with his own crucifix chain, his body left in the trunk of a car at Saint-Hubert Airport, some sixteen kilometres east of downtown Montreal.

Pierre wept: for the Laporte family, and for the choices that he had had to make. He would not negotiate with the kidnappers, and he would confront and close down the terrorist cells—even if it meant curtailing many of the civil and political rights to which Canadians had become accustomed.

Looking back on it, I realize that Pierre didn't want me in any way involved; this was his work, and not something that we debated together. But we did discuss the finer points. I suppose I was one of those "bleeding hearts" he so famously dismissed. I felt a certain injustice that people were being deprived of their rights. But perhaps that's precisely what we needed in our history of becoming the kind of strong nation that we are now.

The War Measures Act was harsh. I understand the outrage over the interrogation and temporary incarceration of so many people. On the other hand, people were being murdered and there was a huge chance that an insurrection would follow, with more exploding mailboxes and more murders. This was the beginning of terrorism, of "us against them" in our own province, our own country, and he had to put a stop to it.

There wasn't an us and them; there was just an us. History has proven Pierre right. The violence ceased in the wake of invoking the Act; such violence didn't cease in Ireland, and it hasn't ceased in many other parts of the world. I think Pierre acted with the kind of courage that set him apart as a leader. Some in Quebec thought this was the worst injustice and they still think of him as a traitor. What are they talking about?

Pierre fought hard and, if cornered, could be severe. But he fought hard for what he believed in, and I respect that. How ironic that some would remember him for taking away rights. This is the man who incorporated a charter of rights and freedoms into the Constitution, giving Canadians rights and freedoms unparalleled in the world. We should embrace and understand these freedoms and be proud of them. Aside from his wonderful children, I think this is Pierre's greatest legacy. It's what he set out to do as a fledgling justice minister, and he succeeded in a grand way.

In time, five known members of the FLQ cell responsible were found, arrested and deported to Cuba; three other members were also later arrested in Quebec. And while I believed Pierre when he told me that without these tough measures, Canada would fall prey to continued separatist violence, these events had a real and harmful effect on our relationship.

Within hours, the security around Pierre intensified mightily. When we next went up to Harrington Lake, we found army trucks and soldiers where previously there had been grassy slopes and clear views. On Thanksgiving weekend, I could see through the mists a neat army tent. On Thanksgiving Day, despite warnings by the police, we took a rickety old boat out onto the lake on our own, then climbed to the top of the hill where beavers had dammed the ponds.

Walking silently through the trees on that rainy day, we heard the crashing sounds of what we took to be a large animal approaching. But out of the bush came a dark, heavily bearded man, and for a second we feared that the security officers had been right in making such a fuss. As he ran past, all he said was, "Do something about nuclear proliferation." After getting lost on the way down, Pierre and I emerged somewhat shamefaced at the water's edge to find a very agitated RCMP officer in a boat holding an umbrella in one hand and a rifle in the other. His gunshots had guided us home. We would never be really private again.

I was, in fact, increasingly unhappy with my life in Ottawa. My work was boring; I had few friends. But for Pierre, I would have caught the next plane home. When I was with him, my gloom miraculously lifted and I simply forgot how lonely I was the rest of the time. As we became more and more content in each other's company, I lived only for the times I could be with him.

But even in our early courtship, I'd felt the chill of isolation. I thought of the day when Pierre asked me to a costume ball at the National Library—our first proper public outing. We had agreed that I would be bored by the formal receptions and diplomatic dinners, but this was to be a more lively occasion. He told me that he would be wearing black tie but pressed me to wear any fancy dress that I wished. I chose to go as Juliet, in a red velvet hippie dress with full sleeves that fell to the ground and my hair pinned up under a net of pearls.

From the instant I stepped out of the car, the evening was a disaster. Not only were we stared at, photographed and cut off from one another, but every group we joined instantly fell silent. Jokes were stopped in mid-sentence; laughter froze in the air. When we danced, people watched. As soon as we got back into the car, I burst into tears. "Why did they treat us that way?" I asked him. "Why can't we be normal?"

Pierre was sympathetic but firm. We had to try again.

This time he took me to dinner at the home of very old friends. I made particular efforts to look my best. The first question I was asked, on walking through the door, was whether I spoke French. Pierre answered for me: of course I spoke French. And so, though all present spoke perfect English, the entire evening's conversation was conducted in French, which I neither spoke nor understood. I had studied French for two years at university and maybe I thought I could manage; I could not. I plastered a grin on my face and pretended to follow. No one actually addressed me. They were interested in themselves and in the prime minister. At 10:30 p.m., Pierre announced that he had to go home to work. I fled with him, once again in tears, wailing that I had never felt so insulted and betrayed. We resolved to try no more social occasions.

I was, however, getting to know his family. On weekends, we would sometimes go down to Montreal, where his mother lived in the original family house not far from his sister, Suzette, and his brother, Tip, who was an architect, and Tip's wife, Andrée. We would spend parts of the holidays with them and I was growing very close to Suzette. Pierre's mother was always immaculately turned out and extremely elegant, but dementia was already clouding her mind.

CHANGING MY MIND | 53

Pierre and I separated then came together again, as the on-again, off-again romance tried for surer ground. I took up briefly with a divinity student and even imagined that I might marry him. Meanwhile, I continued to correspond with Yves Lewis and was still immensely drawn to him. I urged Pierre to take other women out on dates, but I was furious and jealous when he did so. My mother was full of dire warnings: don't be the mistress of a politician twice your age, she kept saying. Pierre is never going to marry you.

After Easter in 1970, I quit my job and decided to go home and live with my parents. I no longer wanted to be Pierre's secret mistress; I wanted to live with him and have his children. For a while Pierre vacillated, but we were both too unhappy without each other, and in the summer of 1970, Pierre finally proposed.

Before committing himself, he told me, he needed to know every single detail of my past life, for fear of later blackmail. At the time, the end of August, we were on a wonderful holiday in the Bahamas, staying at the Small Hope Bay Lodge on the island of Andros, and we walked up and down the beach while I recited the litany of boyfriends, marijuana and past indiscretions.

One of those old boyfriends, Yves Lewis, had sent a letter to me, care of my parents—the only address he had for me. Only later would I learn that my mother burned the letter.

Pierre was drawn to my Scottish bloodlines (ones he shared and understood), and he liked my independence and sense of comfort in nature and in the garden. He liked my homespun skills, how I could cook and sew. My being Anglican was an issue for this devout Catholic, but conversion would solve that. He was looking for a wife and children, and I longed for children. As for my other shortcomings (my lack of French, for example), that too was easily addressed. Pierre thought he could educate me, shape me.

Once he made up his mind, Pierre became the most loving and attentive of suitors. He told me that he had prayed for a long time that he would find someone he loved and have children of his own. He knew what he wanted, but he knew, too, that he had to be convinced our marriage would work. His motto was "Reason before passion."

Now, looking around at his friends, he knew that the moment had come to have children. Because he was passionately opposed to all kinds of drugs and pills, he had persuaded me to give up the birth control pill some months before. As for me, I didn't care where, how or when we would marry; I just knew that I wanted to be with him.

We agreed that I would return to Vancouver and work hard to equip myself to become the wife of the prime minister of Canada. I was to study French, I was to take catechism classes and convert to the Catholic faith, and I set out to become an expert skier—in an attempt to keep pace with Pierre's athleticism. I fulfilled all my promises to Pierre. I proved that I could be faithful through the months of waiting; I gave up marijuana (though, as you will see, that vice would return); I learned to ski well and converted to Catholicism, taking instruction from Father John Schwinkles at St. Stephen's Church in North Vancouver.

In one of his lessons, the priest described the different ways to get to heaven. Catholicism, he assured me, was the jet plane. I was perturbed to be told that my parents' Protestantism constituted a very slow boat. As for learning French, I had done less well—despite ninety-minute lessons every day with a private tutor.

I had also given considerable thought to my appearance as the future wife of the prime minister and acquired a trousseau of ladylike clothes. I had been informed that, soon after our wedding, we were to pay an official visit to Russia. One of the dresses I had made was based on a magnificent sari given to my mother by Jawaharlal Nehru, then the Indian prime minister, when she visited India in 1954.

And I made my wedding dress myself, with a bit of help from my mother and following a round of evening classes with the best haute couture sewing teacher in Vancouver. The dress was a simple, hooded gown made of light ivory Finnish wool and silk, with angel sleeves. I decided to wear no formal headdress but to scatter a few daisies in my hair and to carry a posy of white daisies. I even baked the wedding cake myself, again with the help of my mother. My sister Lin was my maid of honour. For jewellery I had a large silver medallion on a chain, given to me by my parents and made by the same West Vancouver jeweller who made our wedding rings.

The rest of my trousseau came from a designer who had a small shop in West Vancouver. At first he seemed the answer to my prayers—painstaking, friendly and always happy to have another fitting, another minute alteration. Between us, we decided to make the colour scheme of the trousseau centre on three colours: deep royal blue, rust and creamy white. There was, for example, a mid-calf dress in wool crepe, studded with pearls, to be worn with an off-white wool coat with a detachable scarf. I was delighted with all these things, and it was only later that I discovered that this designer was not quite as he seemed.

The moment the marriage was announced, he held a press conference, during which he displayed to journalists the sketches of all my clothes, gave them my measurements and told them personal stories about me, gossipy tidbits about how I came to him like a ragamuffin in jeans and sneakers and how he had guessed the truth at once. This incident should have warned me about what was to come. I had no idea as the PM's wife—the PM's twenty-something wife—what cannon fodder I would become.

What especially upset me, and this may seem small, was the way the designer smugly took all credit for the designs.

My plan was for the evening wedding to be as unfussy as possible. My father had booked a private room at the Capilano Golf Club, ostensibly for the fiftieth-anniversary celebrations of his arrival in Canada, and I had ordered oyster soup, smoked salmon with sour cream and caviar, *filet de boeuf* with Béarnaise sauce, and champagne. There were to be yellow candles set in silver candelabra and, despite the snow, three different arrangements of spring flowers.

We had kept our engagement secret, so I told no one beyond a few members of my immediate family—we did not want the wedding to be mobbed by reporters. To get the marriage licence without alerting anyone, my father drove up to the small town of Squamish, where he found a friendly Mountie who swore to say nothing. Not even Pierre's immediate aides knew the reason for his insistence that the runway at Ottawa be cleared despite the heavy snow and bad forecast.

He had told his aides only that he desperately needed a break and wanted to go out west to ski. Even on the plane to Vancouver, where he began to change into a morning suit, he told his executive assistant, Gordon Gibson, that he had to go to a funeral first. Something of Pierre's sheer determination came across in his absolute refusal to be deflected from making the flight, even in the face of strong warnings from the airport officials. So bad was the blizzard that struck both Ottawa and Montreal—the worst storm in many years—that Pierre's sister, Suzette, and his brother-in-law, Pierre Rouleau, spent five hours trying to cross Montreal and never made it to the wedding. His brother, Tip, and Tip's wife, Andrée, did make it to Ottawa but only after a nightmarish eight-hour drive from their home in the Laurentians. As for Gordon, when he reached the church, he was surprised to see my father standing outside.

"What are you doing here?" he asked. "I'm the father of the bride," my father replied. Gordon was too astonished to speak.

I married Pierre Elliott Trudeau at 5:30 p.m. on March 4, 1971, before thirteen witnesses. Afterwards we had dinner at the golf club in a private dining room. I had spent months preparing for the day. I was very much in love. The country was already feeling a little cooler, sexier and more hip with Pierre at the helm, and now—with his youthful bride at his side—that feeling rose another notch or two. I was a catch for him, as he was for me. As a couple, we were a breath of fresh air.

There was only one thing wrong. Pierre was fifty-one and the prime minister of Canada. I was twenty-two, heedless, not long out of university, a child of the '60s, immersed in the hippie, drug-taking, freedom-seeking culture of the day.

John Diefenbaker, then leader of the Opposition in Parliament, had a good line about the new bride and groom and the age gap between them. I appreciated his humour then and I still do now.

"You can either marry her," he advised Pierre in a rhetorical comment to the press, "or adopt her."

I should, of course, have been warned. Our differences were plain to see; that I chose not to see them said much about my fantasies, my desire to please and my denial of reality. I was not just a product of the '60s; I was, by nature, volatile, oversensitive, quick to take offence, prey to bursts of exuberance and energy soon followed by deep troughs of melancholy.

I was still a very young woman, unsure of who I was and what I wanted to do with my life. I was a romantic with a BA in English; I was scattered and confused, with one trip abroad under my belt and still so, so young. I was a Canadian girl, simple, unsophisticated, nothing special. And maybe that's what Pierre wanted all along, but the expectations of me were huge.

Pierre, on the other hand, was decades older than me, devout, cerebral, rational and clear headed, with a résumé that included schooling from Harvard, the Sorbonne and the London School of Economics and time spent teaching constitutional law at the Université de Montréal. In his backpack travels, he had been to five continents and twenty countries. When I asked him whether he dreamed in English or French, he replied—like a professor patiently explaining a tricky concept to a child—that he dealt only in the abstract.

He was oil, I was water, and we had decided to mix.

What I remember now is that our relationship, until that moment, had been so much fun, so secret, so intense. Now it was about to become public, lonely and extremely scary. After dinner, we were driven up to my parents' ski chalet at Whistler. We were woken next morning at 6:30 a.m. by the telephone. The queen was calling to congratulate Pierre; she had got the time difference wrong. Later came a telegram from the president of the United States, Richard Nixon. Scary, but also the stuff of fairy tales.

My mother had serious misgivings about the marriage, chiefly because of the difference in our ages, though she also worried about how I might fit into Ottawa, with all its constraints. For her part, she had hated living in Ottawa as a politician's wife.

But her nature was to keep her feelings in check and never let them show. My father, the proud, good Liberal, was overjoyed that one of his daughters had married a Liberal prime minister, and he saw how happy I was. (And, of course, when I later left Pierre, my father was crushed and angry and my mother was relieved.)

Since he was very gregarious by nature and found keeping secrets hard, my father had singled out his most discreet friend, who had once worked for the intelligence services, taken him off to a remote beach and spent the evening telling him the news. My sister Jan, on the other hand, had very little discretion. When, just before the wedding, she saw me dressing up in a long white wedding dress, she looked amazed.

"What kind of stupid dress is that?" she asked me.

"My wedding dress," I replied. We had to stop her from rushing straight to the phone, but just the same, when she went off to collect the wedding cake, she stopped at a pay phone and told a reporter friend—who turned up with a photographer at the church. I couldn't really be cross and was later very grateful for the beautiful photographs he took.

The signs of the rifts and the sadnesses to come were all there, on that snowy day in North Vancouver with the crocuses and daffodils just visible. Plain for anyone to see were the oppressive police presence, the end to my independence, the public scrutiny, Pierre's ferocious willpower, the huge gaps in age and character and personality between us.

As March 4, 1971, came and went, all I could think of was the happiness of my life to come. I was so young, so naïve.

CHAPTER 3

HORMONES TO THE RESCUE

"Over my dead body!"

MY RESPONSE TO THE NOTION OF REPLACING THE ORIGINAL WOODEN CLAP-
BOARD ON THE HOUSE AT HARRINGTON LAKE WITH ALUMINUM SIDING, 1972

For a while, we were very happy. We had planned to be away, up
in the mountains in my parents' chalet at Whistler, before Gordon
Gibson made the press announcement. But by the time we set
out from the club, first reports were already circulating. When
we reached my parents' house—where a few friends had gathered
for the immigration-to-Canada "anniversary" celebration—the
circus had begun.

The driveway and entry to my parents' house in North Vancouver were brilliantly lit up by television lights and crammed
with reporters, stamping their feet in the snow and shouting out
their congratulations. I was too happy to care. My siblings and my
parents were suddenly thrust into the limelight and they found
this every bit as overwhelming as I did.

I changed into tweed culottes and a yellow pea jacket and we left for the mountains, pelted with rice, our eyes blinking in the yellow glare of the arc lights set out in a fan all around the drive. We were driven up to the cabin in the back of a police car, Pierre and I sitting in the back holding hands. Next day we skied, and I was overjoyed to discover that in the long months of diligently preparing for marriage, in one field at least I had aced the test. We set off from the top of the mountain and within seconds I was completely outskiing Pierre. He skied the old-fashioned way, using his shoulders to help make turns, whereas I had been taught to keep the upper body quiet, the skis tight together. But the two of us would have been completely mobbed on the slopes had the Mounties not kept people at a distance.

Our wedding, it seemed, had made front-page news in newspapers all over the world. *Time* magazine devoted its cover story to us and described me as a "cross between Doris Day and the Flying Nun." As for Pierre, the magazine remarked, somewhat snidely, that he was a man with a "sharp, almost snobbish sense of the fitness of things" and that he liked to let his own perception of himself show in his dress and "studied presence." His long bachelorhood had apparently been "threatening to become tiresome." I was about to change all that.

We returned to Ottawa from our three-day honeymoon to a tumultuous welcome. We stepped through the glass doors of the

airport into pandemonium: a mélange of reporters, friends, cabinet ministers and their wives, all deeply curious about Pierre's
new bride. I longed to tell them all how happy I was and what a
success I intended to make of my new role.

When we turned into the driveway at 24 Sussex, I observed
that a fresh fall of snow had left the place looking peaceful and
welcoming. We turned into the gates and the guards came to
attention and saluted. Inside the house, a long line of friendly,
smiling people—seven women and one man, Tom MacDonald,
the steward of the household—were waiting to greet me. Verna,
the maid, had arranged flowers in the form of messages all over
the house. "Welcome home, Mrs. Trudeau" was spelled out on a
banner, while roses and carnations decorated the winding stair-
case to the first floor.

During those first months of marriage, we did what we had
always done with what time we had away from Pierre's political
life: we skied, hiked, listened to music together. I often cooked us
Japanese food, which we both loved. We had not had a proper
honeymoon immediately after the wedding, so we made several
trips during the spring and early summer of 1971—scuba diving
in the Caribbean and sailing around Newfoundland on a naval
icebreaker.

I was able to set aside the fact that my French was getting no
better, that the hours and hours of private lessons had achieved
very little. This meant that at the French-speaking dinner parties and receptions we gave and attended, I often understood
almost nothing of what was said, and simply sat smiling and

nodding politely, hoping to make no gaffes. The French teacher we employed to come to 24 Sussex Drive gave up in despair.

The halcyon days didn't last very long. The warmth and sense of approval that had greeted my marriage to Pierre did not survive the long Canadian winter. I was used to living in a family of five girls, constantly dropping in on each other with young friends in an atmosphere of noise and laughter. Pierre himself was a relatively young member of the Liberal Party, but his colleagues and friends were all closer to his age than to mine—some considerably older. In Ottawa, I was far from my family in Vancouver, though my father, who as a retired businessman/politician sat on the boards of different companies (the Bank of Montreal, Alcan, Cominco—ten altogether), often flew east for meetings and I saw a fair bit of him. That was great, and he would later spend time with his grandsons. But I missed my mother and the brawling Sinclairs.

I soon began to feel closed away in a tower. I had no young friends of my own and I certainly didn't fit in with the association of parliamentary wives, who were all older than me. I have a twenty-one-year-old daughter now—just one year shy of my age when I was first ensconced at 24 Sussex with a husband almost thirty years my senior. Were my daughter to come to me as a twenty-two-year-old and seek my blessing to marry a man of fifty-two, I would react with horror. But wild horses couldn't have stopped me then. I simply had no idea what my life would be like, how, like a goldfish, perhaps, I would come to resent my glass bowl.

Pierre would work all day, returning only in the evening to jog through the governor general's estate at 1 Sussex Drive, across the road. The eighty-eight-acre property is a splendid, and uniquely Canadian, place to run—roads and pathways meander through sugar bush, open parkland and many gardens. Foreign dignitaries who visit the governor general are asked to plant a tree; that and other tree-planting campaigns mean that some ten thousand trees now dot the property.

The jog done, Pierre would then eat dinner before returning to his papers. During the few hours we had together, he seemed reluctant to discuss his work, and though I read the newspapers, I was often at a loss as to what filled his days. He abhorred chit-chat, and when we dined out had me phone ahead to find out what time we would be sitting down to eat. Pierre drank very, very little—he would have one sip of wine just to taste the fruit of the vine, and he particularly liked a white dessert wine from Bordeaux called Château d'Yquem. And he loved caviar, which we would eat on toast, along with good Russian vodka poured into tiny vodka cups that Mrs. Michener, the wife of the governor general, had given us. But Pierre refused to waste time standing around drinking before the meal.

The first year of my marriage to Pierre was filled with won-der and delight. I had never been happier, but perhaps I was see-ing my new world through rose-coloured glasses.

I don't wear those glasses anymore. I see now with clarity how opposites and contradictions can coexist in a human being, how a generous man can also be tight fisted, how a husband can say adorable things one minute and hard things the next, how a sweet, sweet husband can turn on his wife. It was all so simple, and all so complicated.

One fine June day Pierre suggested that we drive down to see his mother in Montreal. He said that he wanted to stop on the way to visit his lawyer because there were some papers for me to sign. I asked him what they were for.

"It's to ensure that if anything happened to me and I went bankrupt," he said, "you wouldn't be affected." The papers were waiting for us, and, over a pleasant cup of tea, I signed them. As I handed the pen back, the lawyer said to me, "Well, Margaret, you just signed away your rights to be a very wealthy woman."

His words meant nothing to me. I had no idea how much money Pierre had and I didn't care. Only at his funeral would I fathom the scope of his wealth, measured in the millions of dollars. Looking back, I see that he had an issue—a mental issue, an obsession—with money. It would cause me trouble all during my married life and all the while we parented our children together. Pierre had huge trouble parting with money. It was his Achilles' heel.

When the issue of money came up, I tried to reason with him, and I suppose there were tears. I accepted that this was simply how it was. He didn't like to be criticized or questioned. Pierre was a bit of a bully, and I didn't know about bullying fathers (my father was not one) or bullying brothers (I had none), so I didn't know how to fight back. And I became quite isolated as well; he cut me off from a lot in my life and he kept me to himself—where he wanted me.

But he adored me as the mother of his children because I loved my babies with all my heart and he loved that I loved them.

He could never look away from that through the long years that we had together. What I gained—and in hindsight I can see that the price I paid for this was not too great—was his respect and his enduring love. And had I gone into the courts and demanded "my fair share" of his money, he would have stomped on me so hard.

And yet he was a kind, sweet man. He would say lovely things to me when they were due, and horrible things to me when they were due as well. I was pretty unsophisticated, not like him. We were so different. He would say, "Margaret, for someone with so many needs, you have no avariciousness."

Pride usually stayed my hand.

One day soon after signing the documents, I asked Pierre for some money for something I needed, and he reluctantly went to the safe and took out an enormous pile of Canada Savings Bonds, carefully peeled one off and gave it to me. Pierre never had any money in his pocket and was always borrowing from me or his aides when we went out. I was beginning to notice that he seldom repaid it.

I was noticing other things about Pierre's frugality. He had grown up as the middle child in a household with little money; only when Pierre was about ten did his father—a lawyer and a businessman—make his fortune. Charles-Émile Trudeau did so by acquiring gas stations and later selling them to Imperial Oil. His death, when Pierre was only fifteen, hit the family hard. They were now exceedingly well off, but Pierre's mother, who carried both Scottish and French blood in her veins, was parsimonious by nature and never ceased to instill in him a horror of waste and needless luxury.

When I arrived at 24 Sussex, I found him berating the staff for changing his towels every day, saying that all he needed was one small hand towel, and that it didn't matter how old it was. My father had always trusted us with money, and when Pierre insisted that I write down every single item I bought, including shampoo and stamps, and then show him my list of expenses, I was both astonished and humiliated. Pierre did not want me to have an allowance or a credit card and insisted that I ask him whenever I needed anything.

One of my aunts later gave me a card for Harrods, the luxury department store in London's west end. My "aunt," Lady Molly Sinclair, was married to my "uncle," Sir George Sinclair— two very colourful Scots. George was actually my father's cousin and the two men had studied at Oxford together. Like my father, George was a member of parliament (he sat on the Conservative bench), but before that he was deputy governor of Cyprus and was knighted in 1960 for his service to the colonies.

I used my aunt's gift card to buy things for the family, but Pierre was outraged when he learned of this and forced me to tear the card up. I began to see his meanness as a sort of sickness, and some of my resentment spilled over into arguments. I felt that his attitude was paternalistic and patronizing—never mind hypocritical. For himself, Pierre always bought and wore the best: a gold Rolex watch, a vintage 1960 Mercedes-Benz roadster. But he was downright stingy with me. Perhaps because he had inherited his wealth, he believed himself to be its steward and felt reluctant to use it freely, preferring to pass it on.

The battle royal really started with 24 Sussex. I inherited the house complete with cooks, maids and gardeners, and they had long since developed their own patterns and routines. The new mistress of the household was not only far younger than they were but completely inexperienced in the duties at which they excelled. They had been looking after a single man, a man of austere, modest tastes, for more than three years and there had been relatively little for them to do. And I knew myself to be a perfectionist, determined to turn Pierre's grey existence into something comfortable and homey. As the newspapers had suggested at the time of our wedding, my role was to "throw open the curtains of 24 Sussex Drive, and let the sun shine in."

My first fight was with the cooks. I love cooking, an interest that dates back to my father's starting to work for Lafarge, the Paris-based cement conglomerate, when I was twelve years old. Trips to France, wining and dining in fine restaurants and acquiring books on French cuisine, had dramatically changed our lives. Nutritious but bland meat-and-potato meals gave way to food with both finesse and flavour. And because my sisters and I as children were sous-chefs in my mother's kitchen, we all learned how to prepare these wonderful meals. Julia Child's *Mastering the Art of French Cooking* was my mother's kitchen bible.

But at 24 Sussex, I was immediately made to understand that I was not welcome in the kitchen. The two cooks—both of the plain, old-fashioned English school of cooking—wanted to make steak pies, meatloaf and chocolate chip cookies. Two days after I returned from my honeymoon, I started work on the menus, emboldened by the story that Pierre told me about Golda Meir's recent meal at 24 Sussex. He had carefully explained to Margaret and Rita that everything had to be kosher, but what turned up, calling itself sole au gratin, was a great greasy casserole of fish, complete with its bones, lying in a deep, unappetizing bed of sauce and cream. Another fiasco was when Caribbean leaders came to lunch and were served frogs' legs—no delicacy in that part of the world.

I set to work, went out and bought a dozen cookbooks, and began to make lists and study recipes, comparing ways of cooking fish and sauces and meat to come up with those that sounded most delicious and most nutritious. From here, I drew up a series of healthy, balanced menus. Then, braving the wrath of the cooks, I insisted on being present when a new dish was tried out and refused to order anything for a dinner party until we had tried it several times ourselves. This was a battle. While one cook was pleasant and helpful, the other was—less so.

Verna, the maid who had arranged the flowers in words of welcome, did her best to help and protect me. She was a cheerful, good-hearted woman who had children of her own and treated me just like one of them. "Don't get involved. You are the lady of the house," she advised. But it was impossible for me not to, and it was soon clear that the one cook who was the architect of so much misery had to go. She was a very difficult woman and it took great courage on my part, but go she did. For a while, the other cook was in sole charge, but later I found a French-trained chef called Yannick Vincent who was not only a superb cook but a family man who raised sled dogs and painted in his spare time.

I loathe braggarts, but friends have pointed out to me that I was often ahead of my time (and was teased and mocked for it) on nutritional and other issues. I was a foodie before that term was invented. I insisted that my husband be there for the birth of my children, I breastfed my children, I baked bread and cooked international cuisine, I served raw vegetables at state receptions (which raised eyebrows), I raised the alarm on cigarette smoke and fought the use of pesticides. These stands are now seen as progressive and are taken for granted; they weren't then.

My battle to budge the status quo did not make me any less lonely at old 24 Sussex. On snowy mornings in winter I would put on my boots and stride around the gardens. But then would come a week of blizzards, when an icy wind came roaring up from the Ottawa River, and I was trapped indoors, chafing at the restrictions and nagging away at the staff.

And I was bored. I had few real friends in Ottawa, and though I received several requests to involve myself in charities and foundations, Pierre was reluctant to let me take them on. My role was to be his wife. My isolation was increased by the fact that he had decided that there was no need for me to get involved in politics and had ordered his staff not to pester me or to ask me questions. I was to give no interviews, though I found myself an object of ceaseless curiosity—often of the perfectly friendly sort, but curiosity just the same. Everything I did, wore or said was instantly repeated around town.

I found both managing staff and running a large establishment daunting, as well as the extreme formality that now surrounded me. The transformation from easygoing, peasant-skirted hippie into gracious first lady did not come naturally to me—not least because on almost every occasion I was the youngest person in the room by far. At the tea parties and luncheons for the wives of visiting heads of states or Liberal Party dignitaries, I was continually put down. I found several of the wives of Pierre's colleagues to be ambitious and snide, quick to mock the slightest mistake. Pierre's closest friends were suspicious of my English education, as if it didn't measure up to theirs.

One exception was Nancy Pitfield, wife of Michael Pitfield, the head of the civil service. She was calm and friendly and unflustered, and had a wicked sense of humour. She made me laugh rather than cry. Another great friend I made was Lyn LeBlanc, the wife of Roméo LeBlanc, who was then Pierre's press secretary. Lyn's intelligence and wit kept me from feeling completely out of place.

One political wife who was immensely kind to me from the day I entered 24 Sussex was Norah Willis Michener, wife of the governor general. Somewhat regal in both appearance and style, Mrs. Michener (as I always called her) set out, kindly and firmly, to coach me in the art of protocol. She was a small, elegant, immaculately groomed woman, with a crisp, intelligent voice, and over tea in her house she would coach me on what to do when. "Protocol," she explained, over my protestations, "is learning all the things that you have to do, however much you find them unnatural and trying." If, for example, I found myself sitting next to the wife of a head of state and she lit up a cigarette, I was to do likewise. I abhorred cigarettes and cigarette smoke, but this was my theatre of the absurd. (I did, though, take up smoking when I was forty-eight.)

I am both an optimist by nature and a perfectionist at heart, but I fear I wasn't a very good pupil for Mrs. Michener. I would hurry home from her teas with lists of tips and full of good resolutions. I still have the pamphlet on protocol she gave me. What I could not reconcile myself to was the way that everyone, from policemen to Pierre's colleagues, from the mayor to every visiting dignitary, would pat me on the shoulder, take my arm, press me forward, move me to one side—as if I were a mannequin.

One day I could bear it no longer and said to Pierre, "If one more person touches me, I am going to scream." The word went out: don't touch Mrs. Trudeau. This worked fine with the police and the staff, but the message could not go out to the wider world. There were many times when I just had to grin and bear it.

Even today, I have a strong sense of personal space. I remember one time not long ago at a small northern Ontario airport where I had been picked out at random by security for a patdown. I stayed perfectly still for this procedure, my hands outstretched, but I found it so invasive that the tears were streaming down my face.

The woman in uniform was a nice person, and she asked me, "Are you all right?"

I told her to continue, but then I said, "I find this surprisingly invasive. Usually the only people who get to touch me are those who love me." I just reacted with a Big Brother shudder to this laying on of hands in the name of security.

The other person who showed me great kindness when we sat beside each other at state dinners was Bora Laskin, who served on the Supreme Court for fourteen years, ten of them as chief justice. Because of protocol, at every dinner across the street at Government House—or Rideau Hall, as some call it—I knew exactly where I'd be sitting. On my right would be the wife of the governor general, and on my left would be the chief justice or the dean of the diplomatic corps, representing all the diplomats. The latter was a little man from Haiti; he had been there so long I think he'd been forgotten. He also spoke no English, and I spoke little French.

That left Bora, who was such a beautiful man. I loved him and his wife, Peggy, and their darling daughter, Barb. We all became very good friends. Bora was so educated, such a mentor to me and such an amazing conversationalist, and he really taught me how the parliamentary system works. I had read about all this in books, but he taught me the nuts and bolts at the very moment that Pierre was pushing the Just Society. Pierre respected Bora's deep intelligence—and his humanity. He was another father figure in my life, and I was very sad when he died in 1984.

———————

Given my discomfort with formality, how ironic that some of my best times with Pierre were on formal, official visits. We had more time together, and were able to laugh and also to work as a team, something I was longing to do. Right after we got married, we were invited by Premier Alexei Kosygin to the Soviet Union. At university, I had been immersed in Marx, Lenin and Engels, and I was now fascinated by the thought of observing communism in action. And though the fascination quickly turned to dismay at the sight of Russians I observed on the streets, who looked for the most part pinched and unhappy, the visit provided many delightful moments.

Soon after midnight on a cold May evening, we flew out of Ottawa on a Canadian Armed Forces Boeing 707 for Moscow. This first state visit to the USSR by a Canadian prime minister in office had been widely billed as "a sparkling foray into international diplomacy." In the plane with us were eighteen aides and civil servants, three members of parliament and forty members of the press. We landed to a Soviet honour guard band playing "O Canada." For the next twelve days we made a kind of royal progress—Samarkand one day, Norilsk the next—on a roller coaster of eighteen-hour days. Trudeaumania seemed to have followed us to the Soviet Union: in Norilsk, half the population appeared to be on the streets, standing ten deep along the roads as we swept by in our motorcade.

On one of our first nights, we were taken to see the Bolshoi perform *Swan Lake*. The theatre itself was an extraordinary edifice of gilt and grandeur, though nothing to the feast that followed. Between acts we were shepherded into a dining room with more exquisite and priceless plate, crystal and silver than I had ever seen in my life, with gold dishes, goblets and chandeliers, all sparkling and taken from the collection of the czars. More extraordinary, the ending of the ballet had been altered. The swan did not die.

I asked the unsmiling minister of culture why Tchaikovsky's ballet had been changed. "In Russia," she replied, "our people suffer enough. They do not need to see more suffering when they come to the ballet."

Next day, we went to see some of the Soviet Union's collection of Impressionists, but not for very long. We were rushed past the Matisses and the Renoirs to get to the point of the visit: the "real" art—renderings of sturdy Soviet peasant women working in the fields.

I had never, in all my dreams, imagined such a trip. Whenever we left our palace, the roads were cleared for our cortège. I was both overwhelmed and appalled by the pressure, and Pierre was wonderful, letting me sound off, but only in the bathroom, with the water running, since we had discovered that our every word was monitored. We had checked this out soon after we arrived.

Shutting the bedroom door behind us, I had said loudly and emphatically, "Oh Pierre, what wouldn't I give for an ORANGE! My kingdom for an orange, a fresh orange." Five minutes later there was a knock at the door. Outside stood a waiter, holding a tray; on it sat a banana, an apple, and in the middle, occupying pride of place, an orange. Not a word was said.

What I found most trying were the banquets—and this for a happy reason. Not long before leaving Ottawa we had been at a ball given by the Micheners. Halfway through the evening, the head of the household, Colonel McKinnon, had asked me to dance. He was a wonderful ballroom dancer and we whirled around the room until suddenly I found myself overwhelmed by nausea. A few weeks later, on holiday in the Caribbean, the same queasiness returned. The day my pregnancy was confirmed there was no happier woman in Canada. I've done it! I thought. I have really done it. The doctor, working out my dates on his calendar, looked up and said, laughing, "Your baby is due on Christmas Day." Overnight, none of the things that had been upsetting me seemed to matter anymore. Hormones—mother love—to the rescue.

My pregnancy, however, made the state visit to Russia difficult. When faced with mountains of stodgy food, I felt ill, and I couldn't face a drop of alcohol. The only person who knew that I was pregnant was Mr. Kosygin's daughter, Lyudmila Gvishiani, a gentle, tactful woman of whom I grew very fond. I begged her to keep my pregnancy a secret, for we had decided that if the baby was announced too early the Canadian people would have a long wait. Lyudmila was kind and considerate, and she found a marvellous way of stopping my morning sickness—by carrying a lemon in her bag and giving me slices to suck in the car between our official visits. The day that I was presented with a great Russian speciality to eat—horse—was nearly the end of me.

Because of my pregnancy, Pierre was touchingly protective of me, and the press had been asked to respect my privacy and not crowd round me, though they were not given the reason for this. This led to some resentment, with reporters noting that I was permanently surrounded by "at least half a dozen Russian and Canadian women," most of them "twice my age and thrice my girth." A pity, some reporters remarked, that I didn't mingle more, because they had all been prepared to "embrace" me with something like "fervour." They believed me to be "as unharried by internal turmoil as the bride on a baby-oil ad." Little did they know.

I did try hard to be appreciative and pleasant. I made friends with Premier Kosygin, whom I found to be gentle, considerate and graceful. Obviously a family man, he talked to me for hours on end, in English, about his children and grandchildren, and I was struck by the twinkle in his eyes and by his well-tailored clothes. Leonid Brezhnev, on the other hand, reminded me of faceless civil servants and politicians you see the world over, intent on giving nothing away. The Soviet leader gave the impression of being a hard, rigid, brusque man, like a great sleek and somewhat menacing bear. Neither of us could think of anything beyond banalities to say to each other. (Some years later, Mstislav Rostropovich— the eminent Russian cellist and staunch humans rights advocate, who was a good friend of Pierre's—whispered to me during the interval at a concert, "I luff your husband. I luff Willy Brandt. Brezhnev is a shit.")

When we got married, Pierre had promised me a visit to Newfoundland—part work, part pleasure—and I was delighted when, not long after the trip to Russia, we embarked on a naval icebreaker at Lunenburg, Nova Scotia. I took with me a sack of licorice, having developed an insatiable craving for it. Though not exactly luxurious, the captain's cabin was set aside for us and we were very happy. Unfortunately, much of the coast was shrouded in fog and many Newfoundlanders were disappointed that our boat was often unable to get into the small outports where celebrations were waiting for us.

What we had not reckoned on was the extremely protocol-conscious nature of the French governor of Saint Pierre and Miquelon in the North Atlantic Ocean south of Newfoundland. I had imagined a very informal visit, so I was wearing a cotton shirt and a loose peasant skirt that I had made myself. When we docked, I saw to my horror that the governor's wife was in a Chanel suit with hat and white gloves. We were ushered into a vast, gleaming open limousine to head a motorcade on a tour of the main island. There was just one other problem: once more the shore was hidden by fog. Our host kept describing, without the shadow of a smile, the splendid coastline, beautiful bays and famous rocks. Pierre and I, trying to keep a straight face, peered through the whiteness and admired all that we couldn't see. On occasions like this, with Pierre by my side holding my hand, I felt I could handle anything.

The summer of 1971 was a happy one for me. I forgot my sense of isolation and loneliness. I felt wonderful when I was pregnant; I wasn't alone and suddenly I had a sense of purpose in my life. Being so happy was almost unreal.

I helped renovate 24 Sussex, which was badly run down and furnished in many shades of grey. Though the decorator hired paid very little attention to my suggestions, I did get to create a beautiful sewing room on the top floor, where I would spend hours making clothes. The room had sloping ceilings, four large windows and stunning views over the garden to the river.

Though the decorator preferred beige and brown, I was able to insist on yellow silk for the walls of the master bedroom. It was hard work battling this woman, who was actually not a designer at all but an architect and was very condescending to me. Still, I had the greatest fun. Within months, I could see the house turning into a place I actually wanted to occupy. The living room we painted in soft neutral colours, with thick beige pile carpets, modern sofas and Georgian furniture. We papered the dining room in a Fortuny print, an orange-red Italian cloth, in order to highlight the splendid moulded ceiling, and we borrowed paintings, which we changed every so often, from the National Gallery. I loved the days when I would be taken into the bowels of the art gallery to select great Canadian paintings with the curators. I learned a lot about our art history.

I also turned my attention to the gardens at 24 Sussex, which were attended to by a small army of employees of the National Capital Commission, whose responsibility the gardens were. In their heavy aprons and garden gloves, they would lay out row upon row of tulips—the same size and shape and colour. When the tulips grew tired, the beds would all be stripped and replanted with something else, maybe impatiens—and they, too, were uniform in the same way. You would think the military had taken up gardening.

I convinced the wary staff to inject some randomness and spontaneity into the mix. To one side, a place that got full sun, I created an English garden—the kind I had been used to growing up on the west coast of Canada. I had staff plant lupins, dahlias, delphiniums, daisies, roses, foxgloves and snapdragons.

Meanwhile, Pierre had given me a puppy, and I spent the months of my pregnancy walking for miles as exercise.

After the first months of morning sickness, I felt wonderful. I didn't smoke, I didn't drink and I refused even an aspirin. I converted one of the guest rooms on the second floor at 24 Sussex into a nursery, painting it a robin's-egg blue—homage to my grandmother's house, I now see—and installing an antique rocking chair and table and a patchwork quilt. I also had a plain crib carved and upholstered.

Husbands were not allowed to be present at the birth in those days at the Ottawa Civic Hospital. When I learned of this fact, five months into the pregnancy, I was outraged. There was no way Pierre was not going to be there for the birth of his first-born child. I protested and threatened to have the baby at home. Finally, my doctor sought special permission from the hospital's board of directors, who promptly changed the rules for all fathers-to-be.

Pierre seemed as happy as I was and we spent many idle, contented hours dreaming about our future as parents. Though everyone laughed at me, I knew for certain that the baby would arrive, as forecast, on Christmas Day. Pierre and I worked it all out: we would go to midnight mass on December 24, sleep in on Christmas morning, open our presents, have lunch, then go and have the baby.

And so it turned out. We had breakfast and called the doctor. He told us to go for a walk with the puppy, and when the contractions began to come fast we went to the hospital. Justin's arrival was as uncomplicated as the nine months he had spent inside me.

We gave the baby Pierre as a second name and then James, after my father. Justin was an enchanting child, loving and very bright. He could not have been given a warmer welcome. The people of Canada seemed to rejoice as much as we did over the birth, the first to a serving Canadian prime minister in 102 years. There were announcements on television, telegrams and phone calls, and thousands of letters of congratulation. My collection of hand-knitted sweaters, bonnets, bibs and booties was soon crowding me out of my room. And as soon as it was known that I was breastfeeding Justin, thousands more letters poured in congratulating me for my decision.

We settled into a happy routine. When I felt that the moment had come to wean Justin, I asked one of our staff, Diane Lavergne, a young, good-tempered country girl who had come to us as a maid, to help me with the baby. She adored Justin and would later help me with all the children.

And there were soon more foreign visits and more formal encounters. In June 1973, Indira Gandhi came to Canada on a state visit, and I began to feel that I was growing more efficient at hosting these elaborate, lengthy meals. Mrs. Gandhi and her entourage were staying with the governor general, just across the road from

24 Sussex. I worked really hard to make the official dinner delicious and enjoyable.

Then, not long afterwards, in August, just as our redecoration of 24 Sussex was completed, the queen and Prince Philip arrived, though their visit provided me with a spectacle of celebrity that I did not much care for. I was excited about the visit, as my grandmother had been a passionate monarchist who owned countless books about the royal family.

As part of the royal visit, a stroll through the city had been planned, with the queen and Pierre conversing with crowds on one side while Philip and I walked along the other, the four of us swapping sides from time to time. I have great compassion and admiration for Prince Philip. My hat has always been off to him. Ever the bridesmaid, never the bride, he has his job to do and he does it well. I could never have done it.

Pierre, who as a fervent French Canadian might have been expected not to feel very welcoming towards a British queen, quite admired her. They spoke French together, and he appreciated her intelligence and the way that she, like him, did her homework well.

Because Harrington Lake—the one place where we really got away as a family—was becoming so important for my peace of mind, I felt even more strongly than I did at 24 Sussex about preserving its privacy and intimacy. No one, but no one, was going to be allowed to ruin it for me.

One day, I got a call from the man in charge of keeping up the property. Pierre and I were about to go away for a few weeks, and I was informed that the decision had been taken to modernize the house. As the man put it, the plan was to replace "all this hideous old clapboarding and put on a nice modern smooth facade." I was outraged.

"Over my dead body," I yelled. He was soon back. How about replacing the old wooden window frames with aluminum ones? Again, I refused. Then came a really comic battle, which became something of a *cause célèbre* in Ottawa.

We were up at the lake one day, and I was baking bread in the kitchen when I heard what sounded like the noise of an invading army. I hurried to the window. Down by the lake was a group of men with an enormous machine pumping out insecticide. I dropped the dough and, without pausing to wash my hands, rushed from the house and down the hill, brandishing the rolling pin.

"Stop it!" I shouted as I ran. "Go away." The men looked at me and their mouths dropped open. The foreman ordered the machine to be switched off. I begged, cajoled, threatened. They scowled and muttered. Finally, seeing that I had no intention of backing off, that I would rather lie in the mud and have the insecticide truck run over me, they went away. I was convinced that the insecticides they were using might hurt my baby and damage the ecological balance of the beautiful forest. They were more interested in keeping mosquitoes from eating us alive.

And the day came when I rebelled against the excessive security, the time-consuming requirement of calling down for someone to accompany me each time I wanted to leave the house and then having to wait while something was arranged. Childishly, I decided to fool the guards and slip out on my own—with Justin. One afternoon, I put Justin in his pram and left the house, passing the policemen as they were looking the other way, and set off down the road to visit my friend Nancy Pitfield a few blocks away. But I had been spotted, and when I got home Pierre was furious. He told me that I had to get two things immediately and absolutely straight: that if Justin or I were ever kidnapped, there would be no deal made to get us back; and that, as the prime minister's wife and child, we were extremely vulnerable to terrorists. I was forbidden ever to do such a thing again.

I was then informed that I had to take a course in self-protection. Pierre asked me to get a stuffed animal from the nursery, pretend it was Justin and walk along the road. At a given signal, I was to throw myself down by the curb, lying at a particular angle and cradling the baby in such a way that kidnappers would find it extremely hard to pick us up, while at the same time screaming for help at the top of my voice.

This was a necessary lesson, but one that sent a deep chill through me: I finally understood how vulnerable we were in Pierre's world, how unsafe my children would always be, and that from that day on, wherever I went and whatever I did, there would be large men with earphones and guns not far away. This marked the end of some kind of innocence.

———————

Our vulnerability was further brought home to me by a terrible incident that took place around this time. One day the *Vancouver Sun* ran a full-page article under the headline "The wealthy elite that dominates Vancouver life." Among the names of the top ten leading businessmen, ranked according to the assets of their companies, was my father's. The following week, five young teenagers borrowed a truck and drove down to a deserted beach on the Fraser River to swim. A man with a rifle emerged from the bushes and shot four of them dead; the fifth, a boy, escaped and raised the alarm. When the RCMP arrived, they found the bodies but not the truck, which had vanished.

Some time elapsed before the man was traced. Under questioning, he revealed that he had read the article in the *Vancouver Sun* and had decided to kidnap one of the men mentioned in the article, ask for a ransom, then use the money to tour the world. But to do so he needed a truck, and he had used it to drive around Vancouver casing the ten businessmen's homes. Most turned out to live on busy streets in the Shaughnessy or Kerrisdale neighbourhoods.

My parents, however, lived on a quiet street, shielded by high hedges. When the police arrested him, the man admitted that he had selected my father as his target and that he had planned to kidnap him, keep him tied to a tree in the forest and demand a ransom. Since I was often in Vancouver and had left Justin on occasion with my parents, security police expressed considerable concern for our safety.

Here was a stiff reminder that my position as the prime minister's wife now made everyone in my family vulnerable. My

1. My father (right) served in the Canadian Air Force in the Second World War as a flight lieutenant. They downed this German plane in Tunisia.

2. An early election campaign photo for my dad, who represented the riding of Vancouver North in the House of Commons. From left: Heather, Janet, me, Lin. Betsy would complete our family in 1951.

3. Me at age three, among the tulips on Parliament Hill. We lived in Ottawa for six years; my father was minister of fisheries from 1952 to 1957.

4. The "brawling Sinclairs."
From left: Heather, Janet, Lin, me, Betsy.

5. Juliet to Romeo at the National Library costume ball in Ottawa, on October 31, 1969.

6. Taking Pierre up to Roberts Creek on the ferry to meet my grandmother Rose Bernard, in the summer of 1970, just after we got engaged.

7. On my wedding day with flowers in my hair. I still have the dress.

8. Signing our vows on March 4, 1971, the first time I signed my name as Margaret Trudeau (with Father John Schwinkles, who performed the ceremony).

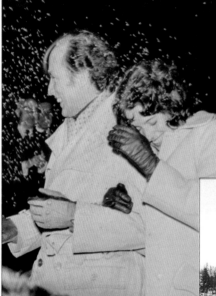

9. Being pelted with rice, leaving my parents' house for our honeymoon.

10. Both athletes, we chose to spend our first day of marriage skiing at Whistler.

11. Dancing with Pierre in a *cabane à sucre* (sugar shack) in a village near Montreal, spring 1971.

12. Justin's first official portrait.

13. Pierre with Justin, then about 18 months.

14. Caught barefoot at the Sparks Street Mall—my first
encounter with a photojournalist (later my friend Peter Bregg).

15. Indira Gandhi,
prime minister of India,
and me, at 24 Sussex Drive.

16. In my role as prime minister's wife, I often hosted luncheons at 24 Sussex.
In this photo, the wives of the prime ministers of the Commonwealth
gather in front of the porch.

17. My first meeting with the queen, in Ottawa. I was so nervous I was wobbling on my high heels; her firm hand held me up as I dipped into my curtsey. From left: Prince Philip, Governor General Right Honourable Daniel Roland Michener, Queen Elizabeth II, Norah Willis Michener, Pierre, me.

18. Was Prince Philip as bored as I was?

19. Visiting the Buddhist Longmen caves, south of Loyang, in autumn 1973. I spent a lot of time with Chou En-lai (far left)—he was wonderful. In this photo, I'm 7 1/2 months pregnant with Sacha, but I found a Chinese jacket-and-pants suit to wear.

20. Visiting a maternity hospital in China, with my entourage.

21. We had the most magnificent day visiting the Great Wall. It was a joy to be a part of history.

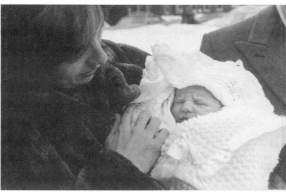

22. Bringing Sacha home from the hospital in December 1973.

23. Zulfikar Ali Bhutto and his wife, Nusrat, in the library at 24 Sussex Drive. Our young sons were constantly being photographed. They soon learned not to fidget!

24. Pierre and I agreed that time outdoors was crucial; we wanted our boys to have a connection with nature. Here we are hiking at Sunshine Mountain in the Canadian Rockies in the spring of 1974.

25. Making a speech on the Toronto Islands at the end of the 1974 election campaign. I did a lot of public speaking during that campaign and discovered that I had a natural talent for it.

26. I've always loved to garden and was proud of the fruit and vegetables we grew at Harrington Lake. Here we are showing off my produce in the summer of 1975.

27. Michel and me.

28. Michel's christening in early December, 1975, in Vancouver. He was about two months old.

29. With my Michel and my grandmother Rose Bernard.

30. Little Sacha with the conductor's hat he always wore. He definitely had his own style.

31. Picking up daddy at the office.

32. With Fidel Castro in Cuba, in January 1976.
Fidel carried Michel everywhere.

33. At the 1976 Olympics in Montreal
with Prince Charles and Prince Andrew.

34. Queen Alia (right) was a close friend.
On our holiday in Jordan, King Hussein (left)
made sure we saw the country.

35. Halloween with the kids (from left: Nadine, the daughter of one of the staff, Justin, Michel and Sacha). Like so many Canadian families, we took our Unicef boxes with us when we went out.

36. Our 1976 family Christmas card, taken at Harrington Lake. My last Christmas card with the family.

family was horrified, for they realized how real the threat was. We now saw the police in a new light—not as a nuisance presence, but as protectors and the first line of defence.

The security wasn't the only thing making me edgy. From the very beginning, I seemed fated to make appalling gaffes that drew attacks and mockery from the press. Sometimes I felt I could get nothing right. Their derision only brought out the rebel in me. When Pierre and I had gotten married, I had had a beautiful dress made—it was studded with pearls and fell to mid-calf—for the reception at which I was presented to the governor general. I was particularly proud of this dress, which I had designed. Years later, when Jimmy Carter was president, we were invited on a state visit to Washington and I decided to wear it to the White House. As it happened, Rosalynn Carter and the other women present that evening all wore floor-length dresses.

The next morning, seeing no newspaper with our breakfast, I asked for one to be sent up to me. After considerable hesitation, a paper was produced. In the newspaper was a long article saying that I had insulted the American public in general and Mrs. Carter in particular by being improperly dressed. Instantly, Rosalynn leapt to my defence. There was no insult of any kind, she announced. On the contrary, my clothes were stylish and totally appropriate. Henceforth, she added, there was to be no discussion or comment about what was worn at White House parties.

The next night it was our turn to host a dinner for the Carters. My reaction to the newspaper criticisms was simply to behave outrageously. I had brought with me something I had bought in Florida—a very short, skin-tight dress made of silver material and covered in sequins. Pierre loved it and approved. As it happened, Elizabeth Taylor was one of our guests, and she had tactfully chosen to come in a short dress.

The press in Canada went to town over my sexy appearance and my seeming disregard for protocol. Pierre and I pored over the papers, which devoted their front pages to this absurd coverage, trying to understand why the political journalists and columnists felt so venomous.

I did have one unexpected ally. The radical American feminist activist Robin Morgan wrote a piece in which she said that she was delighted to observe that women had finally made it out of the society pages and onto the front pages of newspapers, where they rightly belonged. This opinion was, in its own way, just as absurd.

Even with Justin to care for, I felt restless and underemployed. When I first went to live in Ottawa as the prime minister's wife, I was flooded with requests to volunteer with hospitals and other charities, as Maryon Pearson, the wife of Prime Minister Lester B. Pearson, had done before I arrived at 24 Sussex. I could have kept very busy doing that, but Pierre said no. He literally wanted me barefoot, pregnant and in the kitchen. He wanted to care for me and protect me; he knew the world that was out there and I didn't.

In one way, I now see, Pierre was the most tolerant man I have ever met. But his tolerance took the form of altruism aimed at the world. His was an old paradigm that said, "I tolerate you. You're not as good as me, but I tolerate you." His attitude was condescending.

I was then aware that the University of Ottawa had an excellent department of child and developmental psychology and that it had a special focus on children with mental problems. I decided that I would apply to do a master's degree there. Instinct must have warned me that Pierre would not like the idea. I went ahead, applied and only then told him about my plans one night over dinner. He was not only completely opposed to the idea but forbade me even to consider it, saying that I only suggested it because I wanted the company of young men. He was only partly wrong: I did indeed want company, not of young men but of young people, people my own age, with my interests. That these interests included mental illness, which would soon consume my life, was a coincidence, except that clearly I must have had some kind of premonition.

Putting a stop to my plans to study occasioned the first real confrontation between Pierre and me. He thought that by bullying me he could turn me into the perfect wife—in the way that a father might bully a recalcitrant teenager. Unfortunately, Pierre was not my father; he was my husband.

CHAPTER 4

THE UNRAVELLING BEGINS

"I can tell you the secret of my new deal this time.
I have a train, and I have Margaret."

PIERRE ON THE CAMPAIGN TRAIL, 1974

The year before the election, in the spring of 1973, I realized that I was once again pregnant, and the whole question of my pursuing a master's degree in psychology simply went away. But once again, maternal hormones gave me rest and respite from my moods, my highs, my lows.

Just as I had when I carried Justin, I immediately felt content, healthy and full of purpose. We decided to ask Pierre's friend the architect Arthur Erickson to completely alter and redecorate a private sitting room for the family on the second floor, a room that would be absolutely out of bounds to all strangers. When Justin saw it for the first time in the fall of 1973, he was nearly two, and the room was still without furniture. A cheerful, bright, extremely energetic little boy, he looked around the door, burst into shouts of delight and started racing round and round, yelling at the top of his voice, "Freedom! Freedom!" Why that word? I would often sing to him the song that Richie Havens sang so famously at Woodstock in 1969. "Sometimes I feel like a motherless child" is one line, but the one word he sings over and over, the word that set the tone for that rock festival, is *freedom*. And little Justin liked the word. (Later, when the claustrophobia of official life began to suffocate me, I would take off on what Pierre and I called "freedom trips" to places where no one knew I was the PM's wife. He and I laughed at first about those trips. Later still, when it was the suffocation of my marriage that I was fleeing, those freedom trips became the source of great friction.)

From that day in 1973 on, our sitting room was our freedom room. It became my domestic haven and a pleasure to me, with its thick beige carpet, its walls of matching raw silk and its modern Italian furniture—marble tables, leather chairs, sunken stereo and television. In the evenings, Pierre worked here, looking up occasionally to eye the river.

Possibly the most successful and certainly the most unusual trip I made with Pierre was to China in the autumn of 1973. A lot rode on the visit. Although President Nixon had recognized China the previous year, Canada was the first Western nation to visit China officially, and Pierre was anxious to secure an important trade deal. I was seven and a half months pregnant, but my doctor assured me that all would be well. All he insisted on was that I take along someone to help, which was a godsend for it set a precedent, and in the future, especially when ill or pregnant, I was always allowed a companion. I chose Joyce Fairbairn, Pierre's parliamentary assistant. Also on our plane was the deputy minister from the Department of Health and Welfare, Maurice LeClair, who was a doctor himself. The Chinese were so anxious for all to go well that they also had a doctor waiting for me at the airport.

We arrived in Beijing in mid-October. The weather was perfect, warm by day and cool at night. I was amazed by the beauty of the city and the way that it was still like a sprawling country town, with single-storey buildings made of clay, sticks and bamboo poles. Everywhere there was green. When we went south, we found orange blossoms, jasmine trees and cassis flowers.

I had come to China full of prejudices about the terrible health and poverty of the population. My father had travelled there, and he would admonish us as children to finish our dinner because of the starving children in China—"Well, let's send them this meal" was sometimes my unspoken thought. But actually going there as a young woman changed my mind. The people I saw in the streets were not thin and sickly but full of energy and good spirits. I visited a maternity hospital and heard about acupuncture. I asked a woman who had just given birth if acupuncture had dulled the pain of childbirth. I was much amused when she just shook her head. It was agreed that when we returned to Canada we would put the Beijing hospital in touch with the appropriate Canadian medical authorities, for there was as yet no system in China for dealing with Rh incompatibility (when the mother's and baby's blood types are mismatched). At every stop, we were met by a vast, enthusiastic crowd. Little girls with painted faces and tassels in their hands danced for us and sang, "Long live friendship between Canada and China."

Mao was already frail (he would die some three years later), and only Pierre was taken to see him. But I did meet Premier Chou En-lai, who was a handsome, thin, elegant man then in his seventy-sixth year, with warm manners. Chou En-lai, after hearing that I was longing for a meal of Peking duck, laid on a feast of duck in our honour, seating me by his side and speaking to me in excellent English. What astonished me was the freedom of our conversation; we discussed illegitimacy, feminism and the liberation of women.

Chinese women, the premier said to me, were still feudal in their attitudes towards their own femininity, their own bodies and their own sexuality. I immediately felt very awkward about my huge belly, grabbed a napkin and tried to cover my stomach. He laughed.

"No, no, no," he said. "Don't do that. You have come to terms with yourself as a woman. You are proud. Chinese women are trying to become versions of men."

Unlike my first pregnancy, I had a lot of trouble with this second one, particularly towards the end. The baby was lying in an awkward position and I could never seem to get comfortable; I was also far larger than I had been with Justin and could hardly move around the house. As Christmas approached, I became determined to give Justin a wonderful second birthday, one that would be combined with Christmas Day and yet a special day of his own.

We ate Christmas dinner on the 24th, so that the staff could spend the holiday with their families. My mother and my sister Jan were both staying with us. Just as I lifted my glass in response to Pierre's toast, I felt a familiar twinge. Then, soon after, another. Before long the twinges had clearly turned into contractions.

Like many men on Christmas Eve all across Canada, Pierre was upstairs assembling a toy—a plastic motorcycle for Justin. That's all Justin wanted, a motorcycle. So there was Pierre, on the floor, with thirty-six screws and thirty-six washers, assembling this thing. I couldn't waddle up all those stairs, so he would come down occasionally to report on how he was doing and to see how I was doing.

Soon after ten, Pierre appeared to take me to midnight mass. I told him that we would probably need to go to the hospital instead. He laughed: "Trust you, Margaret, to think of having a second baby on Christmas Day. There's no way. Come on, get your coat on, it's false labour."

Wanting to believe him, I struggled to church and then home and into bed. An hour later there was no mistaking what was happening. "Merry Christmas" was all the doctor said when we woke him. "I just knew that this would be bound to happen to you."

Sacha's birth was long and extremely painful. Nevertheless, I agreed with Pierre's thought that the birth should be natural, with no drugs of any kind. Justin had arrived easily, but Sacha was back to front, and much as I pushed, he would not turn round and come out. Pierre insisted that I keep trying. At last, as dawn was breaking, the doctor took charge. He asked Pierre to leave the room and, saying briskly that it was ridiculous that I should suffer like this, told me he would make it easier for me. He meant drugs or an epidural, but I wanted no part of either. I turned my face to the wall and made a heroic effort to relax, though it felt as if my spine was being crushed in a thousand places.

Eventually a rather weary and angry baby emerged. I fell in love with him at once. We decided to call him Sacha, as the diminutive of Alexandre, after Alexander the Great, and Emmanuel, which Pierre insisted on, saying that it meant "God is with us" and that this baby was indeed our second blessing. The British prime minister, Edward Heath, sent us a telegram: "My congratulations on your second Christmas baby."

With two children in just under three years of marriage (I was pregnant for eighteen of the first thirty-four months of my marriage), Pierre and I found that our initially strong physical attraction for one another was being seriously undermined. I seemed to stay broody and preoccupied. Very soon after the birth, I woke up one morning feeling miserable. In hindsight, this was not my first major depression, for I had been strangely low and unhappy after my return from Morocco, which I had blamed on the tremendous culture shock of returning to Canada. But the postpartum depression after Sacha's birth hit me very hard, and it was only many years later that I realized how affected I am by hormonal swings.

Soon I found it impossible to get out of bed and drag myself to the nursery. I possess a deep maternal instinct, and to not feel delight with my own baby in my arms was just bewildering to me. Depression robs you and swallows you down. My one longing was to stay asleep, safe and warm, and not wake up. I wanted neither to play with Justin nor to feed Sacha. I felt frantic when one of them cried, and would burst into tears myself. The world turned quiet and grey and nothing seemed funny anymore. As the days passed and I got no better, and I felt more and more alienated from Pierre, I reflected on the hopelessness and bleakness of my prospects.

My future seemed cast in a dead, colourless light with no possibility of joy. Here I was, alone, with no work of my own, married to a dry, disciplined, rational man old enough to be my father—a man who expected me to bear his children and distract him (looking back, I can see that I was his ultimate distraction) but never to question him or raise issues of my own. When one of my sisters, anxious about my state of mind, said to my mother that I needed clinical help, my mother was furious.

"Certainly not," she said. "There is no way that Margaret can see a psychiatrist. He will only blame me. That's all they do: blame the mother." Her words and attitude spoke volumes about the stigma of mental illness in Canada that persisted well into the 1980s.

South of the border, there were more signs that any candidness about mental illness would not be rewarded. Thomas Eagleton, the Democratic vice-presidential candidate, had been forced to withdraw in 1972 when it was revealed that he had undergone psychiatric treatment, including electroconvulsive therapy.

At last, observing my mounting distress and realizing that something had to be done, Pierre agreed that I should see a psychiatrist, though his rational mind clearly found it all totally bewildering. He drove me to the doctor's office, and I remember sitting in a chair while the doctor spoke kindly and reassuringly about what he called the "baby blues." I look back on this "treatment" and I wonder if a psychiatrist friend of mine was right when she observed that VIP patients get the worst treatment: either impressed or intimidated, the doctor focuses on the celebrity, not the patient.

For Pierre, it was all perfectly simple. My role in life was to be the wife of the prime minister and the mother of his children, and the sooner I could return to my duties, the better for everyone. That there might be some underlying illness, that I might be struggling to cope with a life for which I was totally unfit, was of no interest to him. The question was only how efficiently and how quickly he could make me function well again. I was made to feel as if I were a car that had broken down and had been taken to the garage to be fixed.

Slowly, over the course of several months, the depression lifted. Seeing the state of my melancholy and unhappiness, my gynecologist had given me some Valium, then a very popular tranquilizer. I loved the sense of peace it gave me and I started to function. Only years later did I realize how dangerous a drug it was and how addicted to it I became: leaving the pharmacy, I could hardly wait to get out of the door before opening the bottle and taking one.

But now life once again took on colour and I returned to my duties. The two little boys became the centre of my life, and Pierre and I resumed our loving relationship, though something of our physical passion was still dulled. He had clearly been very worried by my collapse and now listened more attentively to some of my concerns about my life. The staff had all been instructed to try to cheer me up and became more approachable. Pierre himself spent more time with me. The feelings of isolation diminished. One newspaper published a story of us as the "World's Most Glamorous First Family," which struck me as very poignant.

We now settled into a domestic routine. At five to eight, a maid would knock on the door and come in to draw our curtains. If Sacha awoke in the night, the baby monitor would alert us and Pierre would leap out of bed and change his son's diapers and, when I was still breastfeeding Sacha, bring him to me. Pierre may have been the prime minister, but he could not wait to get to his son; it was a source of great joy for him to attend to his infant's needs. The baby would come to me muffled up in many layers of shawls and a wool hat. That was because Pierre was a fresh-air fanatic who insisted on keeping the windows of our bedroom open, no matter the weather or the season. Sometimes, the water in the glass by our bed—from the Constance Cox Brass Bed Company—froze solid. Heavy feather duvets were not the style then as they are now, but in our bedroom the duvet was part of winter survival gear.

By the time I got up, Pierre had already left for the office. Between 9:00 and 10:00 a.m. I read the newspapers, discussed menus and household matters with the staff and planned my day.

Then I telephoned my assistant and together we organized the day's schedule: who needed to be contacted, who invited to this dinner or that reception. Lunch I insisted on making for myself, despite the protestation of the cooks. I would drift into the kitchen around one o'clock, look in the refrigerator and make myself a toasted sandwich of crab, tuna or salmon. During the afternoon, while the babies slept, I wrote thank-you letters, sorted out gifts and dreamed up menus.

We now had a nanny at home, for all the times that I would need to attend an event or a function. This was the early 1970s, the boys were still very small, and whenever I was at home, I looked after them myself. Sometimes, when I was dressing to go some- where, I would hear the nanny making a plan for some wonderful activity that I longed to be sharing in.

If the children and I were at home, the evenings unfolded with military precision. Punctually at 6:45 p.m., Pierre's chauffeur would bring him to the house. "Salut, les enfants!" he would say to the boys and embrace each of them before going straight out jog- ging. Later we added an indoor swimming pool. (Paid for by pri- vate donations, and a great gift to the prime minister's residence, the pool was housed in a separate building, with a tunnel leading to the house.) Pierre would do laps—forty-four, no more, no less. That took about seventeen minutes, and when the children were old enough they would join him in the pool for another fifteen minutes.

The nanny left at 7:00 p.m., so the evening was our time with the children. Justin would sit at the table while we ate, and I often had Sacha on my knee as well, a napkin laid on the top of his bald head so that I wouldn't burn him if I spilled food over him. Dinner was at eight, on the dot.

Obsessively health conscious, Pierre refused to do anything for three-quarters of an hour after a proper meal—the food, he believed, needed time to "digest." So we spent that time listening to music or doing odd light chores. The forty-five minutes up, Pierre returned to work; I was absolutely forbidden to interrupt him unless the circumstance was dire. I was like a faucet, to be turned on and off at will. I learned to adapt, and I had enormous respect for the amount of work he did and for his discipline; I've never met anyone who worked as hard as he did. Often I was with him in the sitting room as he worked, me reading or watching television—with headphones on so the sound would not distract Pierre.

Then we would put the boys to bed, but not before Pierre had read to them—children's stories such as *Goodnight Moon,* a book by Margaret Wise Brown first published in 1947. Dr. Seuss was a favourite, as was Richard Scarry. When the boys got older, Pierre read them Jack London, Alexandre Dumas' *Count of Monte Cristo,* Robert Louis Stevenson's *Treasure Island,* and the Bible. Much later, it was Tolstoy and Dostoevsky and Sartre. The reading over, Pierre and his sons would get down on their knees and pray together at the side of the bed before he tucked them in.

Pierre would then work until midnight, and typically he worked about sixty-two hours a week. Pierre's focus on his work was total. He would wade through his vertical brown boxes—government-issue, leather-bound carrying cases for cabinet documents. When he had gone through the last box, his work was done, but it almost never was.

Now and again, he would break his adherence to his strict weeknight work schedule and we would go out for a Lebanese meal (his preference) or Japanese food (mine), though both cuisines appealed. Insomuch as he wanted to be distracted, it had to be in his time, when he wished it, preferably over dinner or on weekends. That had been fine when we were dating and I saw plays, talked to friends, went to exhibitions—when I could regale him with stories about the outside world.

But now, when I went nowhere and did nothing, there was not much for me to entertain him with, especially on demand. I was very conscious that he wanted me in his life only during prescribed times, and that he abhorred any kind of spontaneity. This confining atmosphere reached its most absurd point when he informed me that we could make love on the weekend, and, if need be, on Tuesdays, but Wednesdays, when there was a cabinet meeting to prepare, were absolutely out of the question.

I felt alone, and most acutely so in a crowd. There was a kind of idolatry at work, a disconnect and distancing by people around me because I was somebody. But I was nobody. My husband was somebody; I was just me. I had come from a family background of friendliness, and I was always amazed at how hard I had to work to fight the assumption that I was stuck up. I was not a fancy pants, and that's why Pierre loved me.

Pierre and I and the babies: we had extraordinary happiness. We were a happy, intimate family—when we were allowed to be. On weekends, when we went up to Harrington Lake, we often went on our own, taking no one with us (excepting, of course, the RCMP officers shadowing us). Just occasionally one of the maids came up for a couple of hours, to lend a hand, but I infinitely preferred the total privacy of being alone. I would often spend whole summers at Harrington Lake, my warm and happy place.

I will always associate that big, rambling wooden house with two things: utter tranquility and the unmistakable fragrances of the countryside. No noise, no cook pestering me with menus, no formalities to follow, no people to please.

The simplicity of the place lay at the heart of its appeal. The house at Harrington Lake was all wood: the walls of wood panelling painted white, the wide pine floors, the kitchen cupboards. The house was set in the middle of a wildlife sanctuary, and was therefore surrounded by forest. Peace was guaranteed, as was privacy. Glass doors separated the living and dining rooms, and in summer we kept them open all the time, accentuating the openness of the place.

I converted the servants' quarters into a children's playroom, which doubled as a sitting room should a nanny or maid come with us. But in the early days, that seldom happened. Here, happily, I was head cook and bottle washer in a kitchen I could finally call my own.

The kitchen at Harrington Lake was huge and old-fashioned, with a butler's pantry—a separate room off the kitchen with a couch. In old Europe, such rooms were used for storage, but some butlers actually slept in them since one of their jobs was to keep the silver under lock and key. The light poured into the kitchen at

Harrington Lake, and the cupboards were ample and fronted in glass. Wood panelling and wainscotting defined the place.

I had had shipped from Vancouver all my old kitchen utensils and pots—brightly coloured cooking equipment that I stored in a work table on wheels, dishes I had bought in Morocco that were displayed on shelves, plus baskets with spices. I introduced natural wood to the kitchen, a butcher's block on a wheeled stainless-steel cart and a huge pine table where we ate all our meals. The result was a kitchen that was warm and open and romantic, and very much my domain.

I would often shop at the local market and buy ingredients for the Japanese and Chinese cuisine that we all loved. The children would help me stuff the wontons with meat and spices at the kitchen table. Around this time, *Chatelaine* magazine asked me to write an article about my life and I chose to describe summers at Harrington Lake and how I grew our own vegetables and shopped and cooked for the family. After the piece was published, several readers wrote letters expressing doubt that the prime minister's wife was cook and gardener.

But it was true. On a patch of land that a local farmer had used to grow turnips for his cows, I had planted a huge organic garden with every kind of fruit and vegetable, from wild strawberry to marrow, from raspberries to corn. We would play a game with the children: the aim was to pick cobs of corn, husk them, race into the kitchen, boil the corn and eat it all in one fell swoop.

We had high chicken-wire fencing installed to protect the garden from marauding racoons and deer. In the fall, I would gather the harvest and freeze it. I once had a photo taken of us perched on a rock with that fall's harvest, and what an impressive sight it was. Elsewhere in North America, a so-called back-to-the-land movement was underway, and gardening was a vital part of that thrust towards self-sufficiency. For me, though, gardening was bred in the bone. My grandmother was a keen gardener, as my mother was, and I followed in their footsteps.

What a contrast Harrington Lake provided for my life in the city. There was something very cloistered, almost claustrophobic about my existence at 24 Sussex, particularly when Pierre was away on a trip and the chef, the only other man in the house, had gone home for the night. We were eight women and two small children, all of us retiring to our cells at night, like in a secluded convent. I sometimes felt more like a mother superior than a prime minister's wife.

Then, in June 1974, the election was called. Only eighteen months had transpired since the last one, but he had had such a close shave that time, with barely a working majority, that Pierre dared not wait any longer. It was now or never: a bid for a real Liberal victory. Pierre's advisers felt that one of his strongest cards with the electorate was that he was now a family man, with concerns about children, eager to build Canada as a country for families.

Initially, he was extremely reluctant to let me accompany him on the campaign trail, but it was clear to me that I did have a role to play, not least in showing him not as a cold and arrogant man—which was how he sometimes came across—but as one with real warmth. We decided that I would go with him on the election tour, taking Sacha with us, as I was still breastfeeding him, together with a nanny to help. Mary Alice Conlon, an ex-nun, was delighted to take the job.

We set out in our campaign plane, the front part curtained off for us, the back full of Pierre's aides and the press. The real daily, not to say hourly, dilemma was how to feed the baby discreetly, so that no one would be shocked. At the start of the campaign, I was extremely modest, retiring behind curtains, into restrooms, empty offices or halls where I could settle down with some degree of privacy. Later I threw all modesty to the winds and became skilled at giving Sacha snacks in improbable places and at odd times. So engrossed, in fact, did I become that I was soon wandering around with him at my breast, answering the telephone, talking, making plans.

There was, however, one major problem. Smoking was then still permitted on planes, and reporters were serious smokers. Separated from them only by a thin curtain, I sat feeding Sacha in wafting smoke, growing more anxious day by day about the effect that this might have on the baby. Finally, with huge misgivings, we agreed that Sacha should stay behind with my family in Vancouver while I continued with Pierre. I hated giving up my baby.

But I was soon caught up in the fever of the campaign. I convinced Pierre to speak from the heart, telling them what he really wanted for the future of all Canadians. I persuaded him that his audiences wanted to know him, hear his enthusiasm and his excitement.

One day, in Humboldt, Saskatchewan, I saw Pierre clutching a folder of papers as he was about to address an outdoor rally.

The audience, picnicking on the grass, were in a relaxed, informal mood. I asked Pierre what the papers were.

"It's our wheat policy," he told me.

"You're going to give them that?" I asked incredulously. "Why?"

"Well," said Pierre, "the media needs it." I took the papers from his hand. "Then give them the speech and you go out there and talk." Pierre walked up onto the stage, put on his glasses and picked up his papers, but just as he began to read, he looked up, put the speech down and began: "My wife says that I must talk to you, not lecture you. So here goes."

I even took to the platform myself, to speak up on Pierre's behalf. In a high school auditorium in British Columbia, I declared that the Pierre I knew was not a politician, but a loving human being "who has taught me in the three years we have been married, and in the few years before that, a lot about loving. Not just loving each other, which is pretty nice, but love for humanity—a tolerance for the individual which reaches out pretty far."

Some people thought he was arrogant, I told them, but the man I knew was not. For me, Pierre was shy and modest and "very, very kind." Some might have thought that this was the politician's wife talking, but I meant every word. The students in the audience cheered. Everywhere we went, the weather was terrible, the warmth of the crowds heartening. In Saskatchewan, when I still had Sacha with me, the crowds had shouted out, "Hurray for the baby!"

Once Pierre freed himself from his written scripts, his whole personality changed, and the people loved it. One of the most

serious issues of the election was the question of spiralling infla-
tion, and Pierre chose to ridicule the Progressive Conservatives'
call for a ninety-day wage and price freeze with his catchphrase
"Zap! You're frozen!" That became the joke of the day.

We did a whistle-stop journey by train across the country, and from time to time I, too, spoke, finding in myself a talent for public speaking and a real taste for performance. What I
knew I could do well was listen to what people were saying and
respond to their needs. I had studied political science, but at
last I was discovering how politics worked, and it was a heady
feeling. We were the golden couple, with golden children, and
everyone seemed to love us. I had made Pierre's aides let me
in on strategy and planning meetings, and I put across views
of my own. It was interesting to be part of the process, to hear
about regional differences and try to match what people seemed
be asking for and what Liberals were prepared to offer. I was
touched and delighted when Pierre announced to a crowd, "I
can tell you the secret of my new deal this time. I have a train,
and I have Margaret."

When election day came, we got a landslide win and Pierre
was back in power. The Liberal Party had won its first majority
government since 1968, largely through the heavy support for
Pierre across Quebec and Ontario.

As Peter C. Newman would write many years later, "Never
would there be a prime minister like that again. He magicked
us. He was the dancing man, sliding down banisters, dodging
picketers, pirouetting behind the Queen's back, vaulting onto
platforms."

The pirouette reference is to a defining photograph taken at a G7 summit conference at Buckingham Palace on May 7, 1977. The photographer Doug Ball caught Pierre spinning a pirouette as an oblivious queen and her entourage walked away. The move was rehearsed and was meant as a silent but playful protest against aristocratic pomp and protocol. Pierre very much liked the queen, but he couldn't abide all the strict rules and regulations that governed any contact with her.

Newman was right. What other Canadian prime minister earned a black belt in judo or went scuba diving? More critically, Newman would also say that there was always a shadow in Pierre's makeup, and that was because he "had an icicle for a heart." Yet that was to misunderstand him. Pierre prided himself on always coming across as rational, in control, governed by reason, but as his behaviour with his own children made clear, he had an exceptionally soft heart.

I had not anticipated the sense of anticlimax that inevitably followed the election of 1974. Pierre returned to his offices, and I to 24 Sussex. Though my reunion with Sacha and Justin was wonderfully happy, I had never been more conscious of the silence and isolation around me. Now that the election was over, I had no further role to play.

I never believed that I had been properly thanked (real thanks would have meant a meaningful job), and I felt I had been used by the Liberal Party machine. Here I was, fresh out of university.

I was adversarial, I knew how to question and I demanded the right to ask what was going on. I had all these tools, and nowhere to use them.

I now returned to my place in the home. The staff were efficient, the security guards polite, the nannies competent. There was nothing for me to do except write letters to all the hundreds of people who had so kindly showered me with gifts for the children. For me, 24 Sussex was rapidly becoming a jail, the jewel in the crown of Canada's penitentiary system, in which I was the sole prisoner. I didn't think the way others around me thought, the way my husband thought, the way the press thought. I didn't fit in. Mine was an unbalanced world. I was angry a lot of the time, and I was furious that this great political maw had chewed on me and then spat me out. One of my psychiatrists would later observe that depression is just suppressed anger—not being able to articulate your feelings and having no voice. That described me to a T.

Pierre himself became the disciplined, hard-working, serious-minded companion he had always been, without the elation and high spirits of the campaign—very willing to have fun, but only at certain times and not very often. When I questioned him about our lives, when I suggested changes, the exchanges had the feel of a teenager giving her father lip. At twenty-five, I wanted more; I know I should not have expected it, but I did. I wanted a role of my own. Only much later, under Mila Mulroney, was the prime minister's wife given some professional status of her own, with her own office and staff.

————————

Then there was a disconcerting episode with Pierre that reminded me all over again about his tightness with money. The owner of the department store Creeds had offered to help me put together a wardrobe for the election campaign. I consulted Pierre, who thought it was an excellent idea, and together we assembled a collection of clothes that were both practical and elegant. I spent about $3,000 and was delighted with the result—not haute couture, but good designers who made me feel at my best.

After we got back to 24 Sussex, the owner sent the bill. I went to Pierre with it. He told me to pay it myself.

"But how can I?" I asked.

"You should have thought of that first," was all he said. Though he did, of course, pay it in the end, I was humiliated and embarrassed. This felt like a slap in the face, particularly when I had tried so hard to help him win the election. He was treating me like a naughty daughter.

In hindsight, the election trail had been a time of elation but the joy was artificial. The invariable depression now followed hard on its heels, only there were no baby blues to account for it. Buffeted by highs and lows and what I now recognize as rocketing brain chemistry, I told Pierre that I needed a holiday. He readily agreed and I took off for Montreal, where I went on a shopping spree—the elation kicking in again—and from there I caught a plane to Paris.

In my distraction I had forgotten to take with me a passport, but I argued my way onto a plane—a measure of the times and the fact that I was the PM's wife. When I reached Paris, I went to our embassy and got myself issued with a new passport.

By now I was flying, my mind out of control, convinced that I hadn't been appreciated and that I was on some sort of mission of discovery. What I now know is that when Sacha was weaned, overnight, at six months of age, my hormones went awry and so did my brain chemistry. For Pierre and me, this was the beginning of the end.

From Paris I went to Crete, where I spent the days wandering, visiting old churches, believing myself to be on a pilgrimage. A state of manic excitement was building up again, and I had managed to convince myself that these wonderful three weeks were time off for good behaviour. I knew that the children would be fine. Pierre was a wonderful father and it was, I argued to myself, his turn. He also had the nanny and staff to help him. I had not, in fact, told him where I was going. He could have traced me if he had really wanted to, but it says much about the state of our relationship then that he didn't choose to find me and I didn't choose to tell him where I was.

That trip opened my eyes. Because I had suddenly been involved with real life, meeting ordinary Canadians all across the country, having a role to play, I felt alive again. I had been a prime minister's wife for four years and a mother for three, but I was still only twenty-six years old: I realized that what I had been missing was my generation, and the songs we played.

Pierre was playing a different song, one that was more staid, more gradual, more stodgy, and never had that song seemed to me so dull as after the excitement of the election campaign. Pierre was widely seen by the rest of the world as a man who did pirouettes. But what he really did was work—hour after hour. Unless it was an official occasion, we never went to the ballet or the theatre. For him, this life was perfect: focus on work and the children. For me, it wasn't enough; I wanted, I needed, to play.

When, three weeks later, I got back to Paris, I called him. He was angry but determined to be pleasant. He reminded me that we were expected in New York, as guests of the Kennedys at the Robert Kennedy celebrity tennis tournament, and he told me to meet him there. Our first encounter was difficult. Pierre was understandably reproachful, but I had nothing coherent to say. Ethel Kennedy kindly sent her maid to iron my dress for the ball in the evening, which was to take place at the fabled Starlight Roof, a nightclub and restaurant in the Waldorf-Astoria in mid-town Manhattan.

Both Pierre and I were soon swept up in the glamour of the occasion, the blinding flashes of the photographers' cameras at the entrance to the building. I was momentarily thrown by it all, but then a strong hand, Teddy Kennedy's hand, reached out and grabbed hold of mine. I spent the whole evening flirting and dancing with him. I found him charming, seductive and warm. He seemed to "get me" and he understood all my confusion about my role as a politician's wife. And because I was in a manic phase, and feeling confident and beautiful, sparkling and vivacious, he was drawn to me.

Teddy introduced me to other people, and I watched how sympathetic and gregarious his manners were. I was swept off my feet. Teddy was then forty-three, recently separated from his wife, Joan, but the death of Mary Jo Kopechne at Chappaquiddick still haunted him, and he had not long before had to cope with his son

Edward's losing a leg to cancer. There was something irresistible about Teddy's humour and attentiveness, but I was not the only woman to see it.

Ted Kennedy seemed much younger than his years, full of fun and good humour, and there was something attractive about his slight air of recklessness. For four years, I had sorely missed the companionship of a large family, and the Kennedys reminded me of my own, able to have open-hearted fun. That's what I was missing, that sense of fun, of being alive, of everything not being so rational, so sensible all the time. Looking back on it, I was manic, desperately in need of help, and should probably have been in hospital. The few moments I spent with Pierre were grim.

"We need to talk about this, but not now" was all he said.

When we got back to 24 Sussex, the atmosphere was rank. On my way upstairs, I grabbed a bottle of vodka, drinking it straight from the bottle as I made my way to the top floor. That evening, Pierre demanded that we talk. My confession was incoherent and desperate. I raved and ranted; Pierre was icy cold and furious.

He accused me of having no self-discipline, of not knowing how to rein in my emotions, of clinging to hippie fantasies. He insisted that I must be in love with someone. I told him that I was—I fancied myself already in love with Teddy Kennedy—that I didn't love him anymore and that I wanted out. Teddy was my means of escape.

Pierre kept saying that he didn't understand, that he assumed I had gone to Europe with another man, that he didn't know what was happening to me. Nor, of course, did I. The words I kept repeating were not so peculiar; what was new was the vehemence and incoherence with which I uttered them. Mania was taking hold. And soon Pierre recognized it. He realized that what I was saying was absurd, that I was simply no longer making sense and that something in me had snapped. I needed a doctor.

CHAPTER 5

DOCTOR, DIAGNOSIS, DENIAL

"Dear Mrs. Trudeau,
I saw you and listened to you . . . on television and I was
deeply moved . . . I also had the impression that . . . you were not talking for
yourself alone but on behalf of all women, . . . all more or less enchained.
Because the moment we love, do we not fall into a sort of slavery?"

A 1974 LETTER FROM THE NOVELIST GABRIELLE ROY, 1909–1983

Clearly, something very wrong had been building up in me for a long time. That it was visible to others, too, was brought home to me when Pierre called me to his office one day to tell me that he had received a letter from Stuart Smith, the head of the Ontario Liberal Party—who happened also to be both a friend and a psychiatrist.

In the letter, Dr. Smith said that he had observed me for some time, how my moods swung about so violently. He feared that I might be manic depressive, and if so, there were treatments to help me. I remember feeling a mixture of amusement and relief: someone, at last, was worried about me. But I also felt that the whole thing was absurd. I wasn't going up and down, rising to highs and sinking to lows: my life was the problem—isolated and with nothing to do one minute, the next dancing with Prince Charles or flirting with Teddy Kennedy. Who, I reasoned, wouldn't have wild fluctuations in moods?

We arranged that I should meet Dr. Smith at the house of Ruth Macdonald, whose husband, Donald, was in Pierre's cabinet (he was then government leader in the House of Commons). On this beautiful day, we sat out in the backyard and talked. The fact that the location had to be somewhere very private, away from all public gaze, says much about the way that mental problems of all kinds were viewed in the 1970s: for the wife of Canada's prime minister to be suffering from depression and mania was not something that could be tolerated.

The trouble was this: I am an actress, and when I have to, I perform. That day, I shone. I gave the best performance of my life. I was graceful, dignified, extremely rational. I talked about the pressures I was living under and the way I was coping with them. Dr. Smith said little, but went away with no further suggestions and no prescription for any medicine. What I would learn only painfully and much later was that denial is simply one stage in the bipolar process, the one that comes before the bargaining begins. I was simply not yet ready to accept the diagnosis.

But by the the fall of 1974, I knew instinctively that I needed help, even if I didn't know what I needed it for. I was miserable, confused, hearing myself say things that made no sense, even to me, and blaming all those around me for my state of mind.

Even Pierre now understood that something in my mind was deeply troubled. I needed proper help. There was no alternative to a hospital.

To avoid all publicity, we decided that I would go back to Montreal and that a girlfriend would take me to the Royal Victoria Hospital. This part was all completely surreal. We had lunch at the Ritz on the way, as if this were just one more jolly day of going to Montreal for shopping with friends, which I did quite often. We ate and chatted, and then she took me over to the hospital. On the surface, I appeared bubbly and confident; underneath, I was absolutely terrified.

I was as skinny as a twelve-year-old boy. My breasts had disappeared. I couldn't sleep, I was never hungry and I couldn't swallow food. Nor could I stop talking. Everything was racing. All I could think was that I wanted help, that I desperately wanted to be back inside myself and not in the mind of this wild and terrifying stranger.

At this stage no one was yet talking about manic depression, as bipolar illness was then called. Doctors in the hospital talked to me, then put me on some kind of medication that quickly numbed my mind. My tongue seemed to swell up inside my mouth, one side of which began to droop alarmingly. Part of my terror was a feeling of being totally alone. I knew almost no one in Montreal and there was nobody with me, no member of my family, no friends. I was alone in every way. The drugs I was given seemed to take away all my ability to express myself. I don't remember what medicine I was given, but this reaction of numbness filled me with horror. I felt completely blank, empty, sedated.

To avoid publicity, I was put not in a psychiatric ward but in an executive suite for men with prostate problems or erectile dysfunction. Only in hindsight can I appreciate the darkly comic side of my situation; there was nothing funny about it then. I had a grey room, a sort of suite, with a little kitchen, and here I felt even more isolated. I was twenty-six years old and felt utterly forsaken.

I didn't know what was happening to me, and no one told me. Had I been put into a psychiatric ward, I probably would have had a better chance of accepting the treatment. I would have seen that there were others in precisely the same condition, with the same problems, and that I was not the only person in the world to possess this apparently rare form of madness. That Pierre, his advisers and the doctors felt this need to protect us all from exposure says much about the way that mental illness was regarded in the 1970s. Looking back, I see a connection between what happened to me and a movie that came out one year later—*One Flew over the Cuckoo's Nest*, which would win five Academy Awards.

The novel that the film was based on was written by American author Ken Kesey, who had worked for a time as an orderly in a California mental health facility. The title derives from an old nursery rhyme:

Vintery, mintery, cutery, corn,
Apple seed and apple thorn,
Wire, briar, limber lock
Three geese in a flock

One flew East
One flew West
And one flew over the cuckoo's nest.

In the movie, a Native American who goes by the name of "Chief" reveals that his grandmother sang this song to him when he was a child. A mental asylum is coyly referred to as a "cuckoo's nest," and a mentally unstable person is sometimes referred to as "cuckoo." To fly over a cuckoo's nest is to go too far, to land yourself in trouble. And that I was in.

After I had been in hospital a few days, Pierre and the two boys came down to Montreal by helicopter to take me out for the day. Justin was now three and a half, Sacha one and a half: for them the day was a wonderful adventure, and seeing them again lifted my spirits. Even at my lowest, I found them comforting and loving, and with them I was at my best. We went off to see an old girlfriend of Pierre's. Though I was frail and vulnerable and confused, I still had the sense to know that visiting one of the great loves of Pierre's life was maybe not the wisest choice. This was a bad decision on his part. His idea was that her place was a safe place.

On the other hand, going there got me out of the hospital for the day. The girlfriend was obviously shocked by my appearance. Even Pierre thought I was completely altered; my voice sounded strange and I didn't really know what I was doing. I stumbled vacantly around, quiet and isolated.

As the days in hospital passed and I seemed to make little progress, Pierre decided that I would do better at home. He came to rescue me and took me back to Ottawa.

All I could think—dimly, through the haze of medication—was that the isolation of 24 Sussex was my real problem. I was isolated from my family, from Pierre. Some of this sense of isolation was, of course, real. Pierre was a very private man. He didn't really have friends, and he certainly didn't see the need for socialization. In any case, the social relationships open to a prime minister are for the most part extremely formal. Pierre would say, "What does it matter what kind of people they are, intelligent or inane? The fact is that you wouldn't get the chance to find out. So why spend time meeting them?"

Before leaving hospital, it was decided that I should hold a small press conference. Keeping a lid on circumstances had failed; there had been endless speculation in the newspapers about what was wrong with me. As I stood up I felt like a terrified deer in the headlights. I explained that I had been ill, that I had been suffering from a mild form of mental illness, but that I was now well on the road to total recovery.

It says much about the climate of public opinion in the 1970s that the reaction was one of slight mockery and derision, even if, in the pages of the *Toronto Star*, a psychiatrist praised me warmly for having been so honest. Jokes were made about the prime minister's mad wife. The stigma surrounding any kind of mental illness was at its height, and I felt reluctant afterwards ever to be so candid again. Only much later would I learn that the dangerous candour of which I was accused is, in fact, a crucial first stage in getting help.

I had left the hospital without a clear understanding of what was wrong with me. Pierre thought it best to bring me home and have me well fed by the staff and let me sleep and hold my babies and for him to take care of me. He was at least partly right. Because that was exactly what I needed. I had to choose to become well, choose not to be sick, and also to fight back myself, though without a good psychiatrist and proper medication it was a lot to ask.

But I did fight back; and gradually I did get a bit better. Somewhere deep inside me I must instinctively have known that choosing to fight was an option. In our new family room at the top of the house at 24 Sussex, with a little kitchen nearby, I was able to prepare meals for the boys, which made me feel more ordinary, more normal.

I was also very lucky in having two friends who now did all they could to help me. One was Nancy Pitfield, who had been at my side so often before and who now listened to me talk and lightened my mood whenever she could. Nancy had been a psychiatric nurse and had a good idea of what I had been through. I spent many afternoons with the boys at her house, which seemed to have all the coziness and safety and lack of pretentiousness so lacking in my own. And there was Heather Gillin, another good friend, the wife of a local businessman. Heather, who lived nearby and who had children of her own much the same age, became a sort of second mother to the boys.

I also received a wonderful letter, from a complete stranger, which made me feel that I had not made a mistake in speaking out about my depression. It came from the novelist Gabrielle Roy.

Dear Mrs. Trudeau,

I saw you and listened to you . . . on television and I was deeply moved by the note of sincerity that rang through all your comments. Television has not accustomed us to such frank and soul-baring remarks.

I also had the impression that you were not talking for yourself alone but on behalf of all women, that you were speaking for each one of us, all more or less enchained. Because the moment we love, do we not fall into a sort of slavery? Doubtless men do, too—who is truly free? but less perhaps than women for whom love is the centre of life and who are thus the most vulnerable of creatures.

I was far from the perfect wife that Pierre had imagined and, as with all who suffer from depression, my desire for sexual relations had vanished. My goal—to get back to my husband, to be a responsive and loving wife and a good mother, not someone filled with sadness, despondency and despair alternating with flights of euphoria and craziness—seemed increasingly inconceivable.

And what neither Pierre nor I seemed able or willing to address was the question of the man I believed myself to be in love with—Teddy Kennedy. I felt that I had fallen so much in love with an extraordinary man. Looking back, I think I did love him. The physical attraction was such a small part of the connection. Ted Kennedy was a compassionate man who really wanted to help me, and I fondly remember his support and reassurance. When he died in August of 2009, I felt a great sadness for him and for his family. Like me, he had done things he regretted and that caused grief and heartache, but he was also a kind man who became one of the great advocates for health care and the patriarch of that huge Kennedy clan.

Since meeting in New York, we had not seen each other again, but we did have long telephone conversations. While I was in hospital, he encouraged me to get psychiatric care. He would phone me and tell me that he was thinking of me. In my mania and confusion, I saw him as a knight in shining armour who was going to save me. Here he was reaching out to me through the universe, so to speak, on an unlisted telephone number. Only many years later would I realize how much I had lost all sense of proportion, all idea of boundaries, that I was merely reaching out to the wrong people in the wrong places, mistaking flattery for love, sexual attraction for commitment.

When I got back from the hospital to 24 Sussex, I found Pierre and the entire household walking on eggshells. Nobody knew what to do with mad Mommy. The children, of course, were very loving, and I was intensely relieved to discover that however peculiar I felt, something in me continued to function as a good, warm, consistent mother. My private pain, my despair, my madness, none of these things seemed to come out in my mothering. Pierre and I tacitly agreed never to fight in front of them, and he begged me to try not to appear too agitated when they were around. They were just little boys, but they were aware of the tension between us. We all resumed our weekends at Harrington Lake, our boating. Pierre was talking of teaching Justin, who would soon turn five, to ski.

Pierre had long since shown himself to be a totally committed father, and there was nothing he didn't do or take on for the boys. He would play "monster" with them in the dark, hiding somewhere in the house and waiting for one of the boys to find him, then springing out to chase them to bed. He would put a flashlight under his chin, fling out his arms and grow tall. The boys were frightened and charmed in the same breath. I sometimes felt jealous, as if the boys had usurped my place in my husband's heart, and at my most bitter I used to think that I had given Pierre what he wanted and that I was now dispensable. But even in the pit of my despair, I could see how happy they made him, and how much they loved him.

In his memoirs, published much later, in 1993, Pierre would write about fatherhood: "I didn't know about this marvellous feeling. It makes you eternally grateful for the miracle of life and for the mother that bore those children." As a father, he was strict but fair; he never raised his voice, and the idea of all physical punishment was abhorrent to him. He wanted his children to read the classics, not watch television, and he wanted them to be able to talk to him about everything, which they did. Inevitably, I felt at times as if I were simply not good enough for him.

———————

Nothing, in fact, had really changed, and I kept looking for a way out. When you are mentally ill, escape is on your mind most of the time. To escape the thoughts in your mind, to escape the people, the way they look at you, to escape the unhappiness of your life. For me, always, the easiest way to escape was with marijuana. What I did not know then was that marijuana, in some people, can trigger mania, and mania, with its rushes of glorious energy and its feelings of power and success, was exactly what I yearned for. A second way was alcohol. A third—extremely common, as I would later discover—was to blame other people (husband, nanny, press, police) for all that was happening to me and not to take any responsibility for it myself (this couldn't possibly be my fault). I did a bit of all three: drinking too much, occasionally smoking too much, and certainly devoting a lot of energy to blaming Pierre.

I blamed him for being such an inadequate husband, for not being there for me, for not understanding me, for being too important a man to find the time to worry about his wife. All that was not true and profoundly unfair. Pierre was deeply concerned and worried, and my woes took years off his life.

One of the worst things, looking back on it, was my lack of real anger. Since my parents had never shown anger with each other, I had no model for expressing myself when I was furious. Had I known how to voice my anger, rather than stifle it, Pierre and I might between us have handled the situation better. There were all sorts of things that I could have been angry about, not least the hostile way the press treated me. And when, later, I learned about anger, the long litany of hurt had already unfolded and our relationship was beyond repair.

To make things worse, after I left hospital, I continued to talk to Teddy Kennedy on the phone. Pierre found this unacceptable; he viewed these long talks as a form of emotional infidelity. The romance escalated, and Pierre was furious and heartbroken at the thought of losing me. I felt so desperate that I told Pierre the marriage was over. Even during the worst of my sickness, I knew there was no future with Teddy; this was the mania talking. He and I fantasized about running away together but then laughed off that possibility as nothing more than a foolish dream.

Pierre was extremely angry that I had given my heart to Ted Kennedy. "Why not a prince of a man?" he remonstrated. "Why someone who cheated on his Harvard exams?"

I look back on our romance and of course I question my own judgment. The prime minister's wife having an affair with an American senator? What was I thinking? But the same could be said of him—what was he thinking?

When, years later, Ted Kennedy visited Ottawa as part of a tour to investigate Canadian medical facilities and learn more about how universal health care works, staff in the prime minister's office were baffled when Pierre refused to grant him even a five-minute courtesy chat. Again, I have to wonder about Ted's judgment. Did he think that Pierre had somehow forgotten or forgiven the transgression? Did he really believe that Pierre would give him the time of day?

With Pierre I just went back to ranting and goading, rising to intolerable highs and sinking into equally intolerable lows until eventually Pierre began to hit back, as any normal man would. And this in turn drove me to such despair that one day I seized a knife and rushed out into the snow. Whether I would have done anything to myself I don't know, but Pierre came after me. This was all absurdly dramatic and intense and inappropriate, and all I could wonder, years later, was why no one had known to help me at the time. Looking back, I see clearly that I bore responsibility for my own illness, but there's a lesson here, too, for those close to me. Knowing my frailties, why did they not intervene sooner? Why did they wait?

However, that sad and desperate day marked a turning point. I was now seen—by Pierre and probably by the staff as well—as a totally deranged, mentally ill person. I felt hopeless, defeated. I capitulated. Pierre said he would put behind him everything that had happened providing I gave up all this nonsense about another man, became a good wife and mother again, and took my place at his side in a proper fashion, with all the Catholic guilt and confession and redemption that my disgrace involved. But he wouldn't love me again. He didn't say as much, but I knew that he couldn't, or wouldn't, ever again. Something had broken. We limped on.

Our official life continued. Of all the state visits I paid, the one to France in the autumn of 1974 was the most difficult. My precarious mental state was a great burden, as was the fact that the formality and protocol were more extreme than for any other occasion of its kind. The contradictions building up all around me were almost impossible to bear.

This state visit to France was the first since Charles de Gaulle had made his "Vive le Québec libre" speech in Montreal during Expo '67, which had effectively cut off relations between France and Canada for almost a decade. On this state visit, we simply had to do not just well but superbly. We had to open the door of good relations again, yet at the same time assert that France could not treat Quebec as a separate, independent country.

My first function in Paris without Pierre—he had been invited to an official, men-only lunch—was a reception given by Bernadette Chirac, the prime minister's wife, a chic woman with nice, soft eyes. The food was superb. The guests were all women, the wives of cabinet ministers, and all some twenty-five years older than I was. There is no doubt that the French can be the rudest, most arrogant and condescending people in the world, and here they were in their element.

Outwardly, all was civility and charm, but not one missed a chance of making me feel illiterate, ill informed and gauche. I had taken with me Marie-Hélène Fox, Pierre's political secretary, a woman who was pursuing a serious professional life. The conversation soon came round to the selfishness of career women and their foolishness in not marrying and having children. I struggled to support Marie-Hélène, but with my lamentable French and my own position as a woman raising a family, there was not a great deal I could do.

I had one afternoon off and planned to spend it at a fashion show. Yves Saint Laurent was changing his neat, tailored look and presenting wild peasant costumes in his new collection. Madame Chirac, hearing of my plan, pressed me to go with her to a more conservative, haute couture fashion parade. I demurred.

Finally, she said she would come with me to the Saint Laurent show. Madame Chirac voiced the opinion that the clothes were hideous. I, on the other hand, loved the collection; Saint Laurent was my favourite designer, and he was freeing women, putting them in pantsuits and tuxedos.

For the French state visit, clothes were even more important to me than for the many other formal occasions I attended: if I felt correctly dressed, my confidence got a boost and, I felt, enabled me to cope. If my shoes were scuffed, I felt distracted and self-conscious. I had asked to take a maid with me to Paris but the expense had been deemed extravagant.

On the night of our grandest dinner, held at the Élysée Palace—the official residence of the president of France—I planned to wear an ultra-feminine pink silk organdy Valentino dress with painted peonies. I kept it for the most important occasions. To show it off at its best, I decided to have my hair done by Alexandre, whose salon was one of the best in Paris, and who kept it open especially for me. His makeup man spent three-quarters of an hour on my lips alone.

The result, however, was a disaster. He had removed all my curls and slashed my hair into what was known as the "mandarin look," all severe straight lines and bangs. With the heavy makeup and the bright red lipstick, I looked like Cleopatra. I came out in tears.

This was not the look to go with a pretty and pink, elegant and décolleté dress. Looking in the mirror, I began to scrub off some of the layers of lipstick, but there was little that I could do about my eyes, which had vanished under more coats of greens and greys than even Elizabeth Taylor wore. In despair, I decided not to wear the Valentino but chose instead a long black evening skirt with a white silk blouse. No sooner did I step inside the Élysée than I realized that I, alone of all the women present, was not wearing haute couture.

The evening started badly and rapidly proceeded to get worse. On one side I had President Valéry Giscard d'Estaing, who wanted to talk to me about hippies and marijuana, as if I were a species from another planet. On the other, Prime Minister Jacques Chirac, hearing the word "marijuana," weighed in with a story about how his own nephew had started smoking it, and how he had been threatened with expulsion from the family.

"We just made it perfectly clear to him," said the prime minister, "that if he carried on with it, he would be disowned, his money stopped, and that he would never be allowed in the house again."

I looked at him. "And has he ever smoked marijuana again?"

Monsieur Chirac looked incredulous. "Certainly not."

The visit, from my vantage anyway, continued its perilous descent. Next day, Giscard d'Estaing's wife, Anne-Aymone, and a group of ladies had invited me to come with them to the Louvre to look at the paintings. My French was still atrocious, and we moved from painting to painting while I tried to summon up suitable phrases of appreciation. Finally I could stand it no longer. I had had all that I could endure. I passed out cold on the floor, my fall broken only by the wife of the French ambassador to Canada, Madame Viot, who was my one ally in all this.

Fainting was an unconscious escape that I had already taken on various occasions, especially when pregnant or very anxious. I had once fainted in Charlottetown and slipped off a chair on a podium when the queen was halfway through an address. President Josip Tito came on a state visit to Canada and I almost fainted then. After the official welcome toast by the governor general, the men got out their cigars and started puffing, and I had to stumble out of the room before I fell over.

Dressing up—as the state visit to France made clear—was not without its pitfalls, but its pleasures were undeniable. Fancy costumes had the potential to take me into a magical fantasy world, a reward for all the boredom and stuffiness of the long social events. I knew I could make myself look good, and that once I threw myself into the part I could transform myself from a girl who usually wore jeans and sneakers into a sophisticated woman. During the pomp and grandeur of these state visits I sometimes pretended to myself that I was in a fairy tale. What made the fantasy easier was the fact that each time Pierre put on his black tie or his tails, I fell in love with him all over again. On these occasions, we were on show, the flower child and the world's most glamorous politician. We acted the part.

Sometimes, the show was of the one-woman kind. One evening when Pierre was away, I had been invited to a dinner party—a rare occasion given Pierre's feelings about parties. He didn't go, so neither did I. But from the first moment, this one was surprisingly fun. There were drinks before dinner, and several different wines with each course. After dinner, I had a glass of Cointreau. Suddenly, I felt extremely dizzy. I made my way uncertainly to the bathroom, was violently sick and collapsed. One guest at dinner was a doctor, and he realized that I was not only drunk but totally dehydrated. I was taken to hospital and given intravenous liquids. Next morning I woke up completely recovered but extremely embarrassed. When I saw the doctor in the emergency room, he reassured me: "Even people with psychological problems sometimes get drunk and have hangovers." I would never again mix my drinks so freely.

As for the psychological problems, things were about to get worse before they got better.

CHAPTER 6

REASON OVER PASSION,
OR PASSION OVER REASON?

"Margaret Trudeau did it again."

THE GLOBE AND MAIL, AFTER I BROKE INTO SONG
DURING A FORMAL DINNER IN VENEZUELA, JANUARY 1976

I was still many years away from understanding the delicate brain chemistry that ruled me, but experience had taught me one thing: I always came back to life when I was pregnant.

During Christmas of 1974, Pierre and I went down to Jamaica for a holiday. He was still angry about my romance with Ted Kennedy, but I worked my charms, managed to seduce my husband and got pregnant. Pierre was not happy to learn I was carrying another child; he didn't think it was the right thing for such an unhappy couple. But the moment I was pregnant I began to feel much, much better. The loneliness, the isolation, the feelings of inadequacy and lack of purpose were all replaced by that complex and mysterious series of hormonal surges—estrogen, progesterone, insulin, relaxin, oxytocin, prolactin. Whatever the cocktail and however it works, I know only that I felt human once again.

Though this was a holiday, Pierre had brought work with him, of course. But with two days left in the holiday, he closed his last brown box of documents.

"I have no more work," he announced. That had never happened. Today, computers and hand-held communication devices mean that the supply of work is endless, but not then. We were in a somewhat remote location and when Pierre closed that last box, he had nothing to read.

"Margaret, what are you reading?" he asked me. Pierre never read fiction unless it was a classic. I rather sheepishly showed him what I had been reading: Erica Jong's feminist novel *Fear of Flying*, about a married woman who takes a trip to Europe with her husband and decides to act on her sexual fantasies with a new lover and perfect strangers.

Pierre could not believe what he was reading. We had lively dinner-table discussions while he was reading that book—one of the first really strong feminist novels, and published just the year before, with millions of readers. Here was a new way of thinking, and Pierre's sense of justice and fairness accepted that women are, in fact, equal to men on so many levels, when it had always been assumed that we were less capable. He knew the truth in his heart of hearts, and yet it was very hard for him to allow that freedom to me or to any women in his life. He was a deeply religious man who totally honoured his Madonna and his mother. She gave him very strict ideas on what was proper and what was formal and possible.

Pierre's mother also gave him freedom, but he lived with her until he became prime minister, so he had a long history of living with a dominant woman. He picked me when I was nineteen: I carried Scottish blood, I was simple, I gardened, I made my own clothes, I was thrifty, I was a good girl. But more importantly, what he was looking for was a wife and a mother for his children. He wanted the whole package. Pierre also thought that because I was so young, he could mould me into the kind of person he wanted me to be. The wife and mother he got; the clay model suitable for sculpting, no.

Just for a while, it was like the old days. I began to function better. In the spring of 1975, I gave my first public speech, to the wives of the Commonwealth leaders at the Commonwealth Conference in Jamaica. I had decided to talk about the place of wives in politics and to touch on my own feelings about getting out of the kitchen and into work, and about how I didn't wish to end up being a rose on my husband's lapel. There were about a hundred people present and I was terrified. Pierre had helped me with the speech. I made them laugh when I quoted a sentence from an earlier edition of Dr. Benjamin Spock's *Common Sense Book of Baby and Child Care,* first published in 1946 and for decades the mother's bible. The sentence, which Dr. Spock removed from subsequent editions, read: "Biologically and temperamentally, I believe women were made to be concerned first and foremost with child care, husband care and home care." Pierre obviously didn't agree. He would change the kids' diapers as readily as I or the nanny would.

Pierre was delighted once the baby, a third boy, was born,

on October 2, 1975. We knew that we would both love the baby forever. Unlike the other two, this one was born in a rush. I had warned the doctors and nurses at the hospital that I intended to do a primal scream. I had read in books about the theory of primal screaming—how the releasing of air, the holler of triumph, was supposed to diminish the pain. But I had forgotten to tell the RCMP officer, Henry Kennedy, who was sitting outside my room and who had become something of a friend. Henry's own wife was expecting her first baby, and the sound of my appalling scream just about frightened him to death.

"Are you all right?" he asked me when I was wheeled out of the delivery room. So loud was my scream that he had thought I was dying.

At first, Pierre and I had trouble choosing a name for the new baby. Then the Italian film director Sergio Leone, who was an old friend of Pierre's, came to dinner, and when I brought the new baby downstairs to feed, Sergio suggested that we should give him the name of one of the angels, since he had been born on the feast day of the angels. Neither Rafael nor Gabriel much appealed to us, but Michael was a definite possibility.

We were just considering it when a few days later I was with Mamie Angus, a friend of Russian descent. While cuddling the baby, she called him "Micha." I instantly rang Pierre, but his aide informed me he was in a cabinet meeting. "Call him to the phone," I said, something I rarely did. Pierre agreed it was the perfect solution. So Micha he became (though formally, his name was Michel), with Charles-Émile as a second name, after Pierre's father.

We had several good times in the months following Michel's

birth. Some years earlier, King Hussein and his wife, Queen Alia, had invited us to their summer house in Jordan. A stretch of highway near the palace had just been completed but not yet opened, and after dinner the king took us to the garage and told Pierre to choose his own Harley-Davidson. Queen Alia climbed onto her pink Vespa and I was put on the back of King Hussein's own Harley, and off we went into the starry night. I had never been on a motorcycle before and am normally terrified of such things, but it was extremely exhilarating. I clung to King Hussein's back and we raced, Pierre doing about two hundred kilometres an hour through the silent darkness, laughing and calling out to each other. During this visit, Alia and I became friends, and once we returned to Canada, we often talked on the phone. She was troubled too, but she was stronger than me.

While I was pregnant with Michel, they had come on a state visit and presented me with professional camera equipment (a Nikon camera and lenses, several thousand dollars' worth) as a birthday gift. This was just what I needed. I went to a local college and took a course in photography and darkroom techniques. I discovered that by looking through the lens I could find another escape path, another way of looking at the world.

I could zoom in on the specific details of beautiful things and become an eyewitness to events. That act of generosity on the part of King Hussein and Queen Alia was a turning point in my life. I cannot remember getting a gift that pleased me more, because the camera opened doors I thought I would never be able to open again. Pierre had tried to talk to me about getting a hobby, but when you are depressed you see no point in doing anything and cannot imagine how you could ever feel connected to anything again.

Being given this fine camera, being taught how to use it and being allowed to go to school—because Pierre now agreed that I could do so—allowed me my first feelings of independence. Here was my first chance at becoming somebody other than the wife of Pierre Trudeau and the mother of his children. For the next two years, I pursued my photography, and Pierre and I struggled to be good parents and to be nice to one another.

One important official trip, though, made it plain how rocky my judgment could be. Pierre made plans to go to Latin America in January of 1976—a major three-week trip to Mexico, Cuba and Venezuela, all the more crucial because the visit was the fruit of Pierre's efforts to expand Canada's ties with the Third World. The visit was doubly important because the United States was still entirely cut off diplomatically from Cuba.

Michel was still only four months old and I didn't want to be separated from him, so I had assumed that I would not be going on this trip. But once again, as with Justin and Sacha, my doctor assured me that Michel could come to no harm. I asked Diane Lavergne, the most easygoing and informal of our staff, to come along with me as nanny.

We flew to Mexico and I immediately took pleasure in all the vibrant colours, the southern light, the smells of the markets. During one of the state dinners, I was presented with beautiful presents from Señora Echeverría, the wife of Mexican president Luis Echeverría. All I had to give María in return was a maple leaf. I was so embarrassed that I gave her the brooch I was wearing—of a killer whale, made by British Columbia artist and goldsmith Bill Reid. Pierre saw my stress. The brooch was worth a great deal of money and had sentimental attachment, but I felt I had no choice.

From that day, I insisted on overseeing the choosing of gifts to be presented on these state visits or when dignitaries visited Ottawa. (I remember, for example, giving to the king and queen of Luxembourg beautiful ladybug pins made of platinum by the distinguished Montreal jeweller Gabriel Lucas.)

Pierre and I stayed in a luxurious hotel in the centre of Mexico City where the butter was brought to our table moulded in the shape of a bouquet of roses. The things we did, the people we met, the places we went to, the warmth and hospitality we encountered everywhere made me feel excited in a way I hadn't felt for a very long time. Michel stayed in our suite with Diane, and I popped in and out to see him. So good did I feel that any caution began melting in the sun.

I had been reading Carlos Castaneda, so Mexican shamans were in my head as Pierre and I toured Mayan ruins near Mexico City. He and I were so athletic in those days that we ran up the entire face of the ruin. The view from the top was so exquisitely beautiful, but both of us ran right back down when we saw that our nanny had parked baby Michel on the sacrificial altar. Bad karma, we both agreed.

Two young Canadian hippies, who had heard about the official visit, somehow managed to break through the tight security when we were exploring the Mayan ruins in the jungle. I was surprised but didn't protest when one of them whispered in my ear, "We've got something for you." I casually left my bag on the ground near the car, where the nanny sat holding Michel, while I went to the ruins. When I got back, a security officer came over to me.

"I think you should know, Mrs. Trudeau," he said, "that Canadian girl slipped something into your bag."

"Thank you so much," I replied. "They must be the cookies she told me about." Opening the bag, I ostentatiously took out a packet of cookies I had brought with me. What the officer didn't realize was that tucked underneath in the bag was a little plastic sack of peyote. That night, at Cancun, I allowed myself a secret taste, one that made me look forward to more.

From Mexico, we flew on to Cuba. My plan had been to land in full regalia: a beautiful silk dress I had bought in Rome, with matching shoes, hat and handbag. Just before we landed I went over to change Michel's diaper. I was just fastening it with the safety pin when the plane lurched and the pin embedded itself in my finger. A drop of bright red blood landed on the front of my dress. Since by now the plane was taxiing down the runway, I had no time to change. Another gaffe: here comes Mrs. Trudeau, on the first official Canadian state visit to Cuba, with blood on her clothes.

When the plane doors were pushed back, a great blanket of steamy heat hit us in the face. Fidel Castro was standing waiting on the runway. I was immediately mesmerized by what I saw: a tall man in green army fatigues immaculately cut and pressed, with incredibly beautiful eyes and a wild, almost fanatical look, which made him physically very attractive. In a voice deep and gruff, he poured out a stream of heavily accented but flowery and romantic English. He quickly endeared himself to me by his attitude towards Michel. He called him "Miche" and carried him around with him. He even procured a special badge that read "Miche Trudeau. VIP Official visitor of the Canadian delegation." From then on, everyone in the family called him Miche (pronounced Meesh), rather than Micha (pronounced Meesha), but to everyone else he was still Michel.

Pierre, Michel, Diane and I were staying in a charming guest house in Havana, built of wood and stone and kept cool by rivulets of water that ran along channels in the slate floor of the house; we crossed rooms by stepping on huge, flat stones. Every window in the house looked out on tropical gardens. So long steeped in the staid, conservative political world of Ottawa, I was soon engulfed in memories of my hippie days. If this is revolution, I thought, then bring it on. Once convinced that Cuba could do no wrong, I found my enthusiasm confirmed everywhere I went. The Cubans struck me as happy people; we took in spectacular entertainments, water displays, gymnastics. I visited daycare centres where I saw the most contented children. The days passed by all too quickly: never had an official visit seemed so enjoyable, or so totally devoid of all stuffiness.

I look back on this trip—taken when I was twenty-seven years old and Ottawa was in the grip of winter—and I fully understand how my depression lifted in the warm sun. Though I love to ski, snowshoe and hike in the snow, winter is hard for me. Seasonal affective disorder is very real, and I now use an artificial light in winter and take vitamin D. When it's grey, cold and dreary, the mood of a depression-prone person can reflect the weather. Small wonder that the Cuban sun put a smile on my face.

The highlight of our visit was a trip out to a remote military installation at Cayo Largo, where a comfortable bungalow had been set aside for us. In the late afternoon, Pierre and Fidel went out to catch dinner. Pierre was a pacifist and would kill nothing, but Castro took a spear gun and the two men swam off in search of fish. They returned with a splendid haul, Castro clutching a large lobster. Under my astonished gaze, he ripped a claw off the still wriggling creature and asked me, "Do you like your lobster with or without lime?" I hesitated, not only because the leg still felt alive but because I had been warned never to eat shellfish raw, other than oysters. But the raw lobster was delicious.

Late that night Diane and I wandered down to the seashore. Soon we were joined by Fidel and one of his aides. It was as well that we were not alone, for he immediately began to pay me a series of outrageous compliments.

"You know my eyes are not very strong," he told me, "so every day to make them stronger I force myself to look at the sun. I find it very hard. But do you know what I find harder? That is to look into the blue of your eyes."

I was sad when the Cuba visit ended, and I was conscious that my time there had shown up very sharply the contradictions between what I felt happy doing and what I was actually expected to do. On our last evening, we ate with Castro, and soon all at the table were clapping their hands and tapping their feet to the loud music that accompanied the meal. When the moment came to leave, weighed down with gifts of three matching chairs for the little boys, I was tearful. Pierre uttered a clever tease.

"I'm glad you're coming with us," he told me. "I thought you might ask for asylum."

Our last stop was Venezuela. Patricia Schwarzmann, our ambassador's wife, had sent me briefing notes on First Lady Blanca Pérez's work with daycare programs, and I was all set to like her. Soon after reaching Caracas, she asked me whether I would like to go with her to one of her centres in the city's slums, where she worked every day with some of the poorer, sicker children.

We set off in a private coach, Blanca Pérez in a simple white dress and sturdy shoes, me in a safari suit with cameras slung over my shoulders. We took Michel with us. At one point, I looked back and saw Madame Pérez's entourage and various diplomatic ladies, all with identical expressions of dismay and distaste on their faces. In their high-heeled crocodile shoes, silk Pucci dresses and heavy gold jewellery, they seemed too terrified even to get off the buses. I liked Madame Pérez all the more. When I got back to our embassy, I felt overwhelmed with admiration for her.

That night, our last in Venezuela, we were to host a dinner for Madame Pérez and her husband. That afternoon, I had been nibbling on some of the peyote given to me by the hippies back in Mexico. Bad decision. Bad judgment. The peyote kicked in as I was dressing for dinner and took me on quite a trip. I was so taken with Madame Pérez—and so high—that I decided to compose a poem to her and recite it aloud over dinner. By now, I believed that I was Eva Perón and Gabriel García Márquez rolled into one.

Mine was a deeply unwise decision, particularly as the nature of the dinner had changed—from small and intimate to vast and formal. The whole of grand Caracas was present. As the meal ended, I rose boldly to my feet and began to sing. The drug was doing its work, and I could pick out every detail in the room, every sparkling petal on every rose.

"Señora Pérez," I announced, "I would like to sing to you a song of love." And my warbling began:

Señora Pérez, I would like to thank you,
I would like to sing to you
To sing a song of love
For I have watched you
With my eyes wide open,
I have watched you with learning eyes . . .

I will spare you the rest. Even in my addled state, I could sense the acute embarrassment I had caused. The Pérezes could not have been more charming, but the Canadian press had a field day. My previous bouts of erratic behaviour had not gone unnoticed in Canada, and next morning the Canadian public opened their newspapers to a feast of scandalous stories about the disgraceful antics of Pierre Trudeau's mad, exhibitionist wife. I wince when I look back at this really stupid, shameful behaviour.

"Margaret Trudeau did it again," *The Globe and Mail* trumpeted. I felt totally disgraced and ashamed at my appalling behaviour. Once home, I promptly compounded the damage. I awoke to hear comments on the radio about my performance, nearly all of them highly critical. Then the talk show host said, "Margaret Trudeau, why don't you give us a call?" So I did. But that was a terrible mistake too, and I came out of it looking still more foolish. I was so lonely, so sad.

The days and the months passed, and the boys continued to grow. Virtually as soon as they could walk, Pierre took them out on the ski slopes, where they soon became fearless, hurtling over the crests of the hills, flipping, falling over, bouncing back, so proficient that especially good skiers from the RCMP had to be found to keep pace with them. But something between myself and Pierre had shattered, and we couldn't seem to put it right.

In the summer of 1976, we were in Rome and had an audience with Pope Paul VI at his summer retreat at Castel Gandolfo. Pierre had suggested that I make a list of questions that I would like to ask him. Kneeling in front of him, greatly impressed and moved by his aura of holiness, I wanted to ask him all the questions that had been nagging me about Catholicism and that conversion had done nothing to assuage. What was a sin? Did thoughts count as well as deeds? (Surely God wouldn't hold my private and inner wanderings against me?) And original sin—how could an innocent child (any of my three sons, for example) be born with the stain of sin on his soul? And where were the women? Why did the Catholic Church treat women so subserviently?

Before I had a chance to ask a single question, the pope patted me on the head and told me that I was blessed among women for having three wonderful sons. Then he turned to Pierre and I was completely excluded from the more serious conversation.

The audience ended with the pope asking Pierre whether he had any questions. Pierre, unlike me, didn't seem to have any. I envied him his certainties. But I was also extremely angry. I left feeling distanced from the Catholic Church, which I felt was failing me as a woman.

Pierre and I had long disagreed over religion. Every evening, when the boys went to bed, Pierre prayed with them. That was fine, and when we married, I had agreed that they should be raised as Catholics. However, I had a real problem with the idea of original sin, and couldn't find any way of seeing sin in a small boy. And I had an even greater problem with the idea of an elderly priest absolving the so-called sins of a small boy, such as eating a chocolate bar before dinner. When I thought about it, I felt that my Anglican God was a gentler one than Pierre's Catholic one.

Some twenty-five years later, Sacha and I had an hour-long audience with His Holiness the Dalai Lama, and it was completely the opposite. He included me in the discussion. The Dalai Lama held my hand to his face and said mothers were the strength and the power.

Both holy men were talking of the grace of the mother, but the Dalai Lama saw me as a person—and not one woman among many. The pope put me in my place; the Dalai Lama put me in the conversation.

In the autumn of 1976 came one of the hardest official visits of my life with Pierre. Looking back on it, I see how tense I must have been. We were invited to Japan, and normally this would have filled me with delight, since I loved Japan and all things Japanese. We stayed in the magnificent Akasaka Palace and everything looked exquisite. However, we were accompanied by Pierre's aide, Ivan Head, with whom I had long been on bad terms. I had the sense that he resented any contribution I might make to Pierre's work. We had tried, but totally failed, to work together during the 1974 campaign, when I knew he had done all he could to keep me from taking part. I found him chauvinistic, and I hated his bureaucratic manner.

From the first, I found the intense protocol of this Japanese visit extremely daunting (such a far cry from our relaxed and convivial time in Cuba). Each small gesture in Japan seemed to carry meaning. The best occasion was lunch with the emperor and the empress, when we talked about photography. Otherwise, one round of formality and starchiness followed another—with one exception. I can still laugh about this one. Pierre and I had gone up north to relax over the weekend in an inn. The charming server in traditional costume brought up steaming bowls of soup, but when I saw bony little fish floating at the top, I told Pierre that I couldn't eat it. "I thought you were the great traveller," he said, deeply patronizing. "You have to be open to new experiences, try things out, experiment." And he set about eating the little fish. At that moment the server returned. She looked horrified. "No, no, no," she said, "you mustn't eat the little fish. They are just to flavour the soup." With that, she scooped them all out with a little net.

By the end of the trip, I had reached a point of acute exhaustion, and something was giving in me. As we were walking down the stairs on our way to the final press conference, with the staff lining up on either side, Ivan Head informed me that I would not be attending it. I had always loved the press conferences at the end of official trips: here was a chance to learn how the trip had gone and what people felt about it. I was outraged. I turned round and began running up the stairs again, shouting "Fuck you!" at the top of my voice. This was a terrible and embarrassing thing to do, and I look back on it with shame. Pierre came after me and said that I could accompany him, but that since the press conference excluded spouses, I would have to sit in a little glass booth on my own.

Towards the middle of February 1977, we made an official visit to Washington. As I sat listening to Pierre address a joint session of Congress, I felt torn between an intense need for him and a longing for Teddy Kennedy. I then attended a State Department lunch hosted by Grace Vance (the wife of Secretary of State Cyrus Vance), and later visited a mental health centre with Rosalynn Carter. That night, at a dinner given at the Canadian embassy, Elizabeth Taylor leaned across the table and said to me, "You look absolutely bored out of your mind. I know precisely how you feel."

Hers was a kind and sympathetic gesture, but I was appalled that I had made my ennui so transparent. I was jolted back into the present and I felt deeply ashamed at this lapse in manners. But the shame I felt was fleeting. Afterwards I arranged a discreet meeting with Teddy. We met in his office and sat drinking cold white wine. I told him that he had not destroyed my marriage but that I had used him to help me destroy a marriage that was already over. I added that to change one's life completely is not an impossible challenge—but a necessity. Still, I couldn't quite bring myself to make the break.

In the meantime, I had a target on my back. I had worn a short dress to the official dinner that night, and as if that wasn't bad enough, my stockings had a run in them. The White House that night was full of celebrities—from Harry Belafonte to John Kenneth Galbraith—but my dress and torn nylons seemed of greatest interest to the press.

Jimmy and Rosalynn Carter were quick to support me. Pierre and I had barely set foot home when we received a hand-written letter from the president, addressed to us both.

"Rosalynn and I really enjoyed your visit with us, and we look forward to seeing you often in the future. Pierre, your experience and naturally frank discussion were very helpful to me as a new president . . . Margaret, you brought a delightful breath of fresh air and charm to Washington. Thank you. Your friend Jimmy." I felt just a little bit better.

In 1977, I heard that Jiddu Krishnamurti, then eighty-two years old, was to hold a conference in California, near Santa Barbara.

I had long been interested in the teachings of this Indian-born writer, speaker and spiritual philosopher, and now that I was so surrounded by formality and protocol, by a way of life that seemed to me so artificial and pretentious, I began to yearn for the simplicity that his words conjured.

I thought of him as a non-guru guru, a wise man without pretensions, and I kept remembering Leonard Cohen's words: "The wise man said, 'follow me,' and he walked behind." Calling myself by my maiden name—Margaret Sinclair—I arranged to go to California to meet Krishnamurti. He knew who I was because we had a mutual friend, a young man with whom I had once been very close, and soon after my arrival he called me over to talk to him. There had been no place set for me at the conference, and he indicated that I should sit by his side during the proceedings.

In the evenings, Jiddu and I walked together in the orange groves and talked. His message seemed to be about freedom, about the need to express oneself and be true to oneself and not to be limited by the constraints of others. "Plumb the depths of your own consciousness," he said. "The only thing that is real is creative love; everything else is a distraction." I went home in a pensive mood. Jiddu Krishnamurti did not believe in organized religion or power of any kind, yet here I was, married to one of the Western world's most powerful and controlling men. Something would have to give, and it did.

Not long after getting home, on a terrible evening full of misery and rage, I attacked a priceless quilt by Joyce Wieland, a piece of art that hung on the sitting-room wall and one that Pierre particularly loved. Stitched on the front, neatly and smugly (it seemed to me then), were his favourite words: "Reason over Passion." I seized a pair of scissors and cut the words off. Taking a box of pins, I then switched the words round, so they read "Passion over Reason." I was in one of my manic phases, and I had concluded that the only way to make Pierre Trudeau listen was to desecrate art.

Pierre's rage was justified. Next morning, one of the maids dutifully repaired the damage, but the real damage—to my relationship with Pierre—was very much beyond repair.

And then the day came when I started to hate Pierre, and now I knew that if I didn't leave I would go insane. I knew, both for myself and for the three boys, that I could not survive in this state bordering on insanity. I could not stay with Pierre for the wrong reasons, and there did not seem to be many right ones. I blamed him—unfairly—for his discipline and asceticism and his lack of intimacy and spontaneity; I blamed him for growing old and for not having the time to look after me, and for the fact that while I was struggling to grow up, he was too busy to notice what was going on.

I turned into a harridan, and a desperate one. The courage that it took me to leave was unquestionably fuelled by the mania that once again was pulsing through me. But deep down, leaving was also rooted in an instinctive desire to survive. I knew that I simply had to find the courage to walk out of 24 Sussex, leave behind the loneliness and isolation and discover who I was and what I could do. My hope, my ambition, was to find meaningful professional work.

All of my sisters worked. Heather had become a widely

respected professor in the Faculty of Education at the University of British Columbia and she would be awarded a medal from the queen for her work with the British Columbia Ministry of Education helping to redefine the provincial school curriculum. Jan would have a long career working first as a dentist's assistant, then as a ticketing agent with Air Canada and, more recently, in the airline's union at the bargaining table. She always was, and remains, a champion of the underdog. Lin had been a very shy, insecure pupil who would retreat to her room and read Harlequin romances, but for grades eleven and twelve, my mother sent her off to boarding school—the elite Havergal College girls' school in Toronto. She came back transformed, and never looked back. She specialized in nuclear medicine, training technicians in the use of new radiology equipment, and had chosen to live in Tucson, Arizona. And Betsy had become a dedicated nurse and hospital administrator. What about Margaret?

In my mind, my calling card read: Margaret Trudeau, photographer.

CHAPTER 7

POOR MAD MRS. ROCHESTER,
HIDDEN IN THE ATTIC

"God, please please help me to know what to do with my life."

ENTRY FROM MY DIARY, JUNE 22, 1977

I recently came across a red leather diary, one I started in the spring of 1977, in the month that I decided to leave Pierre. The diary covers the worst year of my life, my twenty-ninth, and certainly the most destructive. The red book makes for painful reading.

On the first page is this short entry: "March 6. Toronto. Done. I have left Pierre and the children in Ottawa and I am heading out into the world to seek my fortune. Either it will work or it won't."

Two days earlier, on March 4, our sixth wedding anniversary, Pierre and I had agreed on a trial separation. He had made it clear that he wanted me back, but he was going to "let me explore my new freedom," as I noted in the diary, and would help me financially until I found my feet. I was to spend a few weeks at a time away, then return for a long weekend or more with the children, who would be in the care of two excellent nannies and Pierre himself. Justin was five, Sacha three and Michel not quite eighteen months. Looking back on it, I can see I didn't know what I was doing. I just knew I had to go.

I was feeling completely overwhelmed and overpowered, to the point where I was becoming invisible to myself and I thought I was going to disappear. There was just such an imbalance between my desire for freedom—which Pierre completely respected—and his desire for control, which was the way he lived.

The boys didn't want me to go, but they were mostly stoic about it. "Mommy has to work" is how Sacha put it. Justin, the eldest, had figured out that both his mother and father had jobs. His father, he understood, was "the boss of Canada."

The Toronto business was an accident, but it set the tone for what would be two years of mayhem and a prolonged attack on me by the world's press. I had planned to go straight to New York and to start work with Richard Avedon, a high-profile fashion and portrait photographer who had said he would take me on as an apprentice for a week. But then a friend named Penny Royce invited me to spend a few days with her to meet the Rolling Stones, who were in Toronto to play in a small nightclub, the El Mocambo.

The tavern's distinctive neon-green palm tree has graced Spadina Avenue since 1946, and the bar has drawn over the years a wide variety of rock and jazz stars—from Jimi Hendrix to Charles Mingus. The Rolling Stones recorded two live concerts at the El Mocambo on March 4 and 5 of 1977, both folded into their *Love You Live* album.

I took photographs as the band played. At first I felt rather shy, like an aging groupie hanging around the edges, but as I began to work, my spirits rose. Watching Mick Jagger, I liked him, thinking how intelligent and professional he was. Later I met them all individually, and since night and day readily mixed with them, I ended up spending much of the night in their company at the Hilton Harbour Castle Hotel. And all of it, in fact, with Ronnie Wood. Mania is an aphrodisiac, for oneself and for those you come in contact with. The night was fun, an exhilarating start to my new career, but it meant nothing, and in the morning my excitement had been replaced by a sensation of bleakness. I felt sad and lonely and wondered whether I shouldn't just turn around and go home.

What I had not reckoned on was the publicity. My last-minute decision to divert to Toronto had been catastrophic. In my mania, I had failed to understand that Paul Wasserman, the Rolling Stones' publicity manager, would use me as good fodder for the press and that Canadian journalists were sitting waiting for scandals. I had used the Stones, and now the Stones were using me. There were already rumours that Pierre and I had split up; reporters were avid for more news.

I left Toronto and made my way to New York, where I hooked up with an old friend, Yasmin Aga Khan, then twenty-eight. The daughter of actress Rita Hayworth and Pakistan's former ambassador to the United Nations General Assembly, she's now a prominent philanthropist. In those days, she was a friend, and I had need of one. I loved Yas's free spirit and deep elegance, and how she laughed often and sang like a songbird. I had barely settled in with her when the story broke. "Prime Minister's Wife and the Rolling Stones" and "Sex Orgy in Prime Minister's Wife's Suite."

Such treatment was to be expected, perhaps, but still it was both hurtful and terrifying. The March 10 entry in my diary reads: "My life is beginning to spin very fast. I must use all my strength to control the crisis." Bianca Jagger was reported to be furious, my mother was distraught (she told reporters, "If she has any problems, she knows she has a home and parents and sisters who love her"), and the Canadian press were baying for more. Asked whether he had slept with me, Mick Jagger was reported to have said, "I wouldn't touch her with an eleven-foot barge pole." A smart move on his part, but for me the humiliation was total.

When I next returned to Ottawa I found Pierre furious and wretched. He felt a terrible sense of failure and he loathed the publicity. By now I was on the crest of a destructive wave of mania, and I was really acting appallingly. Pierre reached the breaking point. Whenever we argued, he always had to have the last word—and he certainly did that night.

What angered him most, he kept saying, was that I was "bringing shame on the family name." We were due to go to the ballet that night, and by the time we stopped arguing my face was blotchy with tears. I assumed that I would stay at home, and that he would go without me. But he was adamant: he wanted me there, by his side, for all the world to see. He wanted me shamed, and I was ashamed. So I went. The evening was sad and pathetic. After that there was no going back. I was a sick, confused and very angry young woman; staying at 24 Sussex was not an option. I returned to New York.

When I went round to Richard Avedon's studio to start my apprenticeship, I heard, through the intercom, what the reporters camped outside were saying: "Is there a bed in there? Is she sleeping with Avedon too?"

My earlier indiscretions—the embarrassing song in Venezuela, the occasional outbursts in Canada—had been forgivable, but this was different. This transgression, an appalling misjudgment on my part, had transported me into a cold and hostile world where people were out for gossip. Overnight, whatever privacy that remained to me had gone. The entry in my diary that night was defiant: "No one should have to put up with the grossness and viciousness of people's prejudices and narrow minds . . . It is over. I am no longer Canada's First Lady . . . I have had enough of being sad and lonely, bored and aching."

The trouble was that I was no longer in control—either of myself or of the paparazzi. The reporters' hunger for my ill-judged behaviour, brought on by these bouts of overexcitement, was insatiable. Wherever I went, whatever I did, provoked fresh stories. There were not many weeks when I did not appear in *Time* magazine's People column, usually linked to some new man. I became a cover girl, a celebrity in an age before the celebrity culture, famous for nothing except for my scandalous behaviour. From People columns I moved into "notorious" columns. I was quoted as saying that my marriage had been a "total catastrophe in terms of my identity," and that I didn't think a politician's wife should be "a rose on his lapel" (in hindsight, I was more thorn than rose). The fact that Keith Richards and his girlfriend, Anita Pallenberg, were facing heroin-trafficking charges and that my name had been linked to theirs became a "national embarrassment." I could do no right.

Wrong I did in spades. One day, when I had been invited to appear on *The Phil Donahue Show*, members of the audience began to shout out questions:

"Margaret, is it true that you have abandoned your children?"

"Who's your lover?"

"How do you justify doing all this to your family?"

One of the horrors of the show was that the victim was placed on a chair in the middle of blinding lights. I struggled, tried to give coherent answers until I could stand it no longer, and then I swivelled my chair round, with my back to poor Phil and the audience. That provoked laughter, even jeers, but enough was enough.

Another time, a respected *Globe and Mail* columnist wrote that everybody knew Pierre could not wait to get his children away from such a bad mother. I was branded irresponsible, promiscuous, a seeker after celebrity, even half mad. Because my mind seemed to be in free fall, I was easy prey.

One evening, I agreed to do an interview with Jane Pauley for NBC's *Today Show*. I knew and admired her work, and as we sat down she told me that she, too, was "Margaret Trudeau": her given name was Margaret and she would soon marry Doonesbury cartoonist Garry Trudeau (who could, like Pierre, trace his ancestry back to Étienne Trudeau, who had come to New France as an *engagé*, or indentured servant, in the late seventeenth century).

The interview with Jane Pauley started well. But soon the questions about Teddy Kennedy began. I dodged and ducked, but she kept on and on at me. Finally I could bear it no longer. I stood up and said, "I know exactly where you're trying to go and I am not going there." Then I walked off the set. Everyone was furious, but I was just beginning to get a glimmer of a lesson I would need to learn: you have to know when to exit.

You may wonder why I kept going back to journalists who laid siege to my character. I look back and see that it was all part of the career I was trying to build, but clearly I was new and ill prepared, and the madness kept propelling me back for more. With mania comes extraordinarily poor judgment. I thought I was acting properly but I was not. To the outside world, I must have seemed incredibly naïve, but at the time I really did feel that I could make people understand what I was trying to do. And the harder I tried, the deeper the hole I dug for myself.

There is a dark postscript to that interview with Jane Pauley. In 2001, she was diagnosed with bipolar disorder and in 2005 wrote a book about the experience. In *Skywriting*, Pauley describes a manic moment that was all too familiar to me:

> *Feelings came shooting in and out at the speed of bullet trains, along with ideas, followed by phone calls that produced action plans. My mind was racing. Mostly it was good, but I was aware that I was in hyper mode from the moment I woke up at six-thirty and started the day with a bang. When the phone rang at about eight o'clock one morning, it felt like half the day was already done, and I asked my mother-in-law if I could change phones because I was standing in the utility room with a hammer in my*

*hand. Me wandering the house with a hammer in my
hand had become almost a metaphor for my home life.*

I found British journalists, particularly, to be smarmy and
clever and lethal. They practised gutter journalism of the worst and
most abusive sort. I was no match for their seductive ways, falling
again and again for their apparent sympathy only to find myself
portrayed in their newspapers as wayward and publicity mad.

Every harsh word was like a drop of poison, leaving its stain,
and I had no means of defending myself. Even poor Pierre bore
some of the brunt of my wild, irrational behaviour. One day a man
called out to him on the street, "You're nothing but a cuckold."

The publicity began to distort the way ordinary people saw me.
One day, I was introduced to a Canadian man and his wife and
stayed to talk to them for a while. As we parted, the man shook
my hand warmly and said, "It has been really nice to meet you.
I have to be honest. You really scared me. We didn't know what
you might do or say." When I returned to Ottawa for my weekends with the boys, to be surrounded once again by security men,
I felt paranoid. And facing my parents in those days was hard—
really, really hard.

I had not, of course, abandoned the boys, and they were
always on my mind. Every few weeks I returned to Ottawa, to
the top floor of 24 Sussex, which I now made my base. I would
give the nannies a holiday and settle down with the children. The

days I had with them, whether in Ottawa, where the four of us often spent the night together curled up in my big bed, or up at Harrington Lake, were isolated little periods of sanity and happiness. I cooked for Justin and Sacha and Michel, and up in the attic room under the eaves I made clothes on my sewing machine.

I still have it, still use it—a pale green 1971 portable Bernina, the Rolls-Royce of sewing machines. A wedding gift from Pierre and something I had requested, the machine was Swiss made, and, like a Swiss watch, it was precise and dependable. At least something was.

I began to think of myself ruefully as a character in Charlotte Brontë's nineteenth-century novel *Jane Eyre*—poor mad Mrs. Rochester hidden away in the attic.

The boys and I would have our breakfast on trays in bed and play with their new Newfoundland puppy. The boys were growing up with very different and distinct personalities of their own. Justin, the eldest, was always the leader, and though he was at heart loving and good, he could be very rough on the younger boys. Sacha was most like Pierre, very disciplined and hard working. Michel, the baby of the family, had an exceptionally sunny nature.

Pierre and I were always very physical with them, with lots of hugs. I think each generation tries to fill in the gaps from the one before, and if our parents were shy about touch, we weren't.

Because I was no longer part of the formal set-up at 24 Sussex, there were no social occasions for me to attend, and I was free to be nothing but the mother to these boys. Sometimes I felt like I had never been away, except motherhood was far better now than it had ever been—even if, occasionally, I felt as if I were regressing into childhood again.

To the boys, I explained that I was working and needed to spend time at my job but would return for as long and as often as I could. Most of the staff did what they could to help, particularly Hildegarde, the senior maid, a kindly woman who was never censorious, and Yannick Vincent, the French chef, who would leave meals for me when my plane arrived late into Ottawa. Mary-Alice Mullaley was a sister in a convent in the Maritimes when she applied to 24 Sussex as a maid. Her education, her poise and her general qualifications would elevate her to comptroller of the house within a short time. She was an efficient and compassionate manager, and because of her, the place ran smoothly with or without me.

The most important staff members, of course, were the nannies. We were really blessed in that department. The first one we hired was Diane Lavergne, a country girl from a big family living outside Ottawa. She was a loving young woman and delighted in pouring her heart into caring for Justin and then baby Sacha.

When it was her time to move on, after Michel was born, I put an ad in the *Globe and Mail* saying something like "Nanny wanted for a family of three boys living in a government residence." I received more than two thousand responses after an observant editor noticed my ad and put it on the front page. We chose Leslie Kimberley and Monica Mallon, both with extensive training in early child development and play. Leslie's sister, Vicki, took over from her when Leslie went to get her master's in audiology.

The work of these young women was exemplary, and they gave our little ones the guidance and affection they needed. They were all part of our family and, as it turned out, a necessary part of my being able to heal my unquiet mind. As a mother and wife suffering from a mental illness, I was unusually lucky to have such support available to me. For that, I am extremely grateful, and I deeply sympathize with all my fellow sufferers who must cope alone. The time would come when I, too, would be desperately alone in my madness.

Each time I knew I had to tear myself away, I would catch the plane back to New York, tears of confusion and uncertainty pouring down my face. My leave-taking was made infinitely worse by knowing that I was regarded throughout Canada—and I suspect by one or two members of our staff—as the kind of woman who would prefer going to nightclubs to looking after her young sons.

The boys would cling to me when I came home, and Sacha wept when I left. One of the maids was quick to tell me one day that she had heard him whimper outside my door. Pierre and I were careful with each other but distant. He made it clear that if I proved I could run a home, then he was willing to share custody, but he was very reluctant to give me more than a minimal allowance. In New York, I had already sold some jewellery to raise a little money. As for divorce, Pierre, as a fervent Catholic, did not consider it an option.

Never had I felt myself so young and vulnerable, nor had I ever found Pierre so stern. Sometimes I allowed myself to dream that we might find a way of resolving our disagreements, of becoming once again a loving family, a dream that part of me knew could never happen. The difference in our ages—Pierre was approaching sixty, while I was twenty-nine—had never seemed so glaring. Even so, a new relationship was developing between us, one more like father and daughter, and I needed him, wanting to keep him informed about how I was growing up. For his part, he seemed to enjoy some of the tales of the outside world I regaled him with.

Some of my worst moments were when Pierre was entertaining at 24 Sussex. I had been forbidden to show myself on these occasions, and was expected to keep to my quarters. Once the boys were asleep, I would perch on the window seat of my room, listening to the voices of the guests as they arrived, and later watch them in their long dresses and black ties as they strolled in the garden after dinner, the lights from the river glowing in the distance. I would remember all the evenings I had been entertaining them myself, forgetting my misery at the time.

I wasn't always so wistful. When Pierre was not busy, we resumed some kind of family life. Pierre taught the boys to swim while I called encouragement from the side of the pool. At Harrington Lake, we canoed and swam, hiked and had barbecues. Pierre was a black belt in judo and taught the boys how to fall when fighting.

When he started dating, in the autumn of 1977, I was far more jealous than I had expected to be—particularly since many of the women he courted were those who had come as guests and friends to 24 Sussex when we first got married. I noticed that the dinners he asked the chef to prepare for them—lobster and champagne—

were the very ones that he had lavished on me in our first days together. Still, I did genuinely want Pierre to be happy, and even tried to find people whom he might like to meet.

My first bunk in New York was with Yasmin Aga Khan. Later, I was given two rooms on Park Avenue in the fifteen-room apartment of a rich Texan; she wanted a house-sitter while she had the decorators in. Here I camped, spending my days working and my evenings in Studio 54.

The apartment was downstairs from my friends Richard and Lise Wasserman, who welcomed me into their home with tuna-fish sandwiches in the kitchen. Lise, especially, was a darling friend. I did a fair bit of socializing with New Yorkers: Andy Warhol for one. He was a friend, and we were often together at the edge of the crowd, watching the spectacle unfold at Studio 54. Andy sometimes had profound observations; mostly he would just say, "Oh gee." At one point, Fred Hughes, of his team from the Factory (as he called his studio), called and said, "Andy would like to paint you, Margaret. It will only cost you $33,000!" The very idea of asking my husband for that amount never entered my mind. In hindsight, though, it would have been a great investment.

I also hung out with the revolutionary Yugoslavian designer Zoran, Truman Capote, Warren Beatty and Diana Vreeland, the *Vogue* icon. I met Lauren Bacall, Gloria Steinem and many other fascinating characters. Barbra Streisand and I sat on the stairs at

Studio 54 comparing notes. I attended theatre, opera and ballet and took advantage of the sophisticated mecca that is New York. I would have short romances with men whose company I enjoyed but whom I did not really love.

My phone would ring and it would be Steve Rubell from Studio 54: "Maggie, we're going to have a party. All the stars are coming. I'll send a car." And off I would go with my friends, to dance into the small hours. I loved dancing.

I would spend my weekends in the Hamptons, buying clothes with money I didn't have. I went to Washington for celebrity galas, and one night hosted a fundraiser for cerebral palsy in one of the big hotels, feeling that this was really something I could be proud of.

For a while I attended an acting school off Broadway, which gave me skills that, paradoxically, only served to make worse what came later. I learned how to put on a mask, to not show my feelings, to appear perfectly all right when underneath I felt myself to be one step from death. "No hunger, no pain, no fear," I wrote defiantly in my diary. In many ways, I thought I was growing up and learning how to live.

The most important person in my life in New York was Dr. Arnold Hutschnecker, a renowned Park Avenue psychiatrist. He treated people with power and influence. He taught me the one lesson that has proved again and again to be invaluable: know when to exit.

———————

Some days, when I rode the subway, met my friends, planned my work, met the other actors to rehearse, I felt free at last, free to find out who I really was. But when I read my diary now, what catches my eye is a recurring phrase: "under control . . . in control . . . out of control."

Often, too often, I felt used and abandoned, fancying myself in love and then rejected. One night, when I was back in Canada, Pierre and I agreed to issue a statement about a trial separation. He was so angry, and I was trying so hard to appease him.

On May 13 of 1977, word was put out to the press. Pierre, the notice said, was to "take on the major responsibility for the day to day supervision of his children," while "Margaret was to pursue an independent career and give up all privileges and rights as the wife of the Prime Minister." The public were asked to respect our privacy. An eventual reconciliation was not ruled out.

There was at least some truth in the press release. I was, indeed, pursuing a career—the question was, in what? I did some work for People magazine, taking photographs for Perrier in France, and for a while I took up with Perrier's president, Bruce Nevins, a kind and warm-hearted man who tried to smooth my path.

John Dominis, the photo editor of People magazine, gave me other stories to do. I liked John. He and I went on a date once, to the Press Gallery dinner in Washington. John was then fifty-six and he had long freelanced for Life magazine and the Saturday Evening Post; later he was a photo editor at Sports Illustrated. The best assignment he gave me was to cover a professional boxing match—Duane Bobick's fight against Ken Norton in Philadelphia in May of 1977.

But when editors at People magazine heard of my assignments, they took to sending reporters to follow me around and write stories about me taking photographs. My photographs were good and it was fun going to the office, but the job became a circus: I was simultaneously the assignment and on assignment, so there were these absurd scenes where photographers took pictures of me photographing someone else.

I took acting classes to prepare myself for possible film parts. But mostly I rocketed my way around New York, spending my nights in Studio 54 or—after deciding that Bruce was too cold and uncommitted—going off on dates to places like Las Vegas. When I look back now on those days, they fill me with shame and embarrassment. Writing those words so baldly cannot convey the depth of confusion and unhappiness I felt. Much of the time, I lived in a fog, blindly clinging to a plan—that of making a career of my own—acting out of an unconscious drive to survive, not to go under, not to give up.

I thought my break had come when *Good Morning America* invited me to appear on the show with a selection of my photographs, the understanding being that this would be a kind of audition for a job of presenter on the program. But this turned out to be a teaser. Halfway through the program, while I was talking about my photography, the interviewer interrupted me to ask "the question that is on the mind of every one of our twelve million viewers: Have you abandoned your children?"

I wanted to scratch her eyes out.

"How could you?" I shot back. "How could you possibly ask such a question?"

I began seriously to doubt that I was ever going to make it on my own. My entry for June 5, 1977, is bleak: "I am angry. I hurt. I am disappearing. I want to die. I can't struggle any more. I feel awful now—alone and lonely." On June 22 I added, "Stress: boy do I feel it now. On every level I feel vulnerable, alone, pressured . . . being stretched in every way . . . Help . . . I'm not eating, hardly sleeping."

I had lost ten pounds and my emotions were "roller coasting." Week after week, the diary contained the same refrain: "God, please please help me to know what to do with my life . . . help me survive as a good, honest, genuine person who doesn't lie and fake and run away . . . I want to be someone I can live for and live with." By now the highs and lows were coming thick and fast, I was constantly exhausted, kept falling asleep and missing appointments, and was living mainly on vitamins.

More than once, I was on the very edge of packing my bags and returning permanently to 24 Sussex. Slipped inside the pages of the red diary are fragments of paper, torn from a notepad. On each are the beginnings of a frantic letter to Pierre.

"Pierre, please find the time to bring me home. I am begging you, from my heart . . . All I want is for us to be a good family. I need your love . . . I will be a good wife." In February of 1978, just back from a blind date in Las Vegas, I wrote, "Pierre, please help me through this desperation. I am so lonely."

Pierre, for his part, had weathered our separation, politically at least, extremely well. His approval ratings shot up, and he had never been as popular as he was in the summer of 1977. During the previous January, the Conservatives had been leading with a big enough margin to form a majority government, and polls indicated that John Turner would make a more popular Liberal leader than Pierre. Turner, a former justice and finance minister who had left politics two years beforehand to work as a Bay Street lawyer, was waiting in the wings should Pierre step aside. By June of 1977, however, no one doubted Pierre's skills any longer.

Though I continued to spend long weekends back in Ottawa, and though I agonized over my separation from the boys, there was something stubborn inside me, some sense of desperation, that would not quite let me capitulate. I kept hanging on to this notion of freedom, though there were many days when I couldn't understand why—days when I longed for the boys and when I blamed Pierre for what had happened to us, for his coldness, his anger, his hurt pride.

My determination to find my own life and thereby become the mother the boys deserved was greatly strengthened by rare incidents of understanding and generosity. A doctor I had met in New York sent me a present after a bout of particularly bad publicity. With the gift came a wise note: "You must remember, a third of people will love you for what you do, a third will hate you for what you do, and the rest won't give a damn what you do. You have to learn that what they feel is their problem, not yours, their faulty perception, not yours."

Easy to say, hard to embrace. I found it impossible to shake my old desire to please. I had tried so hard to please my parents all through my childhood, then I tried to please Pierre. I could not rid myself of the longing to please everyone, to be loved and admired by all.

I kept repeating to myself, like a kind of mantra, the Ricky Nelson song called "Garden Party." Nelson had been part of a rock-and-roll revival concert in the fall of 1971 at Madison Square Garden, along with Chuck Berry, Bo Diddley and many others. Nelson sang a few of his hits, then switched to a country version of the Rolling Stones song "Honky Tonk Women." Some in the crowd booed, possibly because of police roughing up some members of the audience in the back or perhaps because they didn't like the musical direction Nelson had taken. He was stung by the response and walked off the stage, and later penned a song about the incident—"Garden Party."

My mantra was this line from the song: "You see, ya can't please everyone, so ya got to please yourself."

In the winter of 1977, I got an offer for a film part, to co-star with Patrick McGoohan in a film called *Kings and Desperate Men*. I was to play the wife of a failed actor and controversial radio talk-show host who is kidnapped with her young son by terrorists. The film wasn't bad, but McGoohan and I loathed each other on first sight.

He was a big, surly man with a filthy temper, and filming became a series of bruising encounters. I was not sad when it ended, though I had loved the camaraderie of the set and the teamwork, and the acting had allowed me to give rein to all the emotions that seemed permanently to rage through me. I learned how to pour them out, not rein them in.

On the other hand, acting only allowed me to perfect a natural talent—for putting on a mask, for presenting a happy, reliable, dependable outer self, while inside I felt dissociated, as if I lived on the very margins of sanity. Fake it until you make it: that works for a while. I would pretend I felt great and, for a while, I did. But not for long. The pressure, bit by bit, built up, and then I would explode, in misery and mania.

A second film, *L'ange gardien (The Guardian Angel)*, shot in the south of France, had me as the mistress of a wealthy Canadian businessman. She has a series of light flirtations with other men only to discover that her lover has had her followed by a private detective. Not surprisingly, perhaps, this film was not a success. And it would not have taken a genius to realize that I had been chosen to star not because of my great talents as an actress but because it was a fine publicity stunt to have the scandalous wife of the Canadian prime minister running around Cassis on the Mediterranean coast with a lot of men. Gossip columnists and paparazzi flew into town and followed me around shouting out questions, some new, some very old: Had I left my husband? Had I abandoned my children? What did I think about French men?

My hope then was that word of the movie and my being in France might allow Yves Lewis, my old boyfriend, to find me. I had lost contact with him and always wondered what had become of him. I had an address for him in Paris, and before going south to do the film I went there and knocked on the door, and this beautiful, doleful young woman came to the door. She had long hair and the light was behind her. I asked her, in English, if Yves Lewis still lived there.

No, she replied, and I must have looked so sad at this news that she reached out, touched me and said, "Ma petite fille, l'amour change." Indeed, it does.

I did find Yves, in a way. I was in a makeup trailer on the set of the movie with my co-actor in the film, a very well-known character and comic actor in French cinema named Francis Lemaire. He was a very sweet man, and both he and his wife were very kind to me. But this day he looked stricken and sad.

"Francis," I said to him, "what's wrong? Are you having a bad day?"

He explained that a good friend had just lost his son. "He was the most beautiful boy," he said. "I have known him since he was a child and was very close to him. He had been wandering the streets of Paris wearing a white robe, then hanged himself."

Somehow I knew.

"Is it Yves?" I asked Francis, "Yves Lewis?"

"Ah," Francis said, "you're Margaret."

That was so terribly, terribly sad. Later, I met with Yves' stepfather in Paris for lunch. This man thought that Yves was the most complete human being he had ever encountered—so beyond anyone whom we would label a Renaissance man. A childlike spiritual questing layered over a very serious, disciplined mind. Looking back, I can see that you never get over your first love, especially when taken in this way. I see now that I have no regrets about the choice I made. One look at my family is all it takes.

In the early spring of 1978, I was approached by John Marqusee, the director with his wife, Janet, of a small British publishing house, Paddington Press. He suggested that I write my memoirs, and he offered an advance of $60,000. What with movie and serialization rights, he said, I could hope to make something in the order of $400,000. At last, here was a real chance for financial independence. I flew to London, signed the contract and began work.

I hadn't been there long when I was introduced by friends to Jack Nicholson, who was in England to make *The Shining*. His long-term partner, Anjelica Huston, had not accompanied him. Soon Jack and I were spending our evenings in the terrace house he had rented in Cheyne Walk, a historic street in Chelsea overlooking the Thames. Laurence Olivier, Henry James, Dante Gabriel Rossetti, and Mick Jagger and Keith Richards of the Rolling Stones are among those who have lived on this street.

Under Jack's tutelage I learned how to move calmly and safely through the streets of London—without alerting packs of paparazzi. I knew our relationship could not last: Anjelica kept threatening to turn up, and Jack had made it plain that ours was no more than a passing affair. But for a while I was happy. He was elegant and gracious and talented and kind, and I owe him a lot. I adored him; he was sweet—no, more than sweet. He was fun, fun, fun.

I was enormously attracted to everything about him: his good manners, his soft, slow voice, that twinkle in his eyes, the smile, the way he could make going to a party or a restaurant feel like you had deliciously succumbed to something wild. I had never thought that any man could hold a candle to Pierre, but Jack could. I felt, once more, young and sexy, and what a treat it was to drive around London in Jack's chauffeur-driven Daimler.

One night, after a day of shooting on *The Shining*—about a man's descent into madness—Jack related how director Stanley Kubrick had made him eat thirty-four grilled cheese sandwiches as they struggled to get that perfect take. He wasn't hungry that night.

But Jack also taught me about a lifestyle of no strings, of freedom, of independence. I had talked the talk, but could I walk the walk? Could I have the romance without the commitment? Turns out I could. He taught me how to be free.

The Marqusees had put me up in the Savoy, where I felt pampered. "How strange and marvellous," I wrote in my diary. "Perhaps it is over—the years of pessimism and self-destructiveness. I feel good, alive." But then, I always felt good and alive when I was falling in love. Like pregnancy, the adrenaline of love was and is a powerful antidote to depression.

My diary conveys with clarity just how much of the time I was ricocheting between highs and lows. When something went well, I ascended, and as I climbed, I began to feel invincible and act accordingly. My mind raced and I couldn't slow it down. I would spin around, cooking up wild plans, feeling incredibly attractive and wanted by every man who set eyes on me, whirling out into the night to go to yet more parties. There was nothing I could not do, and no one who did not profoundly desire me. I was the life of every party: I was irresistible and promiscuous. And it didn't matter how much I spent because there would always be more money coming in, and if there wasn't, well, I could make more. Wasn't I a brilliant actress and a gifted photographer?

Then would come a setback—an ugly article in a newspaper, a taunt from a reporter, a slight from a casual lover—and I would sink again. I would come home from a heavy night and collapse into a dreamless sleep, not waking before noon, only to start out again on another round of parties and flirtation.

I was drawn towards celebrity yet repulsed and revolted by it. My mind was awhirl in guilt and fear and fantasy. For a while I imagined myself as Joan of Arc, in a new version of her life, this one ending with her rebirth as a boy child.

A right-wing tabloid inveigled me into doing an interview. Next morning, I opened the paper to find the story. "She walked out on the Prime Minister," it began, "left her three little boys, rocked the world with her weekend with the Rolling Stones." The piece went on to describe me as a "self-confessed" hippie who smoked dope, used four-letter words and didn't wear a bra. I bitterly resented the piece. In her frumpy, superficial, nasty way, the reporter had managed not to understand a single thing I was trying to say. I thought I would die of misery and shame.

An ominously dark diary entry for April 1978 reads: "Again the thought of death (sweet release) comes over me, here, now. Would I not be better off?"

My life in London could not go on and I was lucky to get away. The book was finished and delivered, Jack Nicholson returned to Anjelica and I went back to New York.

But before leaving Chelsea, I met a wonderful man, a Formula One race-car driver named Jorge Koechlin. His paternal grandfather had been an officer in the Peruvian army and his maternal grandfather was a direct descendant of Emperor Franz Josef of Austria. Jorge's family had gone from Austria to Peru in the late nineteenth century. I adored Jorge. In New York, we continued to see each other. We stay in touch even now. He was one of the great knights of my life.

Back in Canada, there had been dramatic changes. With only four weeks left of his five-year term, Pierre had called an election and lost. The cards had been stacked against him: Canadians professed themselves tired of their charismatic prime minister and his patrician ways. While Pierre toured the country with almost arrogant disdain, Joe Clark and the Conservatives wooed them with bonhomie and earthiness.

Early on election night, May 22, 1979, it became clear where the vote was headed. The defeat was overwhelming. Though Pierre himself kept his seat, fourteen members of his Liberal cabinet lost theirs.

Unfortunately for me, I had assumed that Pierre could only win. I was devastated that he had suffered defeat, and humiliating defeat at that. We talked on the telephone that evening, and I commiserated with him on the loss.

"It's true, quite true," he told me. "We're out."

Against the advice of friends who were with me that night, I insisted on going to Studio 54—where the press found me. I was seen to be dancing the night callously away, and it was thus that they portrayed me next morning, pirouetting around with a naked midriff and dishevelled hair, dancing on my husband's political pyre. I could not have felt more ashamed.

My humiliation that summer was complete when I saw the article that appeared in *Playgirl* magazine. One of the first things that happens with the swing from mania to depression is that the body plummets into sickness. I had agreed, after much persuasion, to do an interview with a reporter from *Playgirl*. When still in New York, before news of Pierre's defeat, I had rung to cancel the interview, telling her that I was sick.

The young woman was friendly, solicitous. Could she at least drop by with some chicken soup for me? Foolishly, very foolishly, I agreed, touched that someone would want to go to such trouble. She arrived, was charming, listened to my woes, asked a few kind questions. Before I knew it I was pouring out my woes, the coziness and apparent safety of the situation making me confide in her my deepest secrets. The resulting article was more of a disaster than even I could have imagined. I was in complete disgrace.

Pierre, however, was reassuring. He never blamed my outrageous behaviour for his political defeat. This was one form his generosity took: tight-fisted with money, yet loath to cast blame when that would have been so easy to do. And he was never judgmental about my mental illness, always proactive—he wanted help for me. That is so important for a depressed person, to have the support of one's inner circle.

Pierre was a complicated man, and full of contradictions. He was a kind man who could be extraordinarily mean, a very modest and shy man who could be monumentally arrogant. That's true of all of us: we are all yin and yang, light and dark.

My antics in London that year had not gone unnoticed. Soon after landing back in Manhattan, I went to a dinner party where I was seated next to a fashionable psychiatrist, Dr. Ron Fieve. I had met him before, with his wife, and knew that he worked at Columbia University. He didn't beat around the bush.

"Margaret, you mustn't mind my saying this, but I really think you need professional help. I believe that you are manic depressive. I can help you." I was taken aback, but at the same time deeply relieved. When he suggested that I go to see him in his office, I agreed.

Next day, sitting across from his desk, it all came tumbling out. I told him about the highs, about the days when I felt that I was invincible and immortal and there was nothing I could not do and no one whom I could not attract, and then the days when I didn't want to get out of bed, felt so full of guilt and insecurity and bleakness that I could only cry. I told him about the rushes of joy and elation versus the nights when I wanted only to be dead. I have no real memory now of what I actually said. I know only that once I had started I couldn't stop talking and that as I talked I knew how badly I wanted to find some peace of mind. What struck him was not so much what I said but the way I said it. He listened, then confirmed his original diagnosis.

Then Dr. Fieve told me that he had been working with a new treatment, a salt called lithium, and that it provided stability and balance to people like myself with violent mood swings. Lithium, he said, had been used since 1870 to treat mania after links were established between excessive uric acid and a range of psychiatric disorders. The treatment had fallen out of fashion only to be rediscovered by an Australian psychiatrist, John Cade.

In 1949, Dr. Cade had described experiments using lithium on rodents and in some trials with people. But the medical profession had been slow to follow suit because of lithium's effect on thyroid and kidney function and one other serious drawback— even minor overdoses could lead to death.

However, lithium had at last been approved by the U.S. Food and Drug Administration in 1970, and it was already altering the lives of untold numbers of people throughout the world. Dr. Fieve warned me of two things: one, lithium did not suit everyone; and, two, the nature of the manic depression beast was such that those afflicted often stopped taking it the moment they felt better, only to set off on yet another roller coaster of mood swings until persuaded to go back into treatment. I listened, and agreed to try lithium. He wrote me out a prescription; I took it to a pharmacist and swallowed my first dose in the fall of 1979.

The effect on me was dramatic and almost immediate. Within days, my horizons had ceased to swing dramatically, I

37. At the White House in 1977, wearing the "scandalous" dress.
From left: Pierre, Jimmy Carter, me, Rosalynn Carter.

38. Here I am photographing my favourite photographer,
Canadian Peter Bregg, in Washington.

39. Here I am at 24 Sussex, just before leaving for New York in 1977. Years later, my friends had this picture signed and framed for me.

40. Going off to seek fame and fortune.

41. On a beach with Michel, near my sister's
house in West Vancouver, 1978.

42. Saying goodbye to my boys. Leaving them was always so hard.

43. Dancing with tennis champion Vitas Gerulaitis at Studio 54 in New York.

44. Andy Warhol and me at Studio 54. He and I often stood at the edge of the crowd, in awe of the spectacle before us.

45. Sophia Loren in Montreal, where she was making a film. I visited her on set and took photos all day.

46. On the set of NBC's *Today Show* with Jane Pauley, when I wouldn't answer her questions.

47. My friend Heather Gillin, who was second mummy to my boys, with Sacha and Michel.

48. Celebrating my sister Betsy's wedding. Sacha's not in the picture because he objected to the itchyness of his grey flannels.

49. Michel and Sacha on a summer day.

50. In front of my new house at 95 Victoria Street, Ottawa, 1980. My own house, at last.

51. In the backyard of my house in Ottawa.
Refusing to conform, Sacha wouldn't wear his
stylish matching sweater.

52. The boys being free, playing in the driveway of 24 Sussex.

53. In Jamaica in 1980, with my great friends Mary-Jean Green and Lady Mary Mitchell.

54. Taken in my home, when I was working in television.

55. In Ottawa with Bill Luxton, my co-host on the talk show *Morning Magazine*. I loved the research and preparation before the on-air interviews. I was always curious about people and made natural connections with the guests.

56. My initiation into comedy, on *Big City Comedy Hour*, with John Candy. He was a wonderful, kind man. A great Canadian. The highlight: John pied me during the introduction.

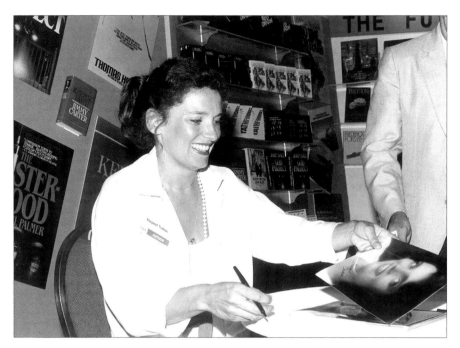

57. A book signing for *Consequences.*

58. With Fried on our wedding day, April 18, 1984. I wore a navy blue coat dress from Saint Laurent.

59. At home with baby Kyle. He was the first baby who was all mine, no nannies.

60. Mother and child, November 27, 1984.

61. Fried could not have been a better stepfather to my boys.

62. Michel and Kyle at Halloween. My three older boys
were thrilled to have a younger brother.

63. My 40th birthday, in 1988; I'm pregnant with Ally.
From left: Karina (Fried's niece), Sacha, me, Kyle, Michel.

64. I had always dreamed of having a daughter. Ally was
born February 2, 1989. She was such a happy baby.

65. Sacha with his little sister.

66. With my mother.

67. Ally, at the age of three, playing on the governor general's fence.

68. Fisherman Kyle, at our cottage on Newboro Lake.

69. My little princess. I loved to sew, and
Ally is wearing one of my creations.

70. Justin and me in my backyard.

was sleeping at the proper hours and I had lost my taste for the wild life. The febrile and dangerous pleasures of New York had lost their charm. I looked around and thought, "What am I doing here?"

For the first time in almost two years, I felt normal. And I knew, with absolute certainty, that I had to go home. Looking back over my wild and incoherent months, I felt overwhelmed with horror and disbelief.

Jorge Koechlin was a great help to me around this time. He was with me in New York and he knew how badly I missed my children. He urged me to go back home and I could see that he was right.

"Peace is descending on me," I wrote in my diary. "I feel grounded." I packed my bags and went back to Ottawa, not as a penitent, seeking forgiveness, but as a mother, restored to some kind of normalcy.

Pierre and I now discussed the future calmly, with affection towards each other. The tension between husband and wife when a marriage is crumbling dissipates dramatically when the two parties no longer have to cohabit. The same opportunities for sniping and venting aren't there. What a relief!

We agreed that I would find a house, not far from Stornoway, the house of the leader of the Opposition, into which he was about to move, and that we would share the boys. By great good luck, a small red-brick Victorian house on Victoria Street—within walking distance of Pierre and not far from St. Bartholomew's, the oldest church in Ottawa—had just come on the market.

I saw the for-sale sign as I was walking along the road. The owners were asking for a $60,000 deposit. Hearing rumours that Paddington Press was going bankrupt, I flew to London and asked for my advance. With great reluctance, but fearing that refusal would push their creditors to close in, they gave me a cheque, which I immediately used as a down payment on the house. Pierre generously agreed to pay the mortgage on the rest.

A few months later, I moved into what was my first real home. Pierre and I, living on government property, had had nothing of our own—save a few sheets, some pots and pans at Harrington Lake and a magnificent yellow Chinese rug, which I had once admired in an exhibition and he had bought for me. With these and other items, I began to furnish my house, turning it into a real home for Justin, Sacha and Michel, for whom I now shopped and cooked.

The moment I moved in I was delighted with my purchase: it was attractive, unpretentious and superbly and totally reno-vated, with track lighting and pine floors. I hung heavy curtains against the winter cold and painted the walls of the master bed-room blush pink, to go with a thick, pale pink carpet and flowery curtains in the Japanese style. I did, and do, love pink for its calm-ing effect, a fact that prison wardens and hospital administrators fully understand and often deploy.

For the little boys, my house was a dream come true. They had bunk beds and they kept their bicycles in the garage and could play and bike for hours in total safety in the lane behind the house with all the other local boys, and there was a yard where they could play soccer and badminton.

The first caller at my new home was a large van from Johnson's Antiques delivering a butcher-block kitchen table. I solemnly laid a picnic lunch on it and proceeded to inaugurate my new life. Many years later, Justin was asked whether there was, in fact, anything in particular that he remembered his mother saying to him. He replied, "She said to have fun," and that, indeed, was what I wanted for them.

In my life, I've been lucky in real estate—I was so pleased with my new acquisition. Above the kitchen sink in my house was a ledge, and here I put a row of African violets. From the street, the house looked small, with its screened-in porch, but beyond the threshold lay a big sitting room and four bedrooms, with a large garden in the back. Pierre, when he came to see it, admitted that what I had finally pulled off was a "real home"—something we had never had.

Pierre, too, had his own house. In the fall of 1979, he acquired an art deco house on Pine Avenue in Montreal, the former residence of architect Ernest Cormier. I found it a bleak mausoleum, dark and chilly with marble floors. On the other hand, it had a water-bed, and the boys whooped when they found that.

On New Year's Eve of 1979, Pierre came to my house in Ottawa and, over champagne, we toasted the joys of house owner-ship. We put the boys to bed and as he was about to leave, I raised the matter of an allowance. I thought I was being reasonable. Pierre would be away campaigning for the next several months and I would have exclusive charge of the boys.

When he took out $50 from his wallet and asked if that would be enough, I felt I was being both mocked and humiliated. Enraged, I went at him and he pinned me to the floor, and my screams wakened the three boys—who were all very afraid and alarmed.

Michel, then just four, saved the day. He asked Pierre to come to his room, and I have no idea what was said but they were gone half an hour. Little Michel, Pierre would observe later, always put sense into him.

Both Pierre and I were mortified by what had happened, and we did get counselling. But there was no repairing our marriage. I had seen hate in his eyes that night, as he had seen hate in mine.

Pierre was not a violent man, and I absolutely forgave him. I look back and I understand that by all my antics I had wounded his pride. Worse, I had broken his heart.

CHAPTER 8

A PLUMP, HAPPY PIGEON

"My dominant emotion was jealousy . . . that she could be so free."
THE PIERRE CHARACTER IN THE PLAY *MAGGIE AND PIERRE*, 1980,
BY LINDA GRIFFITHS

Now began the happiest years of my life. All the uncertainty, all the loneliness, the sense of having no work and no purpose, faded away. I became, at last, the person I had always wanted to be. The relief, to me and to those around me, was enormous. There were a few hiccups to start with, but those I dealt with—or at least, I thought I did.

Though Dr. Fieve had told me that I should see a psychiatrist as soon as I returned to Ottawa, I hadn't really taken in how carefully the lithium would need to be monitored. I was casual about making an appointment, perhaps because I was now, for the first time in many years, calm—too calm, as it turned out. And also extremely hungry. From the moment I woke up in the morning to the moment I switched off my light at night, I thought about food. Dragging myself sleepily from my bed in the mornings, I would start longing to eat. At night, I woke from deep sleeps ravenously hungry and would get up and make myself toast and hot chocolate. When the boys were with me, I baked cakes and biscuits and cookies and pies, as if my life depended on it.

As the days passed, I sank further into a contented stupor. Those of my friends who noticed became worried, but as I made fewer and fewer efforts to contact anyone, I grew fat, and then fatter, largely on my own. None of my clothes fit. This was not life—hibernation, more like it.

Then came the day I was too embarrassed to go out; I noticed that I had begun to shake. At first this occurred just when I lifted something up and I could usually control it, but then I shook if I tried to use a knife or drink from a cup. I did seek medical advice.

The levels of lithium were checked, found to be too high and decreased. That was what accounted for my huge weight gain: many psychotropic drugs cause weight gain by slowing metabolism or fuelling appetite—many taking these drugs can't seem to get enough carbohydrates and sugars. Not all doctors warn their patients to watch their diet, and what happens is this: a depressed patient gets fat, and the flab only worsens the depression. Many patients don't need to take these drugs for years, but some patients do. Since I was complaining of lethargy, a new psychiatrist recommended an antidepressant called Tofranil. Seeing my size, he urged me to go on a diet, something I found virtually impossible. Lowering the dose of lithium had stopped the shaking. From time to time, I would catch sight of my bulk in a mirror and make strenuous efforts to cut the medication down further. Within days my head would begin to clear, but withdrawal symptoms followed, I felt sick and I returned to the old dose.

As Christmas 1979 approached, I felt so comatose that I realized I was not capable of making the necessary preparations. The idea of finding a tree, decorating it, and shopping for and cooking a Christmas dinner was inconceivable. A friend urged me to ring my mother in Vancouver.

"Mom," I said weakly over the phone. "I don't think I can manage without you. Will you come?" She was with me the next day and set about keeping me busy with baking, buying presents and decorating the house.

Aside from our New Years's Eve drama, relations with Pierre had been going well. We had a wonderful Christmas all together, as a family; I had money in the bank, and I was once again imagining that I might get back together with him. We had settled down to a routine of sharing the boys, and if I slept most of the time they were with him, I somehow found the strength to stay awake when they were with me.

For the first nine months of my return to Ottawa, Pierre had been out of government, living in Stornoway—the official residence of the leader of the Opposition since 1950. The two-storey house in the Rockcliffe Park district of Ottawa—the setting for a great many embassies—was built in 1914 for a grocery-store magnate. Sir Wilfrid Laurier, Canada's seventh prime minister, was a godfather to one of the original owner's sons and he had apparently visited often. The house was called Stornoway by its second occupants; their ancestral home had been in a town by that name on an island in the Outer Hebrides of Scotland. The house is bright and well appointed, but I felt no sense of belonging there. Just as I had at 24 Sussex, I lodged in the attic until I moved into my new house.

When Pierre had moved out of 24 Sussex, all our things were carefully packed away into boxes and stored in Stornoway, but Pierre did not bother to unpack most of his as he did not expect to be out of government long. He was, however, frantic when he discovered that a valuable painting by the French cubist painter Georges Braque was missing, along with a precious jar of black truffles. He foraged, like one possessed, in his boxes, but there was no sign of either.

One day, some time later, I was unpacking my own crates in my new house when I found both the painting and the truffles concealed among my own things. Pierre was overjoyed. I discovered that they had, in fact, been put there on purpose by Hildegarde, the senior maid at 24 Sussex. She had despaired when she realized that I was moving into a new house with barely a single possession of my own, and she thought she would slip a few things into my boxes. Pierre had made it absolutely clear when we parted that there wasn't much that I was entitled to.

"After all," he pointed out, "you can't have fifty–fifty of 24 Sussex—since that's not ours." What he didn't add was that he didn't really want me to have fifty–fifty of our wedding presents either, with the result that I had come away with almost nothing.

Pierre had been right to think that his period in the political wilderness would be brief. Joe Clark's Progressive Conservative government had fallen after a defeat on a motion of non-confidence, and new elections had been called. Pierre's exile had mellowed and humbled him into running the best election campaign of his life, and the results had proved it. He had taken 44 per cent of the vote—only 1 percentage point less than in his heyday of 1968. On March 3, 1980, Pierre and a thirty-two-member cabinet were sworn into office at Rideau Hall. Pierre was again prime minister.

The campaign had done something else. Since he had had to be away so much, I had sole care of the boys for a lot of that winter. That this arrangement had gone so well, that I was clearly proving myself to be a responsible and loving mother, made possible our agreement to share custody of the boys.

Spring approached slowly, very slowly, and I began to come out of hibernation. I felt a bit fitter, though I was still desperate for a job. A possible film of my book, *Beyond Reason* (published in 1979), was being talked about, but I refused even to discuss starring in it, knowing instinctively that I did not want to relive a past that I had truly put behind me.

Then one day came a call from Ottawa's local television station, CJOH, asking me to participate in a telethon to raise funds for the Civic Hospital. It turned out that this was something that I was good at, and when the producer asked me to demonstrate cooking a Japanese meal in a half-hour special, I was delighted to do that too.

Out of this volunteer work came a more serious job invitation. Not long before, I would have been offended at the idea of appearing on anything less than *Good Morning America*. Now I was only too happy to accept a job as co-host with Bill Luxton on CJOH's regular weekday show, *Morning Magazine*. The job, I reasoned, would introduce me to the world of everyday television, earn me some money, provide me with a regular job and perhaps lead to other things. Most important of all, I was grateful and profoundly happy to be working.

I wasn't due to start work for some months, and that invitation acted like a wakeup call. When I looked in the mirror, what I could see was a little, very round, very plump pigeon. This was not what the producers wanted.

So one day I got up, said enough is enough and stopped taking the lithium. That was the hardest thing I have ever done. I threw away all my pills. Pierre, suspecting nothing, took the children off to Harrington Lake. Then I closed my front door and weathered the storm.

For ten days, I sweated constantly, I was sick, I had diarrhea. I felt weak, cold and shivery. I was dizzy and paranoid. But I did it. The day came when I woke up feeling better. My head was clear and I no longer felt sick.

Now I needed to get thin. I started a ferocious diet, went running and swimming every day. I am lucky in being able to lose weight quickly. Within six weeks, I was fit and a great deal thinner.

Then came a totally improbable invitation. A Japanese nightclub owner wanted me to come to Tokyo to open a new club, and he was willing to pay the staggering sum of $20,000 for the job. I was a bit suspicious—so much money to do so little? But I needed the money, and Japan was one of the countries in which I felt happiest. A wealthy real estate developer was planning to invest in a club; he hoped to fly me, first class, to Tokyo, where I would make three half-hour personal appearances at his discotheque. The Japanese, he was reported as saying, "think of you as one of the foremost spokeswomen of your generation." How could I refuse? It didn't occur to me that things were not as they seemed.

I went to find Pierre to discuss my plans for the Japanese trip, and he seemed pleased that I was doing so well. I remember saying to him at the time words that would later fill me with horror. "Psychiatry as I experienced it," I told Pierre, "is no more than a gigantic illusion."

I believed myself totally well and I forgot all about Dr. Fieve's warnings. All this talk of manic depression had been absurd. It was just as I had thought: my former life had been mad, not me. That life had made me lonely and down one day, frenetic and busy the next. Yet again, denial was playing its part. There was nothing wrong with me, only with everyone else. And so, for a while, it turned out.

On March 4, 1980—my ninth wedding anniversary, as it happened—I left for Japan. My Japanese hosts had sent me two first-class tickets, for myself and my sister Jan (who came along to keep me company), and a cheque for $4,000, some of which I used to buy new clothes. We were met at the airport by limousines, two charming young female interpreters and our escort, a good-looking young Japanese man driving his own silver-blue Mercedes. We were told that he would look after us during our stay. Our lodging was the presidential suite in the Hotel New Otani. Photographers were kept at a discreet distance. Everyone was courteous, charming and generous.

So began four days that were as enjoyable as they were bizarre. I was thinking of writing a Japanese cookbook and had brought my cameras with me. My hosts arranged that I should be taken everywhere that interested me. On the second evening came my first guest appearance. I had expected crowds, photographers, publicity. Instead, I spent half an hour sitting on a sofa in a fairly modest drinking club high up in a skyscraper, making desultory conversation with a small gathering of Japanese dignitaries. My next two appearances followed the same course. I asked about the music and the customers, only to be told that they were still waiting for their liquor and music licences.

I had also been invited to do a television interview, which I feared would match all the hostility I had experienced with the British and North American press. But the interviewer could not have been more charming. Did I like Japanese food? How many children did I have? What would my book on Japanese food be like? This was all very mystifying.

I spent my days enjoying myself, visiting Tokyo's markets and taking photographs. An unofficial visit had also been arranged with Madame Shigeko Ohira, the prime minister's wife, over cups of tea with Jun Ashida, Japan's foremost dress designer. Moichi Tanabe, a noted Japanese writer who also founded a bookstore chain in Japan, took me to a restaurant where we were served thin slices of lobster and a nest of noodles full of delicious fish. When I had my final encounter with the developer, he tactfully slipped an envelope containing the remaining fee into my hand.

Only on the very last day did everything become clear. My invitation had just been a front. *Beyond Reason,* which had caused such a stir and so much scandal when it was published in Canada, had been bought by a Japanese publisher and was now being launched. Knowing that I would never have agreed to a publicity tour, the Japanese publishers had had the clever idea of hiding it behind something that I *would* do—namely, open a discreet club. I felt only a moment of annoyance. I had had a wonderful time, and I laughed when I looked carefully through all the photographs, taken day after day by a man I had assumed to be the developer's photographer. In every caption appeared the words "Beyond Reason."

I returned to Ottawa feeling rich, appreciated and laden down with presents. My reunion with the boys was happy. Leaving my suitcases unpacked, my cameras scattered around and my fur coat on the bed, I took the boys as a treat to see *The Black Stallion.* We got home at about nine o'clock, and I was irritated to see that the place was in even more of a mess than I remembered. There was chaos indeed. In our absence, the house had been burgled. My first thought was for the boys' security. As calmly as possible, not to frighten them, I tucked them all up in my bed, closed the door and called the children's security force, who were parked as usual outside our door after we got back from the cinema.

The burglars had been very thorough. All my cameras were gone, together with the undeveloped film—effectively nixing my Japanese cookbook. The suitcase with all the presents had vanished. So had the Andrew Grima gold pin studded with diamonds that the queen had given me on her state visit to Canada in 1974, along with a valuable and charming gold cross that Pierre had had specially made for me one Christmas. My $20,000 fisher fur coat was missing.

When I reported the theft to Pierre, he was very droll in his response: "Well, Margaret, it was a magnificent coat—but you no longer live a magnificent life."

(Somewhat to my shame, the jewellery turned up some years later when I was searching for Christmas wrapping paper in my basement. As I pulled a roll off a shelf, a knapsack fell out from behind it. I unzipped it and found all the missing jewellery, which I myself had put there and forgotten all about. But the fur coat was never found).

After Pierre had moved to Stornoway, protection for both him and the boys had virtually ceased, but now that he was back in office, new arrangements would need to be made, especially in light of the burglary. While in the past I had hated and dreaded the guards, now I welcomed them. As long as the boys were with me, I had a police car parked constantly outside my front door. Police accompanied us while we shopped or went to the movies, and each boy, when on his own, had his own guard.

Justin, who was becoming an accomplished skier, took a guard from the RCMP security detail ("the children's squad," we called it) along with him on the slopes. Pierre, me, the three boys:

we all had designations when security communicated with each other on their walkie-talkies. Pierre was Maple One, I was Maple Two, and the boys were Maples Three, Four and Five.

Security tightened still more when, not long afterwards, John Lennon was murdered in New York and there were fears that other cranks might copy the murderer. Though I resisted turning my house into Fort Knox, complete with iron grilles and gates, I did agree to stronger locks and reinforced doors, and I soon learned to appreciate the joys of not having to park my own car on a freezing day with three cold and impatient small boys in tow.

The protection also made me feel a lot safer. One extremely cold snowy day in midwinter, I was at home with a friend, Gro Southam. We were sitting talking when the bell went. I opened the front door and there was a dishevelled, barefoot man who spoke almost no English but managed to explain that he had seen a picture of me in the papers and that I had looked very sympathetic. He put his foot in the door and began to push his way in. At this moment, Gro, who is forceful, rushed up behind me, edged him out and slammed the door. We then used the newly installed black phone—one connected directly to the police—and within minutes squad cars were racing down the street. The man was found not far away, wandering in his bare feet through the snow. He turned out to be a Polish émigré with mental problems. The whole episode taught me how sensible our precautions were.

———————

The moment had now come to talk to the boys about our lives. Justin was eight, Sacha six and Michel four, and they behaved like all brothers do. Justin was the golden boy, very bright and quick and loving, though he tended to lead the others astray; Sacha was disciplined and serious, like Pierre; and Michel was always cheerful and lively. We had been able to get away without explanation until now because one of us could always be away "working."

Before that moment, I had thought—from time to time and rather wistfully—of returning to Pierre. Not long ago I found a letter that I wrote to him in the summer of 1982 but never sent. "I am a happy woman," I had written. "I am not turning to you in desperation and loneliness but rather in a positive, loving need . . . Do you think we could begin to even think about reconciliation, Pierre? I would do anything I could to allow the possibility of us all being together again as our whole family. I'm not too old to even think of adding to our size—but what a dreamer I am!" It was not to be.

For the moment, we had settled into a pattern and we both agreed that it was better for the boys if they understood what was going on. Pierre and I had had a few sessions with a family counsellor, which cleared both our minds and proved to us how fundamentally different we were from each other. Together, we explained to the boys that while Mom and Dad would always remain friends, we were better off living in two separate homes. This talk was especially hard on Sacha, and I hated having to tell him. But as the counsellor put it, Pierre and I were like two trains running in the same direction but on parallel tracks and those tracks would never converge.

Meanwhile, Pierre maintained discretion. When reporters asked him to comment on the state of his marriage, he turned the question around and asked them to talk about the state of their marriages. Asked about his party-girl wife, he said only, "She's a good woman," and he accepted part of the blame. In his book *Memoirs,* he conceded that he was in his fifties when he was learning about marriage, parenthood and the workings of politics, all simultaneously—"So perhaps it was a little too much for me and, regrettably, I didn't succeed that well."

In 1980, I decided to be brave and watch a play called *Maggie and Pierre.* The one-woman play was written by Linda Griffiths, who played both parts. Explaining that she saw us as "epic characters" in that we contained "all the elements of humanity, magnified," the writer and actress justified the play by saying that our story had already been shared by all of Canada, and "actually by a lot of the world as well." I thought the playwright had caught Pierre's aloofness and obsession with himself.

The play starts in Tahiti, with me telling Pierre that I had no need to read about Bacchanalian rituals in Edward Gibbon's classic history text, *The Decline and Fall of the Roman Empire,* because I had already "been there."

It continues:

PIERRE: *That sounds like a long journey. How much farther do you want to go?*

MAGGIE: *Forever. And you? . . . I want to be world renowned, to shape destiny, to be deliriously happy. You might say, I want it all.*
PIERRE: *I want to be world renowned, to shape destiny, to be deliriously happy. You might say, I want it all.*

Griffiths got it right: I had wanted it all. There was another bit in the play that felt very close to the bone. Maggie is leaving Pierre and begging him to come with her; not willing to abandon his political career, he refuses. Pierre is talking to a journalist called Henry (this is one spot where the play erred, for Pierre would never have spoken to a journalist this way): "You know something, Henry? As we were going through all those horrendous fights, my wife was at my feet, and she was crying and screaming and wailing and literally banging her head against the wall, and I stood there, frozen, in the classic pose of man, locked in my own gender, not knowing whether to go to her and comfort her, or leave because it's too personal to watch, or hit her, or what to do. And my dominant emotion was jealousy . . . that she could be so free."

I actually liked the play, and so did many critics. In *The Globe and Mail* Ray Conlogue wrote, "The trouble with reviewing Maggie and Pierre is to know where to start admiring it . . . What lifts the play above expectations is its compassion. Griffiths explores our erstwhile first couple without ever taking a cheap shot." At long last, someone had written about us without taking a cheap shot.

Justin, Sacha and Michel took the separation of their mother and father very well. Soon they were like several others of their friends at Rockcliffe Park Public School (where I had studied for two years as a child in grades one and two), with two parents' addresses and telephone numbers on the school list. What differences Pierre and I had over the boys' upbringing—I was more indulgent when it came to television and occasional snack food but more demanding over their clothes—we worked out calmly between us.

Pierre was a wonderful and loving father and now took to getting one of the boys to accompany him each time he went abroad on an official trip. In due course, Justin would go to Russia, Sacha to the Middle East, and Michel to Washington.

On one of those trips, Pierre was huddling with Anwar Sadat at the presidential palace in Cairo, along with Léopold Senghor, the president of Senegal, and later UN secretary-general Boutros Boutros-Ghali. An Egyptian who was translating for Pierre introduced Sacha to the three men. Sacha, then seven, had just returned from the zoo. He gleefully reported that earlier that day, he had seen four giraffes and three elephants, "and now I'm meeting two presidents." Senghor understood English and he burst out laughing.

A battle that I did have with Pierre concerned the children's clothes for these trips. He saw no problem in taking them in the jeans and T-shirts given to them by well-wishers wherever they went. I insisted that they be properly dressed, as a mark of respect for their hosts, so I got them polo shirts and khaki pants and blazers. For the colder weather, and for the memorial ceremony on

November 11, when they always accompanied Pierre, I found trench coats for them. From those days forward, they would look well turned out.

We agreed that for the moment they would stay at Rockcliffe Park Public School, one of the oldest and most respected local schools. Generations of politicians' and ambassadors' children had been educated since 1922 at the school, which boasted an excellent French immersion program. I felt strongly that the three boys should be part of their local community and not somewhere apart, in a private school.

But I had to accept that when they reached ten or eleven years of age, they would move into the French stream and have the kind of rigorous academic education that Pierre valued. As for sports, neither Pierre nor I were much in favour of team sports. We decided that they would play soccer, so as not to lose out altogether on team activities, but not hockey, which I thought violent and brutish. Instead, they would ski, canoe, hike and swim.

We were delighted with our arrangements. They now had the best of all worlds and our individual concentration when we were with them. As the boys insisted on going to school by bus with their friends, we had their police escort follow the bus. I missed our times at Harrington Lake dreadfully. The lake was where I had been happiest, but Pierre took that away. A little revenge.

Though I missed Pierre, I knew that we were doing the right thing. Our ages made us so very different, but we were also completely different people, with almost no tastes or ideas in common. Pierre was a devoted father and an exceptional man, but I now realized that I had always felt emotionally bullied by him. And I had accepted it because deep down I felt that I was no good and that I deserved it.

That spring of 1980 I began to go out with other people, and for about a year I had a serious relationship with a man called Jimmy Johnson, a lawyer and businessman who had two children of his own. As children, he and I had lived on the same street in Ottawa, though we never kept company. Jimmy was Irish Canadian, a great guy and a great skier and a good role model for the boys, and I believed that he and I shared the same beliefs. We both loathed cocktail parties and organized events, and we both loved spontaneity. But I was in Nassau, hosting a special for the Ottawa TV station, when I realized that I couldn't go back to Jimmy. On the whole, I was living a quiet life in a very dull city and I didn't meet many people. Daunting to some men was the fact that I had been married to Pierre Trudeau and been the prime minister's wife.

When I got home, I took off with the boys and friends to ski at Mont Tremblant in the Laurentians. And there something wonderful happened. We had stopped in a brasserie for dinner. In the bar, I met a charming, good-looking German man called Fried Kemper. He invited us over to dinner at his chalet the next night and it was lots of fun, with all the children together. We played charades. As with all the important men in my life, one look and I knew. He felt the same. We skied together, we talked, we fell in love.

Fried's parents, John (Joachim) and Mary Kemper, had escaped from East Germany at the end of the Second World War.

They described the terror as they were trying to get away, hiding in ditches and in the woods and hearing the Russian soldiers filing by. The Germans had invaded Russia earlier in the war; now the Russians were returning the favour. The Red Army cut a horrid swath, countless German civilians were raped and murdered, and many Germans committed suicide rather than face being caught.

Applying for a visa at the Canadian consulate in Berlin, the Kempers had been promised a farm in their new country. They arrived to find that the farm didn't exist and that they were entitled only to a flat in a tenement building. John got a job selling vacuum cleaners. But he prospered, and Fried, his brother and his sister were given good educations and a happy childhood. John had gone on to build up a successful real estate business. By the time we met, Fried was in partnership with his father.

I felt us to be very well suited. I was now thirty-four, Fried thirty-three. He had never been married and he loved children. Though he had different interests from mine—he was an entrepreneur and a jock, never finished university and rarely read books—he was good and honest and straightforward and neither formal nor grand. He also loved to cook, as I did, and it was with him that I started to make osso bucco, an Italian dish that would become my trademark meal. Above all, Fried made me laugh. Fried had a quick wit and he knew how to tease without hurting.

Living with Pierre, who was by nature very serious and whose one kind of humour was slapstick and pratfalls (he loved Charlie Chaplin), I had forgotten how important laughter was to me. Fried had a crude sense of humour, but he was outrageously funny and he had me laughing all the time.

Soon, Fried was like a delightful elder brother to the boys, joining in their sports, teaching them about the land and how to build—docks, sheds, a cottage. He was very handy. Before long, he sold his house and moved in with us. He wanted us to get married, but Pierre, as a Catholic, remained totally opposed to a divorce.

By now, I had been given my own television show. In the winter of 1984, I invited a fertility expert, a doctor, to be my guest. To ask the right questions, I had done a considerable amount of research on the subject. I learned that after the age of thirty-six, the chances of getting pregnant drop dramatically. Even though I had three children, these statistics alarmed me: I realized that somewhere in the back of my mind, I had thought I would have children with Fried. After the show, I consulted the expert. I was using an IUD as contraception, so what did he advise? The doctor suggested that I visit his clinic, and twenty-four hours later, he removed my IUD.

The night before, Fried and I had shared a hot tub out on the deck. It was snowing hard and as we sat in the bubbling hot water we drank a bottle of champagne. That romantic evening was momentous in both my life and Pierre's, for he had spent it out walking through the blizzard, trying to decide whether or not to step down from politics. I, on the other hand, was conceiving a child.

Pierre had reached the decision that his political days were over. He was sixty-four and had spent almost his entire life in politics; in all, he had been prime minister for fifteen of the last sixteen years. He wanted time to read, to see his friends, to listen to music. He decided not only to leave politics but to move to Montreal, to get back to his childhood roots and to his French life. There was nothing sadder, we agreed, when he told me what he was going to do, than an aging former politician hanging around the fringes of political life.

Several weeks later I was in New York, where I had gone to record interviews for my show, when someone handed me a glass of red wine. I took a sip and found it tasted very peculiar. Since with all three boys the same thing had happened—one sip of wine and I felt sick—I knew that I was pregnant.

Fried was delighted. My first act was to tell Pierre. We both cried. We had loved each other, but life—his wisdom, my capriciousness—had gotten in the way. Not wanting the new baby to bear his name, Pierre now agreed to a divorce. He thus became, as he told friends, the first prime minister to become a single parent as a result of divorce, though he had few weeks left to serve in office.

Fried and I were married very soon afterwards. On the day of the wedding, our car was stopped by Pierre's chauffeur as we drove towards the registrar's hall. He handed me a huge bunch of roses, with Pierre's love.

While Fried and I had been in Jamaica on holiday, my father had died—on February 7, 1984. He had had heart problems, and surgery, but he was only seventy-six; I was sad, but looking back on it I realize I did not mourn him properly. At our wedding dinner, a simple family occasion with a close friend as maid of honour, I was immensely touched by the way that John Kemper welcomed me into the family. He announced that since my boys had recently lost their grandfather, he would like to ask them to allow him to be their new one.

On November 17, 1984, Kyle was born—a big baby weighing well over eight pounds, with lots of dark, curly hair. He was the most perfect baby in the whole wide world.

I had chosen to have him in a birthing room, and Justin, Sacha and Michel came to view their new brother within minutes of the birth. They were now thirteen, eleven and nine years of age, and this new baby was an object of great excitement to them. For them, this was better than a puppy. The obstetrician had given me a shot of Demerol after the birth and I remember that I felt as if I were a bird, perched high in the corner of the room, looking down on the wonderful scene of Michel in his round granny glasses and old jeans, holding the baby in his arms.

We hadn't been able to decide on a name so we had leafed through a then-popular baby book, *Never Name Your Baby Bill*, and had come across Kyle in the K's.

For his second names, we called him after our fathers, James and Joachim. The day before, my sister Jan had had a baby girl she called Jamie, so there were now two cousins who were almost identical ages. I had given up my television show, having simply assumed that pregnant women could not appear onscreen; and, in any case, I intended to look after Kyle myself. I wanted to put behind me the years when my busy schedule as the prime minister's wife meant that there were times when my babies were cared for by nannies.

This was my second chance at happiness, and at being the kind of person I wanted to be—and I was allowed to be that with Fried. Those first years, we were so happy. I was in love with my husband and this newborn, who was everything I wanted. He was beautiful and he was mine. I was not obliged to attend any fancy parties and there were no nannies to contend with—which was a good thing because Kyle didn't like even a babysitter. We were besotted with him. Fried was playful and funny with him, Fried and I were working together on our dream summer house, and we had good friends. Everything was good.

Fried was part of a huge and loving extended family, and I realized how much I had missed the bustle and the affection of family life. We used the money from the sale of Fried's house to renovate mine and put in a new kitchen, family room, and master bedroom and bathroom. In 1971, John Kemper had bought 350 acres, with five miles of waterfront, on Newboro Lake. In the nineteenth century, engineers had built the Rideau Canal and a series of locks, thereby allowing boat access to a number of lakes and rivers. Newboro marked a dividing line, with all waterways north of the town flowing up towards Ottawa and all waters to the south flowing down to Kingston. John had sold off most of the waterfront land but kept two bays next to each other, and he had given each of his children the right to build a cottage while retaining the land himself in case of any splits in the family. Here, on an island just off the waterfront, Fried and I built a house.

The place was exactly what I had always wanted. We made it

very cozy, with a wraparound deck and a hot tub, and I put in a show kitchen that I had been able to acquire at half price. Wood defined the cottage: cedar on the outside, golden pine inside. I decorated the long, narrow house in some of my favourite colours—white and yellow and blue. There was a children's room with bunks, a spare room for friends and a loft where we put futons for more children. Fried already owned a chalet at Mont Tremblant in the Laurentians, a ski resort first made fashionable in the late 1930s. That was my idea of bliss: day after day of skiing with the family.

On Saturday nights, wherever we happened to be, we played card games and board games, and we built space stations out of Lego. On Saturday mornings, as a treat, the boys were allowed to make their own breakfasts while we slept; on just this one day, they could have as much sugared cereal as they wished and they ate it sitting in a row before the television, watching cartoons—Spider-Man, Bugs Bunny, the Road Runner.

I like to think that with Pierre and me as parents, Justin, Sacha and Michel got the best of both worlds—and I think they would agree. They had a wonderfully old-fashioned, strict father: no television in the house, they had to read the classics and discuss them at dinner, they had to put a penny in a jar when they didn't speak correct French. Pierre was generous with them, with his time, with his love. They had a wonderful outdoor life up at the cottage at Morin-Heights, north of Montreal.

And I had them on the weekends. Fried was the best possible stepfather they could have had. The boys would take the train down from Ottawa when they were at school from fall to spring.

Where Pierre had high expectations of them—their education, he believed, was his responsibility—I was the empathetic one. What could I do to ensure they grew up strong?

And Pierre and I would talk constantly on the phone. How did Justin do on that test? How was Sacha eating? Had Michel's cold cleared? There was no snarkiness between us, no getting even. That was all behind us now. We had done our fair share of horrid battling. I wince to think of the ferocity between us, of words and emotion, but that was gone. At last, there was peace between us. We had failed as husband and wife, but as father and mother, we succeeded.

From spring to autumn I was based on the lake with the children, though we also went to the lake in winter, when, on magical, blue sparkling days, we skated and tobogganed. Life was perfect. Before the snows arrived in January, the frozen water of the lake was so clear that you could see through the transparent ice down to the pebbles.

By now the older boys had moved for their French schooling to Montreal, where they stayed with Pierre at his house. On weekends, a police driver brought them up to us.

"When are the brudders coming?" Kyle would ask as soon as he could talk.

Around this time, when Sacha was in his early teens, he invented a game called Survivor, which we played at the cottage on Newboro Lake. All the kids, adults and house guests would play, though the company sometimes disappointed.

I remember one of the kids complaining to me, "She's such a wuss. I don't want her on my team!"

The game worked like this. Sacha had written with indelible ink on plaques the words *water* or *food,* and placed these plaques throughout a two-acre perimeter in the woods that defined our play space in the huge property. Once you found a plaque, you took a token as proof you had located the station. And before the game began, we all plucked tokens from a hat to determine whether we were herbivores or carnivores. Sometimes I was a bunny—so there were lots of creatures out for me. The herbivores had to hide and the carnivores sought them out, and once the former had been spotted, the latter took their tokens. The herbivores could win the game by picking up food and water tokens without being spotted. It was a wonderful game, and players really got into their roles: I remember a shy little girl being transformed when she picked a bear token—did she ever assume that role!

Meeting Mary, Fried's mother, for the first time, I had discovered how completely inadequate I was as a housekeeper. She taught me how to keep house, to become organized. As a family, the Kempers excelled in celebrations—every birth, every occasion, every season—and Mary took immense pleasure in thinking up perfect presents and making cards out of pressed flowers to go with them. On Friday nights, the men came from the city, bringing steaks and beers with them. We had barbecues and bonfires. Fried's father had an accordion; every member of the family played a different musical instrument, and at night they played and we all sang. We picnicked, kayaked and canoed. By the age of two, Kyle was an excellent swimmer.

Then, on Monday mornings, the men would leave again, the boys would go back to Pierre—if it was still school time— and the women and small children would stay on at the lake, the little cousins running backwards and forwards along the tracks between the houses. Sometimes we packed lunch and took off for the day across the lakes, moving from one to the next through the locks. We would anchor the Bayliner underneath the cliffs from which the children could jump into the deep, clear water. Fried used to grumble that I kept hitting the shoals. The plastic kayak was more suited to me.

I was a keen gardener, and grew strong by planting out vegetables and flowers and moving boulders. Fried's father kept praising me, telling me how impressed he was by the energy I put into doing everything well. I revelled in his admiration, and I realized that no one had ever really told me that I did anything well.

In the winter, when the snow came, we spent our weekends up at the chalet, and there the boys would join us after school. Sometimes Pierre came with them and we all skied together; I had once been better than all of them, and now I struggled to keep up. Pierre and Fried got on well, and Pierre was extremely generous at sharing the boys and making everything as easy as possible for us.

When Kyle was two, Fried taught him to ski by snowplowing down the slopes, pulling the little boy on a leash. Occasionally we took all the children away somewhere hot for a holiday. Fried's business was flourishing and we seemed to have enough money for everything. We were a little team: Fried and I and the four boys.

I felt that I had been given a second chance at life and I was determined to take and enjoy it. There were no more bouts of mania, and the days of medication were over. I had found balance, one that was natural, not drug induced. Life with Fried was so good, and I was eating well, living well, playing well and loving well.

I weathered even potential disasters without too much fuss. One day, when Kyle and my niece Jamie were two, I was out at the cottage on my own with the boys. We were all in the water, all of us naked, when I noticed that a tree not far from the house was on fire. I put the babies somewhere safe and rushed up, still naked, to the house.

By sheer good luck, I had insisted that one of the first things we put in when we built the house was a hose on the deck—not to put out any fires but to water my plants. There was no phone to call the fire department. What had happened was this: a friend who had stayed the night before had flipped the butt of his cigarette onto the ground, which was as dry as tinder and rich in decaying pine needles, leaves and twigs. The butt had smouldered, become red hot, and then set fire to the peat, the fire travelling along the roots and then spreading to the dry wood. I trained the hose onto the flames, then realized that I had to soak the peat as well, because the fire continued underground and little fires kept bursting through here and there. The experience was terrifying, and it was an absolute miracle that the house did not catch on fire, but no serious damage was done.

———————

On February 2, 1989, Groundhog Day, I gave birth to a baby girl. Such a blessing, finally, to get my little girl. I had always longed for a daughter, and with each son had felt a pang of sadness. We called her Alicia, after the older boys protested that our chosen name—Mary Rose—was taken. The boys had studied British history, and they knew that in the sixteenth century, Henry VIII's favourite warship was one called the *Mary Rose*.

I kept Alicia with me in my arms almost every second, terrified that she might get sudden infant death syndrome and that I would lose her. She never cried. She was a sweet, easy baby, with a lot of her father and her grandfather in her, a tidy, well-organized child, who was soon swimming and skiing with her brothers. Like them, she was fearless, and when we went skiing I had to watch her, for she was prone to fly off down the slopes, wild and carefree.

During the hot summer months, my five children lived in the lake, spending all day in or on the water—water-skiing, canoeing, wakeboarding. Fried was a wonderful cook and I woke each morning to the smell of bacon sizzling on the grill. His sister Tini and his brother Michael's wife, Lynda, had become like sisters to me. On July 1, Canada Day, we lit fireworks and had a gigantic pig roast. Because the edges of the lake were marshy, we had brought in loads of sand to create a beach, and here, summer after summer, we lived. I could hardly believe my own happiness.

CHAPTER 9

SLIPPING

My mind was fizzing, racing, jumping from thought
to thought, scheme to scheme, idea to idea. I felt as if I had a
thousand-volt charge surging through my head . . .
I had been here before.

VANCOUVER, 1998

A book I cherish is Katherine Ashenburg's *Mourner's Dance: What We Do When People Die*, published in 2004. This is a scholarly book on mourning traditions through the ages and one written by an author with a personal stake in understanding the process: when her daughter's fiancé died, everyone in that young man's circle, including Katherine, scrambled to cope.

What Ashenburg found is that we have become detached from death, unlike our ancestors, who embraced it. Time was that families stayed with the dead from time of death to time of burial, they photographed the dead with the living, and families took responsibility for cleansing and clothing the body in preparation for the funeral.

During my early forties, a number of deaths and other misfortunes rocked my life, and whatever equilibrium I thought I possessed soon vanished. Anyone who has owned and loved dogs knows how the death of a dog feels, how losing a cherished pet is like losing a member of the family. I have had six dogs in my life and I know the sorrow all too well. But in 1991, the death of our dog felt like a dark metaphor for a life spinning out of control.

In 1990, we had bought a Labrador puppy for the children. Raven, as we called her, was fourteen months old—a charming, jet-black dog with a sweet nature. We all doted on her.

That summer was intensely hot. One muggy day in August, we were up at the lake and I had returned from shopping with the children and began to unload the car—we had a Ford Explorer and I was unloading from the back hatch. Raven had come with us, of course, and she got out of the car when we got out.

After carrying the parcels into the house, I called for the dog. When she didn't appear, I assumed that she had done what she often did during periods of great heat: wriggled under the raised part of the house, where it was always cool. I shut up the car and Justin and I took the younger children off in the boat to swim.

We got back an hour or so later and were surprised when Raven failed to greet us. We called and searched. Then I went over to the car. There she was, lying on the back seat, dead, having suffocated in the awful heat. Unbeknown to me, while the hatch was open during the unloading of groceries, Raven had crawled back into the car and under the seat, drawn to the coolness that the air conditioning had offered, and fallen asleep.

I loved that dog so much, and Kyle, then six, was especially heartbroken. My grief at this death was out of all proportion. I cried and cried. This was just one loss during a time in my life that felt defined and framed by loss—acute, unbearable loss. I had suffered from postpartum depression after Ally (as I called Alicia) was born, but the black dogs of despair had just begun to hound me.

Not long after Ally's birth in 1989, Fried began to have financial problems. The business his father had started had grown rapidly and enjoyed some extremely successful years, but now, with the recession that hit North America in the early 1990s, everything to do with building and housing began to suffer. Fried had moved too quickly in expanding his office, and he had made a few mistakes with his investments.

At first he said little about it, wanting to protect me. And because I was so engrossed in the family and in bringing up the two small children, I didn't really take it all in. I had an uneasy feeling that we were communicating less and less, but I didn't press him. All he would say when I asked him was that there was less money but that he could still provide for us in the same way.

When the recession deepened, Fried announced to me that there was no choice for us now but to make some cutbacks in our lives. The first thing to go was the ski chalet at Mont Tremblant. Then the holiday trips were given up. We weren't alone, of course; all around us, friends were striving for the same kind of savings. And we still had my house on Victoria Street in Ottawa, and the cottage on Newboro Lake. But the markets kept tumbling and Fried was forced to sell his main company. Then he went into bankruptcy.

I had first starting smoking marijuana in the 1960s, and it had always had a wonderful effect on me. Cannabis relaxed me, made me stop worrying and also seemed to help me concentrate better. In my moments of greatest frenzy, a joint was the only thing that somewhat calmed my racing mind.

With some of my friends, marijuana acted as a soporific. They would sit for contented hours staring at the wall, but the drug had always energized me. I really loved the way it opened up a huge world for me, allowing me to experience sights and smells and sounds that I had never known existed. Marijuana seemed to put me exactly where I wanted to be—somewhere safe and happy, with the past somehow dealt with and the future optimistic.

I smoked not to escape but for pleasure. And though I felt a great sense of loss whenever my stash got low, I didn't really see myself as dependent. I told myself that dope never prevented me from functioning, only enabled me to live more decisively, in the moment, perceiving the good things, forgetting the bad. But there, of course, lay the rub. I forgot not only the bad things but much else besides—my chores, the bills to pay, the meals to cook. Later, as the children grew up, I used to say to them, "Smoke pot for fun, but it will never let you get ahead. All ambition will be driven away."

While married to Pierre, I had had little opportunity of obtaining marijuana. The occasional joints I smoked, and the occasional experiments with mushrooms, had been few and far between. The cocaine I had tried while on my benders in New York had left me convinced that it was not the drug for me; I had seen too many friends destroyed by it. Cocaine is the master thief: it steals everything, including your life. But with marijuana, which I now smoked whenever I wanted, in spite of Fried's disapproval, I felt safe. Too safe, as it turned out.

One morning, as I was leaving to drive Kyle to nursery school, I bumped into our local postman, who told me that a parcel had arrived for me and that there seemed to be quite a fuss about it at the post office. My first thought was that it must be something from my mother in Vancouver. But when the postman delivered it next morning, I saw that it had no address or name of sender. I unpacked it, and inside—as I soon discovered—was the most wonderful marijuana.

With great delight, I hid this great gift away in a cupboard upstairs and threw the packaging into the garbage. That afternoon, returning from collecting Kyle from nursery school, I found two police cars waiting outside my house. As I put the key in the lock, several policemen surrounded me. I was, they told me, under arrest for possession of drugs. I was clutching Kyle in my arms and felt so terrified that I wet my pants.

A friend of a friend had sent the marijuana to me anonymously. But this other person had let slip in a public place details of the delivery and the RCMP had caught wind of it. They informed our local police, and the packet had been detected by police dogs that had picked up the unmistakable scent of the marijuana.

When I had unwrapped the package, I had noticed that it had been curiously marked—by what I now realized were the dog's teeth. To my considerable embarrassment, I was informed that I would have to appear in court. I was fingerprinted and photographed.

In the event, we got an excellent lawyer and I was let off with a stay; my lawyer pleaded a defence of entrapment. If ever caught again, I was told, there would be serious trouble. Just the same, the press, which had had nothing scandalous to say about me for several years, now had a field day. Even so, I managed to make light of it all, telling myself that everyone gets busted at some point; I went off to a friend's chalet and talked it over with friends who managed to make me feel better.

Bob Dylan had written, "Everybody must get stoned." Ergo, I reasoned, everyone, at one time or another, must get busted. The whole episode seemed to me more absurd than worrying.

Around this time, a very close friend, Mary-Jean Green, was diagnosed with breast cancer. Her mother, Mary Mitchell, an eccentric, clever, talented Scotswoman, had been a wonderful friend and mentor to me. Mary-Jean's father, Sir Harold Mitchell, had been in Winston Churchill's war cabinet and had married Mary while she was in the Women's Army Corps.

Mary Mitchell and I had first met when Pierre and I took Justin, then a tiny baby, for a holiday to Jamaica. Two days before setting out, the Jamaican high commissioner had come to 24 Sussex to ask whether there was anything that could be done for us by way of preparation. I told him that it would be lovely to find a girl who could look after Justin while we had dinner.

The high commissioner looked appalled. "You're taking the baby?" he asked. The Jamaica Inn, where we were booked to stay, did not allow babies. However, his good friends, the Mitchells, had a guest house on the beach, an old fort that they had redecorated and made charming and that they now offered to us. I loved Mary from the moment I met her and remained close to her right up until she died, many years later.

Mary-Jean, her only child, had learned Japanese so she could communicate with business people in Japan, and after the death of her father she had run a multi-million-dollar international coal corporation. She and I had had our children at the same time and spent many happy hours raising them together. Mary-Jean and her husband, Peter, were among our closest friends. She was generous and considerate and never talked about her own problems.

Mary-Jean was thirty-eight when she first heard about the cancer, and she fought it with everything her strong character and considerable fortune permitted. She had always been very health conscious and constantly made me feel guilty about my eating habits and lifestyle.

She tried every new treatment, visited every clinic, travelled to places where she had heard of new cures. One thing I really minded was that our financial troubles prohibited me from going with her.

I could comfort her only with this: some years earlier, I had persuaded her not to send her boys, Alexander and Andrew, then aged five and six, to prep school in England. I convinced her to keep the boys with her in Bermuda, where they went to school on a nearby island. What this meant was that her boys were with her in her last two years. Mary-Jean was younger than me but she was a very close friend and had a huge impact on my life. Now she was gone.

Two years later, Mary's turn came. She had bought a house in Boston to be near her grandchildren, and Fried and I often used to visit her. One day she said to me, "I have a little problem in my chest." She was coughing and coughing. "Chest," it seemed, meant "breast." Soon after, she was dead. I bitterly mourned this very dear friend. She was such a cosmopolitan person, very liberated and suffused with extraordinary spirit.

My losses were now mounting. Not long before Mary-Jean died, I had been at home one afternoon with Ally when Heather Gillin, another close friend, bicycled over to see me. She told me she had terrible news: she was dying. She, too, had cancer. When she left, I was so angry and upset that I kicked a tree. I thought I had broken my toes.

Heather wanted no visitors and I never saw her again, though we talked often on the phone. One day, I was up at the cottage and I went into town to get a newspaper. There I found a notice of

Heather's death. The funeral was that same day, and it was too late for me to get to it. I began to feel that I was never there at the right time for the people I loved.

Fried worried constantly that I might get pregnant. I was in my early forties but had always conceived very easily. Given our financial problems, and the fact that we already had two children of our own, Fried was adamant that we should have no more. His idea at first was to have a vasectomy, but something in him balked at the prospect and he found he couldn't go through with it. I, too, resisted the idea of taking steps to eliminate any possibility of conceiving. I was not seriously thinking of having another child, but the idea of making it impossible appalled me. Being a mother had been the essence, the best part of me, the most fulfilled part, perhaps because I felt so very unfulfilled at everything else. Being pregnant had been the happiest times of my life.

Then fate intervened—twice—to make my decision for me. One day I found myself pregnant, and I was overwhelmed with happiness. But when I made an appointment to see the doctor, he informed me that the placenta—the organ that connects the developing fetus to the uterine wall—had not attached properly. Next day, I had to have a dilation and curettage procedure. That afternoon, when I let myself into the house, the phone was ringing. Justin was calling to tell me that Mary-Jean was dead.

I felt completely devastated: I had not even been with her, and I had given her no support and friendship at the end. I couldn't stop myself thinking that while her life had been vanishing, so had all thoughts of another new life growing inside me. Two terrible events had occurred at the same time, and something strange was beginning to happen to my mind. A bleakness was starting to consume me, as if the golden years were over and we were no longer the happy family we had been. I began to slip.

As the days passed, and Fried and I resumed our increasingly distant marriage, so, slowly but surely, I slipped more. Because I had been happy and free of symptoms for so long, I simply failed to understand. I had forgotten, in the way that people often do forget real pain. All I knew was that every day my mood was becoming darker and that every day I was moving a little further from my husband and children. I continued to cook for my children, to help them with their homework and to play with them—these joys and obligations helped keep me going—but I began to wonder how long I could do it.

The sunniness and light all around me began to dim; my surroundings and everyone in them took on soft grey tints. Our finances were growing steadily worse and I began to feel guilty that I had contributed so little to the household. I felt sad, exhausted. And I began to do what I now know, in one form or another, I always did—I began to look for people to blame for my unhappiness, and I dreamed of escape.

My darkness wasn't my fault; it was someone else's, and, in this case, Fried's. In the red diary, I had written: "I do not want to be married any more. I do not want to be co-dependent on a man for my life. I have my own road to travel and I must do it alone."

I was in this state of grey despair when Raven, our young dog, died. Mary-Jean's death, my miscarriage, my increasing estrangement from Fried: the tragedies—and that's how each one felt—were piling up.

And so the slide quickened. At first, my bleakness felt like a comforting escape from the menacing world. In my mind, I had found a safe, dark place to be, a cave in which the light faded beyond the entrance and I could retreat in my mind into the darkness.

It was only much later, when I heard Leonard Cohen's words from his song "Anthem" ("There is a crack in everything / that's how the light gets in"), that I realized that for a depressed person, the light can be a tiny flame. Just recently, a friend asked me if I would write a letter to her daughter, who was wrestling with severe depression. What I told her was this: At the darkest hour, you will see a tiny shaft of light in the form of the love and compassion of others. I urged her to reach out for that light. I know that now; I didn't know it then.

My cave was not a safe place at all, but a deep, bottomless pit, into which I fell deeper and deeper. I had no energy, made no plans. I slipped through the days, loving the children, trying my best to look after them and doing all I could to stop anyone noticing what was happening to me. For a while, I thought I would feel better if I found a job, but what job? I was too old to work in television, and although I had a vast pile of photographs I couldn't think what to do with them.

There were days when I felt as if I were in mourning. I sat on the floor, making collages by cutting up photographs of my past, searching for meanings in the pictures. I spent hours in a shed at the bottom of the garden at Newboro Lake, painting the inside white and red, longer and longer there each day. This was my escape hatch, my way of holding on, of avoiding facing up to the depression that, each day, enveloped me more firmly in its grey, bleak light. But the cost to my family was huge.

We struggled on. Then, in the summer of 1995, when we were again back at Newboro Lake, I woke up one morning with an excruciating pain in my neck. When the pain failed to get better, I feared it might be the onset of arthritis.

One evening, I found that I could no longer lift a saucepan or open a tin without extreme pain. I saw a general practitioner and described my symptoms. He listened, then told me to stand up while, one by one, he put his fingers gently on various parts of my body. When I had let out a squeak of pain each time he touched sixteen of eighteen pressure points, he told me that he thought I had fibromyalgia.

My first reaction was one of relief. Here was a clear medical problem and something that could quickly be treated. I was wrong about that. Fibromyalgia, the doctor informed me, was an illness that came from the mind, not the body. What I was suffering from was referred pain, and it was manifesting itself by travelling to different parts of my body.

The brain, he told me, has a very clear picture of different parts of the body, but no clear picture for anxiety, sadness, low self-esteem or loss. And because the brain doesn't know where to send the signal, it sends pain wherever it can. What had to be treated was not the pain itself but what lay behind it. And this, he said, was clearly depression. This all made horrible sense to me. Looking back on the previous few years, I now realized that what I had been suffering from was indeed all too like my earlier bouts of depression. Why had I not recognized this before?

Apart from a period in the early 1980s, when I was also taking lithium, I had never been on antidepressants. By the 1990s, Prozac was widely recognized as an extremely effective drug, and for most people it had very few side effects. The doctor wrote me out a prescription. I went to the pharmacy and came home relieved.

With some reason: within a few days, I felt as if spring had come again. The world regained its colour, the grey bleakness dissolved and energy flooded back into me. I started baking, gardening; I began to laugh again. The world, which had seemed empty of joy, was once again lively, funny, full of laughter.

The doctor had put me on a fairly high dose of Prozac. I kept the dose high and stayed on it for several years. What I was to learn only later was that with bipolar illness, Prozac can act as a trigger for mania. To me, at that point, that pill felt like a miracle drug, and I kept the dose high and stayed on it. I did a bit of research into the brain and discovered that the general medical view was that in depression the brain is depleted of serotonin, and that antidepressants, when they work well, restore serotonin.

And when, from time to time, I had little bursts of mania, I was relieved, not frightened, taking them for glimpses of even greater happiness and energy. That was in the early days. But before long, the bouts of mania became more frequent, the intervals in between shorter, and as their intensity increased, so I became more and more alarmed.

All through this period, Fried and I had been growing increasingly apart. Partly because he loved golf, and partly because golf was a good way of meeting the kind of people he needed to meet for business, Fried had taken up the game seriously and joined one of Ottawa's more exclusive clubs. But the membership was expensive and we did not have the money for me to join as well. In any case, much of my time was still taken up with Kyle and Ally and the three boys, when they came to stay, though now that they were older they were often away doing things on their own.

Prozac had caused me to gain weight once again, and when I looked in the mirror, I didn't recognize myself—in every way. I had become boring, to others, but also pretty boring to myself. So I took the course I always took: I looked around for someone to blame. And just as I had once blamed Pierre for everything that was wrong with my life at 24 Sussex, so I now blamed Fried for my restlessness and perpetual dissatisfaction and my unbearable sense of defeat. I blamed him for the recession and for losing all our money.

I blamed him for being so self-controlled and so unloving when I had lost the baby and for the ease with which he moved on from trouble. I blamed him for not reading more books. I blamed him because I was fat and unattractive and he didn't like me much anymore.

Blame began to fill my days. Fried and I had almost totally ceased to communicate and I moved out of our bedroom and into a separate room of my own. Then my menopause began; and just as the hormones active in childbirth and pregnancy had once triggered in me violent swings of mood, so too did the hormonal changes of menopause.

When I went to see a doctor and told him about the ungovernable seesaws in my moods—from despairing to ecstatic in just a few hours—he patted my arm reassuringly.

"It will pass," he said. "You just have to wait." And then he added, in words that now strike me as funny, "You are shrinking quite nicely."

He was referring, of course, to my diminishing bones and indeed all my parts save my nose—one of the changes that menopause induces. At the time, all I could think of was this: Who wants to shrink?

Everything now seemed to conspire to make me vulnerable—every casual remark, every disruption, every untoward event. My weight was still increasing and the Prozac no longer made me feel better. My energy had sunk to almost nothing once again. And so I took a fatal turn. I telephoned the general practitioner, who told me to stop taking Prozac and to start something else. This was a mistake. The drug was new, and perhaps doctors were still trying to get a handle on its use.

I came off the Prozac all at once, without reducing the dose bit by bit, choosing to forget Dr. Fieve's words about the dangers of coming off medication too suddenly.

Deciding that I needed a break, I left the children with Fried and went off to see my mother in Vancouver. I had hardly set foot there when the mania began to rise. I became involved in one of those ridiculous and dangerous pyramid schemes then doing the rounds. The principals involved would later do time in jail. I had gone to a dinner and heard someone boasting about the dizzying profits she had made from porcelain figurines that practically sold themselves. I swallowed the bait.

Dopamine is a chemical naturally found in the brain, and it gives high energy and creativity under normal circumstances. But what I was experiencing were surges of dopamine, great, all-powerful waves so that I could feel the energy coming out of the tips of my fingers. I had racing thoughts, most of them disconnected. This is called "impaired insight": you think you know everything but you don't. You can't eat, can't sleep, can't function. You're almost touching heaven, but not.

I can remember excitedly telling my mother and my sisters that these porcelain figurines would make our fortunes. I kept urging my family to come in with me, to buy hundreds of figurines and store them in our garage. By now I knew, as did my mother and siblings, that things were getting out of hand. They could tell by my restlessness and rapid speech.

One of them urged me to call the doctor who had prescribed Prozac, and when he returned my call he expressed worry that I had come off the drug too suddenly. I told him how I was feeling. He was appalled and told me to go at once to the local hospital and get them to look at my eyes. His great fear was that I was now in the grip of full-blown mania.

When I got off the phone, I told my mother what the doctor had said. Her reaction was the same one as she had had many years before. I needed a cup of tea and a good night's sleep. In any case, the hospital would only send me to a psychiatrist, who would blame her for being a bad mother. What my mother did not realize was that I was wired, not tired. She was right in one sense: I did, indeed, need a good night's sleep, or any sleep at all. I had barely slept for several weeks because my frenetic, racing mind gave me no rest. I felt full of ideas, confidence, exuberance. Since there was nothing I could not do, why not sell porcelain figurines?

The next morning I went skiing with an old friend named Ross MacDonald. My energy and my courage knew no bounds. I was like an eleven-year-old girl, leaping over blind drops, and my friend kept urging me to slow down. He was also mystified by all the peculiar things I kept saying. I told him that I had decided to change my life, that I was leaving Fried and would buy a house in Vancouver.

When I got home that night, I felt possessed by feelings of power and insight. I was convinced that whatever I wanted to do, I would do brilliantly. My doodles were works of art, my sentences were brilliant turns of phrase that would fill prize-winning books. My mind was fizzing, racing, jumping from thought to thought, scheme to scheme, idea to idea. I felt as if I had a thousand-volt charge surging through my head. Those around me, meanwhile, were plodding, dull, unadventurous. I also had an irresistible urge to laugh, to sing out loud, to dance around the house. I believed that every man around me found me irresistibly attractive. I had been here before.

But no one can live for very long at that fever pitch. Next morning, I was taken to St. Paul's Hospital and put into a psychiatric ward.

CHAPTER 10

ONE FLEW OVER THE CUCKOO'S NEST

"Look at all this. You've got the most beautiful life
and the most wonderful children who love you very much.
Why are you so sad? Why can't you just love your life?"

MY SON, MICHEL, ONE NIGHT IN A CANOE ON NEWBORO LAKE, SUMMER 1998

I had not been in a mental hospital since my brief stay in 1974, almost twenty-four years earlier. There had been good times and bad times in between, periods of happiness and periods of acute misery, and spells on lithium and Prozac. But this was different. This had a horror all of its own.

On my wild day on the slopes I had fallen and hurt my knee. In order to get me to see a doctor for my manic and terrifying moods, my distraught family told me that I needed to have my knee checked. When I realized that I had been tricked into a seventy-two-hour observation stay at St. Paul's Hospital, I was furious, paranoid—and terrified. Above all, I felt betrayed. My mother, though she did visit me, was appalled that her daughter was in a psychiatric ward. She was afraid of mental illness and never really accepted what I had gone through. Surely, she would have thought to herself, life has its ups and downs and everyone feels sad at one time or another?

(Much later, in the summer of 2008, I gave a speech as part of a Unique Lives and Experiences lecture series. Jane Fonda, Lily Tomlin and Diane Keaton were all on the bill that summer. I gave the talk at the Orpheum Theatre in Vancouver in front of a huge crowd, and there, in the front row, sat my mother. She heard, really for the first time and in crushing detail, what I had been through. What I remember about that night was how tender my mother was with me after that speech. Her eyes had been opened.)

My sisters, nervously, came from time to time to visit me in hospital. Justin, who was teaching in Vancouver, was there constantly.

The first thing the doctors did when I was admitted was to put me on strong tranquilizing drugs to bring me down from the mania. I was given Epival (valproic acid), which contains sodium valproate—an anticonvulsant used chiefly to treat epilepsy by stabilizing electrical activity in the brain but also sometimes as a mood stabilizer and to control episodes of mania. I fought my handlers the whole way. So violent did I become that I was put into a straitjacket and locked into a padded cell. There, I sang "Michael, Row the Boat Ashore" continuously for two hours until they agreed to let me out. I have no idea why I chose that song. I only know that that was the most humiliating moment of my life; I have always had a fear of being imprisoned, so that experience will remain with me until the day I die. My strongest emotions were defeat and loneliness: never, before or since, have I felt more alone or more abandoned by the world.

I was under constant observation—CO, it's called. Someone sat at my door and watched me twenty-four hours a day, even as I slept. This was unnerving, but I accepted it. I had been the prime minister's wife and I was used to being guarded.

The psychiatric ward was pleasant enough. I had my own room and there was a well-lit, homey common room. But there was nothing at all for the patients to do, and we were strongly discouraged from discussing our problems with each other. In any case, we were, for the most part, too heavily drugged to talk, and I have always had a horror of communal living. My time in Morocco in those hippie camps, growing up with cousins—both had instilled in me a love for privacy. When I felt strong enough, I shuffled around the ward, trying not to bump into other patients who were shuffling along their own desperate paths. As the drugs began to work, I felt increasingly confused, lacking in all energy. One morning, I was told I could go for a walk if I wished. I shuffled my way around the block and came back. I could have escaped, but I was so sluggish that I doubt I could have gone far.

Along with my feelings of abandonment was a conviction that I had been turned into a prisoner—with no rights, no friends and an indeterminate sentence. That initial seventy-two-hour observation period had been extended indefinitely, though now I was a "voluntary" patient: I could have left had I insisted, but I had neither the will nor the courage to do so. All I could think about was my children, and how I longed to be with them. Fried was in Ottawa with Ally and Kyle, and didn't come to see me; nor did the children come, since he felt that a mental ward was no place for a nine-year-old girl to see her mother.

At the height of my mania I had written terrible and abusive letters to Fried, blaming him for everything. Michel, on the other hand, hearing what had happened, immediately got into his car and drove eight hours from Rossland, in the interior of British Columbia, where he was then living, to see me. He brought me a notebook in which he had written, "Your family loves you very deeply."

The food in the hospital was totally unappetizing and seemingly lacking in any kind of nutrition. There was no privacy: we were checked every few hours all through the night and there were no doors on the shower stalls. I was sick, sick to death, of being so sick.

A young doctor had been put in charge of me, and from the first moment, we neither trusted nor liked each other. I found her unsympathetic, verging on cruel; she clearly found me impossible. Everything she did or suggested I fought against. When my sisters came to see me, I begged this doctor to let them take me home. I told her that I could be put in their care and that they would fly with me back to Ottawa.

She was adamant: I would not be discharged until she said so. Only later did I learn how important it is to like and trust your psychiatrist and to feel that he or she is in your corner. Not all psychiatrists are brilliant, and not all like every patient, but there was no connection between the two of us. The weeks passed. I wandered, zombie-like, up and down the corridors, growing more and more sedated, more and more indifferent.

I ate less and less, and began to spend as much of the day and night as I could in bed. I stopped begging for release: I no longer cared what became of me.

Seeing my new tranquility, the young doctor decided that it would now be safe for me to go home. I had been in hospital for two and a half months; it was May 1998 when I was allowed out. I could have left before, but leaving against medical advice would have adversely impacted both my therapy and my relationship with my family.

One of my sisters, Jan, came to collect me, and flew with me back to Ottawa. I felt defeated and very small, but my reunion with Kyle and Ally filled me with delight. Still only thirteen and nine years of age, respectively, they had found my absence confusing; trying to reassure them was now my priority. The older boys, though worried, were now away pursuing their own lives. Justin was studying for his teaching degree at the University of British Columbia, Sacha was away travelling in Africa and Michel was in Rossland. When he saw me, Fried—understandably upset by my vindictive, accusatory letters—was cool.

In order to be released, I had had to undertake to check in, as an outpatient, at our local hospital in Ottawa. I was extremely fortunate not only in the hospital, Queensway Carleton, which was everything that a psychiatric hospital should be, but in the psychiatrist who took my case. The contrast with St. Paul's in Vancouver was overwhelming. But something else had changed, too: I was more accepting of the notion of treatment, more ready and willing.

Dr. Mary Brown was not only an excellent doctor but an extremely nice woman. The first morning, as I was sitting in her office answering questions, she suddenly stood up and came over to me. "Margaret, come here and stand in the light, where I can see you properly." I followed her over to the window. She looked at my skin and pulled back my eyelids, which were bright yellow. I had developed jaundice from unmonitored doses of Epival, the substitute I had been given for lithium.

I am hypersensitive to medication, and often need a small fraction of what others are routinely prescribed. I am, unfortunately, also one of those people whose liver function is affected by Epival (valproic acid), and none of the normal tests—on blood cells, liver and clotting time—had actually been done. Tests were now rapidly done and I was informed that I had lost 80 per cent of my liver function and that I would have to stay in hospital for at least three weeks in hopes of getting it back. Doctors at the Vancouver hospital had to have known that Epival may compromise liver function, but the appropriate tests were never taken. I was furious when I found out and months later tried to see that young psychiatrist—who refused to see me.

Seeing how fragile I was, Dr. Brown very gently urged me to stay on the psychiatric ward and not in the ward with people suffering from liver disease, many of them dying. This was the right decision. The psychiatric ward was full of light and gave onto a garden with picnic tables under the trees. Patients were encouraged to take walks outside the hospital grounds. The common room, in sharp contrast to St. Paul's, offered all kinds of activities and hobbies. But if I was tempted to think that this was a happy place, I got my reality check. Not long after I entered the hospital, a friend sent me twenty-four roses in a cut-glass vase made by

Lalique, the French crystal manufacturer. Wanting to share them with the other patients, I put them in the common room. Soon after, a young girl found the opportunity to smash the vase and cut her wrists before being rescued by staff.

One of the worst aspects of my jaundice was the unbearable itching. Every inch of my skin throbbed and tickled. I was put into baths of oatmeal, where I spent much of my days. At night I was given gloves to stop myself scratching in my sleep. Slowly, my liver function returned. I was put on a strict diet, with lots of water and fresh vegetables. I was fortunate: I recovered fast and suffered no lasting damage.

While these treatments continued, Dr. Brown talked to me about my mental state. She tried various medications until she was satisfied that she had found one that suited me. My bouts of mania alternating with depression were, she told me, a clear indication that I was suffering from bipolar illness. Dr. Brown assured me that these mood swings were normal in bipolar patients, and that the condition was treatable. But, she said firmly, you must co-operate. I was only too willing.

And during my stay in the hospital, Dr. Brown went to considerable lengths to make my life bearable. She put me on Wellbutrin, an antidepressant that not only suited me well but had the added advantage of not causing me to put on weight. She allowed me out to the store to buy lengths of material, and arranged for my sewing machine to be delivered to the hospital. I began, once again, to make clothes.

As always in psychiatric wards, our main caregivers were the nurses, kind and knowing men and women who had seen this illness a thousand times. As Dr. Brown put it, she could help me with drugs and she could teach me how to monitor my moods myself, but the nurses were the ones who would really chart the course of my illness and my recovery.

Finally, I had a clear and unambivalent diagnosis, one that I was able to take hold of in a way I hadn't been able to before. I was bipolar, which explained the ups and downs, the erratic and destructive swings my life had followed. I had been told as much before, but never with the same clarity and finality. Somehow, I hadn't fully absorbed the diagnosis—until now. In this, Dr. Brown had been excellent, leaving no further room for confusion.

But there were two key components to my recovery that no one told me about. This education I would have to acquire on my own and over a period of years. The first hard lesson was that a cure could not be simply imposed from without, by means of a mere pill. Recovery was more complicated than that. I would have to take a hand in my own recovery, to decide to get well, to explore and then put into practice all the different aspects of healing—diet, exercise, therapy, meaningful and purposeful work. The second vital piece of information that I then lacked was the crucial relationship between bipolar disorder and marijuana.

Not long after I got home, Michel had an accident while driving along the Trans-Canada Highway near Portage la Prairie in Manitoba with his dog, Makwa (named with the Ojibway word for "bear"). A young man, driving carelessly, made a left turn without looking and his pickup crashed into Michel's car. Michel was cut and bruised but otherwise unhurt; his car, however, was a write-off and his much-loved Makwa had gone missing.

When he called to tell me, he added that he was going to stay and search the area, a vast open plain with wheat fields as far as the eye could see, and ten kilometres or more between one farmhouse and the next. He hoped that the dog might have run off and was somewhere licking his wounds not too far away, for Michel was pretty certain that in the crash or the aftermath the dog had been hit.

A local pharmacist loaned him a car and for the next five days Michel scoured the countryside, whistling and calling Makwa's name. He put up leaflets and posters in the neighbouring villages. Michel was heartbroken that his search had yielded nothing and he was on the verge of giving up when he received a call from a campsite not far away. That evening a young woman had checked in and seen the poster about Makwa. Sitting by the campfire and seeing the first star appear in the sky, she had recited the familiar words "star light, star bright" and wished that the boy might get his dog back. A little later, a dog crawled out feebly from the undergrowth and the woman felt a wet nose and a tongue licking her hand. She recognized Makwa's picture from the poster. The dog had been hurt but he would recover, and the reunion between Michael and Makwa was, of course, joyful.

That summer of 1998, Michel and I looked after each other up at Newboro Lake. His cuts and bruises took a long time to heal, and I was fragile too. I made us chicken soup; he took me canoeing on the lake. Fried, who is a man with a deep well of generosity, had forgiven me, but I was still feeling bad, and he was still very distant. He found it hard to understand just what had happened to me to make me treat him so horribly. What made me most wretched was the way I had been tricked into going into hospital in Vancouver, and I was haunted by the memory of the ward with its shuffling, grey people. My family had intervened, and I'm grateful they did, but what I felt most acutely at the time was a sense of betrayal.

Michel kept telling me how lucky I was to have all this—the lake, the children, Fried—but I couldn't somehow take it in. Coming back across the lake one night in a canoe, Michel said to me, "Look at all this. You've got the most beautiful life and the most wonderful children who love you very much. Why are you so sad? Why can't you just love your life?" The trouble was: I couldn't. I made meals, I swam, I went boating, but there was an emptiness inside me.

As the summer wore on, "with a little help from my friends," I occasionally managed to obtain some marijuana. Only when high did I seem to feel better, more able to cope. And bit by bit, I did begin to feel more balanced. The children stopped watching me so anxiously, friends came to stay. The crisis seemed to be over; life was getting back to normal. I was shaken, but I was going to be all right. In any case, my mask was holding fine.

CHAPTER 11

NO, NO, NO, NO

Sweep, sweep, dear Mama, for your work is not yet done,
Sweep and weep, dear Mama,
For your lost young son
Sweep, sweep,
Weep, weep,
Mama, your day has not yet come,
Sweep and weep, Mama, for your dead son.
MY POEM *"For Michel,"* SPRING 1999

When September of 1998 came, we packed up and moved back to Ottawa, for Kyle and Ally had to return to school. The summer had been one of recovery and it always made me happy to see how close Michel and Fried were. From the moment I was first with Fried, they had found great pleasure in working together; neither was an intellectual in the way that Pierre was, and they loved doing things with their hands.

I used to watch them in the garden in their blue coveralls, cutting down trees with their chainsaws before going off fishing in the lake. Fried was an affectionate and generous stepfather, and Michel, knowing what it was like to be the youngest boy in a family of brothers, had always been particularly kind to Kyle.

Michel had just finished his degree in marine biology at Dalhousie University in Halifax and, while with me at the lake, spent part of the summer completing some English papers. He was particularly pleased when one of his professors wrote across the bottom of an essay on Emily Carr, "Michel, you may have picked the wrong major. You're a born writer." In fact, he had plans to write for the skiing magazine *Powder*. Skiing remained his passion and he had decided to move out west. He couldn't wait to get free, to get on with his life. Though the three boys had inherited money from Pierre's father, Michel liked to live like a ski bum— working in a steel mill in the summer and as a "lifty" (operating a chairlift at a ski resort) in the winter. He was the only one of our family with a union card.

Of the three older boys, Michel was the one most like me, not rational and cautious like his father but free spirited and too bold for his own good. From a very early age, he had felt no awe towards Pierre, and he was the only one who ever stood up to him. Michel's character was completely honest and straightforward. Not surprisingly, he and Pierre had had many confrontations, particularly over Catholicism, but they loved and respected each other. Michel was perhaps the one who best understood my differences with Pierre, because he had shared them. Like me, his motto was "Passion over reason."

I remember one time when Michel was seventeen and working as a camp counsellor in Algonquin Park for the summer. Pierre
and Sacha, meanwhile, had set off from Montreal in the Volvo.
They were bound for a rock concert in Texas—though Pierre
insisted on calling them "jazz" concerts. Sacha had just returned
from Africa, where he contracted malaria, and had already suffered three twenty-four-hour bouts of the illness. After Pierre left
Sacha in Los Angeles and came home, Sacha proceeded to Salt
Spring Island, where he stayed briefly with my sister Heather—
and had another recurrence of malaria.

My sister took Sacha to the hospital, where it was discovered
that he had no health card.

"Where's your health card?" Heather asked her nephew.
Turns out Michel had it. I called the camp, where they insisted
they had no one on staff named Michel—until finally my contact
said, "Oh, you mean Mike?" Michel came to the phone and the
health card was duly sent off in the mail to his brother.

Later, Pierre called me.

"Why did Miche have Sacha's health card?"

"So he'd have ID," I replied.

"What do you mean?"

"So Miche can get served in bars. He's underage, of course."

"Michel drinks in bars?" Pierre was aghast.

I love that story. It's a story about a father's naïveté and
a son doing what sons—especially sons who are free spirits—
invariably do.

———————

Late in October, on a perfect early autumn day, very blue and still, Michel said goodbye to me in front of my house on Victoria Street in Ottawa. He was taking Makwa, of course, and he asked to borrow the bicycle rack for his car. We stood talking in the bright sunshine on the sidewalk. He was elated, full of plans. After a few minutes, he got into his car and drove off down the street, but when he got to the end, he suddenly stopped, jumped out, ran back, hugged me and told me how much he loved me.

The second week in November, a girlfriend and I decided to go down to Montreal for the night to do some Christmas shopping. We stayed at the Ritz-Carlton on Sherbrooke Street. Sacha came and had dinner with us in the hotel's Café de Paris, and we laughed because he was very casually dressed and had trouble getting past the maître d'hotel (the restaurant's web-site advises that "sophisticated casual attire is recommended"). Sacha, too, was heading off on a trip, up to the Arctic. We had some caviar and soup. Life, I was beginning to think, might be all right again.

Next morning, at 7:30 on Friday the thirteenth of November, there was a knock on my hotel bedroom door. Two police-men from the RCMP stood outside.

"I'm afraid there is bad news," one said. I thought at once of Sacha. "No," they said, "it's not Sacha. But Michel is missing. There has been an accident." I didn't even know that Michel and three of his friends were on a skiing trip in British Columbia, in Kokanee Glacier Provincial Park in the south-central interior. The police explained that Michel had been skiing on the edge of the glacier when a small avalanche was thought to have swept him over the ice and into the lake. I can remember falling to the floor, shouting out, "No, no, no, no."

I got dressed and they drove me to Pierre's house. Pierre and I lit a candle and sat waiting for news. Michel's friends had been found and airlifted out by a national park service helicopter, and Sacha went up to join in the search. Andrew, Michel's closest friend, had been lucky: he was caught in the slush and the other boys had been able to save him, and they had kept him alive all night in a raging blizzard, clinging together in the partial shelter of an outhouse. By sheer good fortune, for the boys had told no one where they were going and they had taken no cellphone with them, there had been another party of skiers not far behind who had been able to sound the alarm.

Snow kept falling and there was a danger of more avalanches, but on the seventeenth of November, RCMP divers managed to reach the lake. Part of it was already covered in ice, so their inflatable boat had to be towed by helicopter to open water. Michel's body was never found. The water was icy and no one could have survived in it for long. With his heavy boots and backpack, Michel had had no chance. Sacha came home alone, without his brother.

And just as Michel had searched for five days for Makwa on the prairie after the car accident, Makwa and Andrew's dog, a part Huskie called Yukon, circled the lake for five days looking for Michel. The two dogs had refused to enter the rescue helicopter, so food was left for them. The dogs made a snow cave and continued their futile search.

When it was clear that there was no further hope, my life slipped away from me. I felt that I, too, had died in that avalanche.

And if not dead yet, death was all I wanted. When I got home to Ottawa, Ally was waiting for me. We clung to each other and cried and cried until at last she stopped and said, "I can't ever cry like this again. It hurts my head too much."

She was nine years old and far too young to have to grow up so painfully. Later she said she would make me a cup of tea. I couldn't get off the floor, so she put it down next to me and we sat there together, on the hard floor, drinking our tea.

What I regret most now is that I didn't think enough about how much everyone else was suffering. Justin, Sacha, Kyle and Ally had lost a brother they adored, Fried a stepson, Pierre a son. Years of battling the different stages of bipolar illness had made me so self-absorbed that I was little help to anyone else. The pain came in stabs; I hadn't known it was possible for anything to hurt so much. I begged my doctor to put me into a coma so the pain would go away.

"Margaret, I could do that" was all he said, "but then at some point you would have to wake up and you would still have to face the reality. Michel is gone."

I don't remember much about the funeral held in Saint-Viateur Church in Outremont, a Montreal borough on the north side of Mount Royal. It was here, in this church, that Pierre had attended mass as a young man—and prayed that children would come into his life. And they had. But now we both faced the torment of enduring the loss of a beloved son.

Justin, who had become our spokesman, read a Mohawk prayer, Sacha gave the eulogy in French, and Fried read some verses from the Book of Job. Pierre, in a short address, said, "If there is no resurrection, no heaven, then nothing that I have done in my entire life has any meaning." I said nothing. Someone had given me a book about grieving—*The Healing Journey through Grief*—and it was actually very helpful. But I scribbled in the pages these words: "How can I survive without my Miche? Miche is dead . . . He is dead and I am alone now. Come home, Miche dear . . ."

I just could not face the fact that Michel was dead, and I looked for various ways to deal with my grief. Probably the most important work I did was at the Wabano Centre for Aboriginal Health in Ottawa, where a Native elder named Sister Irene helped me—by meditation, chanting, visualizing, channelling— to release my son's spirit. For so long I could not face that he was dead, but I got to a point of clarity and ease. I could see the spirit of Michel as a bird soaring away and I didn't have to worry anymore about his material self.

Michel's brothers felt the same impulse. After the memorial service, they built a sweat lodge at Morin-Heights, Pierre's cottage in the Laurentians north of Montreal. The tribe gathered. A good sweat lodge, run properly, is very cleansing and good for the soul. We were looking for anything to ease our pain and we all had the same sense—that the ceremonies so long practised by those who were in this land before us still have meaning today.

It was decided that Makwa would go with Andrew and his dog; there seemed sense in that, though I wondered whether Andrew would ever see Makwa without seeing Michel.

In my extreme grief, I gave little thought to Fried, from whom I now felt more estranged than ever. I couldn't cook, I couldn't shop, some days I couldn't even breathe. Nor could I handle his sadness. My old trust in him, my feeling that he was there to protect me, had gone. He had been the rock on which I had thought I would always lean, and now that rock had turned to dust—and I had done the crushing. Had someone been on hand to see what was happening to me, how Michel's death had sparked a depression that only medicine could help, then Fried and I might have hung on. But we were unable to comfort each other. The grief I felt was normal; my handling of that grief increasingly was not. Many marriages do not survive the death of a child.

The one person I did feel close to was Pierre. Pierre, now seventy-nine years old, was absolutely devoted to his sons. With Michel's death, he seemed to shrink into himself. Having raised them to be fearless, having constantly urged them on to ever greater physical challenges, he was now haunted by guilt. Without his encouragement, would Michel have been so reckless? Had Pierre brought up the boys to be less trusting, more cautious, would the accident never have happened? Sacha, who lived with Pierre, reported that in the evenings his father no longer bothered to turn on the lights; Sacha would find him sitting in the dark. He seemed to grow both small and old.

Pierre had always taken the greatest trouble with his appearance. Now he lost all interest in what he was wearing or what he looked like; he barely ate and turned away from his friends. Every time I saw him, he seemed to have withdrawn a little further into himself. I should have noticed more, taken more heed, but I was too consumed by my own misery.

The first year after Michel's death passed in a cloud of grief. I clung to Pierre as we both tried to accept this hideous loss. Meanwhile, Fried and I were struggling. On the first anniversary of the day Michel died, we held a memorial service for him at St. Bartholomew's, the church across the street from my house. Pierre came.

As a teenager, Michel had gone to summer camp at Algonquin Park, and once he grew up he had repeatedly been back as a counsellor. I had not expected so many people in the church. Dozens of friends he had made at summer camp came to the memorial service, and seeing their young, hopeful, shining faces filled me with acute feelings of sadness that Michel's was not among them. In the pages of my diary, I wrote, "Since my son's death, I feel horrified, shaken, helpless, forsaken, detached from reality, numb with outrageous grief." I made myself speak at the memorial service, and later read my eulogy on the radio.

The spot where Michel had died became the site of a pilgrimage for me each year, when I would hike up the three hours from the nearest road on foot and sit by the edge of Kokanee Lake. I think of this lake in the Selkirk Mountains as his grave, and what a lovely place it is. This alpine lake is deep and cold, one of thirty lakes in the park, and surrounded by precipitous cliffs.

Kokanee Lake is also the place that has brought me signs that I have found immensely comforting. When Michel was a small child, we went together on a trip up country to Haida Gwaii—the Queen Charlotte Islands off the coast of British Columbia. Pierre had been made an Eagle Chief, and the boys Children of the Raven. Since an Eagle Chief cannot be married to someone outside the tribe, to my great honour I was made a Sister of the Raven.

Kokanee Lake is a place where eagles and ravens gather. More than once, on my visits to the lake, eagles have swooped and seemed to lead me down a road. On one occasion, when I was with my nephew Rob, I said to him that I wished that I could have some sort of sign before we left the lake. He was deeply skeptical.

"What," he asked, "would you consider a sign?"

"Anything," I replied.

As we walked up the path, I heard a loud screeching. Looking up, I saw to my delight an immense eagle swoop over the lake, its wings almost touching the waters where Michel had died. From that day, the sight of these huge birds has given me a sense that the spirits of those whom I have loved and who have died are soaring.

Out of Michel's death has come a powerful sense of renewal and rebirth. Every summer, when I hike to Kokanee Lake, I collect water and bring it home. When a grandchild is born, I use that water in the christening, so Michel's spirit can touch the child. Michel is the one of my five children I don't have to worry about now on a daily basis. It's the same with Pierre. There's a peace that comes when you give your loved ones their place. We keep them alive by telling lovely stories about them.

As a family, we tried to find some comfort in working with the Canadian Avalanche Foundation, raising money to help build a chalet for back-country skiers and hikers, with all the latest equipment for providing weather bulletins, avalanche warnings and information about the current safety of conditions. We told ourselves that we would do everything we could to prevent this kind of death happening to other parents. Canadians were so generous: some $1.5 million was raised. It was magical. Every bit of lumber, every window and door, every nail had to be helicoptered up to the building site. The $7 million project was a wonder.

On July 12, 2003, the Kokanee Glacier Cabin was formally opened. It's a stunning three-storey post-and-beam cabin set on the shores of Kaslo Lake, just north of Nelson in the West Kootenays of the Selkirk Mountains. The cabin sleeps twenty in summer and is a stepping-off point for hikers who want to explore this jewel of a park.

The cabin pays tribute to Michel and sixteen others who have died in avalanches in that area. The families of all those victims—and they came from all over North America—were there for the dedication ceremony, so seventeen pairs of scissors all cut at the same moment into that long red ribbon. And at that moment, ravens swept down on us. They were messengers. The generators are never off at the cabin, and a light always shines, like a beacon. I take some comfort in that.

One day my sister Betsy found a rose seedling in her garden. The plant was a deep plum colour, a thorny *Rosa rugosa*, but she could not identify it in any horticultural encyclopedia. Finally, she named it the Michel Trudeau Memorial Rose, and the proceeds from its sales all go to the Canadian Avalanche Foundation. My brother-in-law Robin says that it is the most vigorous rose he knows, and that it will grow anywhere. I want it to flourish all over Canada.

Not long after Michel's death, two blows struck in succession. Nancy Pitfield, a close and dear friend, finally succumbed to breast cancer after fighting the illness with every ounce of her strength. I was made numb by her loss.

Then Pierre was diagnosed with prostate cancer. At first, he didn't tell me. Later, I learned that his first reaction on getting the news was to say, "Good, now I can die too. I can be with Michel." Though the cancer was at a very early stage, he refused all treatment. After he left politics, Pierre had resumed his work as a lawyer and continued to walk every morning to his offices overlooking the St. Lawrence River and the mountains.

But now he seldom ventured out. I only realized how sick he was when I saw him, on June 21, 2000, at the annual party Sacha always gave with friends to mark the summer solstice—the longest day of the year. I hadn't seen Pierre for a while and my first thought was that he was dying. He had lost a lot of weight and looked thin and gaunt. We sat by the campfire, and I held his hand. Even in the summer heat, Pierre got cold very quickly and wanted to sit close to the flames; when he stood up to leave, he needed help walking to the car.

That summer, feeling very shaky myself, I accepted an invitation from Jane Faulkner to visit her in Switzerland. When I got back to Montreal, on my way home, I rang the boys to ask how Pierre was feeling. Sacha answered, and his voice was etched in worry, "Thank God you're back, you must come quickly. Dad is dying." Pierre had announced that he wanted to die at home and it had been decided that loved ones would be with him all the time, and that we would take shifts so that he would never be alone. I was pleased to be a part of it, and I also wanted to be there to help Justin and Sacha. We all knew that Pierre did not have long to live.

The first night I was there, Pierre felt well enough to come up to the second-floor dining room for dinner. It was almost like old times. My role was to be mother again, to cook and make sure the boys were all right. We laughed and I told Pierre about the Van Gogh exhibition I had just seen in Europe.

But soon he was too ill to finish a meal or even climb the stairs, and we would eat our meal round his bed at a small table. Then we converted a bedroom downstairs into a dining room, so he didn't have to face those stairs. Every day, he grew a little weaker. During the shifts I spent with him, he sometimes wanted to talk, but mostly he liked to lie in silence. One afternoon, I lay on the bed next to him and he wanted me to hold him in my arms. When his body became so frail that it hurt if anyone touched it, I sat holding his hand.

Pierre was not frightened of death. For a while, after Michel died, he had questioned his faith, but now he seemed to embrace his religion again and talked of joining Michel. We talked about Michel a lot. When I was with Pierre, I often wore the pearls that his mother had given me before our marriage. That seemed to please him. The only thing that the living can do for someone who is dying is to remind them of all the good things that happened in his or her life. Pierre and I shared beautiful memories of our happy times parenting our sons.

Looking back, I can see that we took consolation in the fact that we had loved each other once, loved each other deeply. He was kind and thoughtful, and he threw away his heart to me. But my catch wasn't very good; it's true what George Bernard Shaw said about youth being wasted on the young.

Several years after Pierre died, Peter C. Newman told a story about him in his book *Here Be Dragons: Tales of People, Passion and Power.* Stuart Hodgson, then commissioner of the Northwest Territories, was flying over the North Pole in the winter of 1974. As they passed over the pole, Pierre took control of the plane and called 24 Sussex, where a housekeeper answered. Maybe he wanted to share the excitement of the moment. He asked for me, and (this I find hard to believe) I apparently refused to come to the phone. At this, Hodgson told Newman, Pierre "sobbed."

"Why did you marry her?" Hodgson asked him, I gather with compassion.

"Because I love her," Pierre replied. "I truly love her."

Pierre died one afternoon in the early fall of that year, on September 28, 2000, after not having spoken for nearly a week. In many ways, Sacha was the son that Pierre was closest to. He had always lived with his father, and they were very alike: disciplined, loyal, a bit gruff, unwilling to waste time on banalities. Towards the end, Pierre was unconscious and both Sacha and Justin stayed by his side, comforting him until the very end. They let him go very peacefully with their enormous love for their fine father. I slipped deep into sorrow.

From the moment it was known that Pierre was dying, the public concern and support throughout Canada had been overwhelming. The press were camped out all around and, to our horror, a satellite dish had suddenly sprouted on a telephone pole not far from the house, clearly visible from the bedroom where Pierre spent his days. He found the sight of it distressing and Sacha had the dish taken down.

For many Canadians, Pierre was the politician who had shaped modern Canada, the man who had made multiculturalism work. Now that he was nearing the end, they wanted to honour him, and when the news of his death was announced, there was an outpouring of grief. For four days, Pierre's body lay in state in Ottawa in the hall of the House of Commons, and Canadians queued to pay their respects, in a long line that wound right round the square.

On October 2, four days after Pierre's death, I went down to the square with my sisters. A TV reporter, a man well respected as a shrewd political pundit, caught sight of me. Thrusting his microphone in my face, he barked out, "How do you feel today, Mrs. Trudeau? Have you remembered it's Michel's birthday?" I was so taken aback, so shaken, that I dropped to the ground. Later I got a profuse apology from his news organization.

What that reporter did was so extraordinarily inappropriate and insensitive. That's the hardest I have ever been hit publicly by anyone at any time anywhere. These journalists dare to judge, they dare to pontificate. It makes me so mad.

The casket containing Pierre's body, draped in the Canadian flag, was taken by train from Ottawa to Montreal, where the funeral was to take place in the Notre-Dame Basilica. Sacha and Justin, who at twenty-eight was emerging as the strong figure in our family, travelled with it. All along the tracks, there were people standing and waving, and many of them were crying. I felt that Pierre, the man who never went out without a red rose in his lapel, and whom the press had always described as a man of "reason over passion," would have been touched by the piles of red roses and by the fifty thousand Canadians who had filed past his coffin.

I had gone down to Montreal the previous day. Early on the morning of the funeral I had a brief meeting with Fidel Castro, who was to be one of the pallbearers, in his hotel. This was the only time, apart from a visit to Russia, that he had left Cuba, and I hadn't seen him for some years, though we had remained friends from my first visit to Cuba in 1974. I found his kindness and sympathy very comforting. Heads of state, political dignitaries and former leaders had all come to Canada for the funeral. Justin delivered the eulogy with eloquence and passion. He thanked his father "for having loved us so much" and went on:

"My father's fundamental belief never came from a textbook.

It stemmed from his deep love for, and faith in, all Canadians, and over the past few days, with every card, every rose, every tear, every wave and every pirouette, you returned his love. It means the world to Sacha and me. Thank you . . .

"We have gathered from coast to coast to coast, from one ocean to another, united in our grief, to say goodbye. But this is not the end. He left politics in '84. But he came back for Meech. He came back for Charlottetown. He came back to remind us of who we are and what we're capable of. But he won't be coming back anymore. It's up to us, all of us, now."

And then he ended with the lines from the Robert Frost poem "Stopping by Woods on a Snowy Evening"—a poem that we had often recited to the boys when they were children. But for the eulogy, Justin changed the words slightly. Instead of the traditional ending, Justin said: "The woods are lovely, dark and deep / He has kept his promises and earned his sleep. *Je t'aime, Papa.*"

I suddenly felt myself begin to slip, to do what I always do in moments of extreme emotion, a form of collapse I can't control. Instantly, I felt a strong hand on my shoulder. The hand belonged to Jimmy Carter, who whispered words of encouragement into my ear.

Then, seeing Justin so sad and distraught, looking almost as if he had fallen on his father's coffin, I tried to rise to comfort him. Immediately I felt another strong hand, keeping me in my place. The hand was Fidel Castro's.

"He's a man, Margaret. He's a man, " Fidel told me. Let him be, was the message. Justin must rise on his own.

Leonard Cohen was there as an honorary pallbearer, as was the Aga Khan. The support was extraordinary, so extraordinary.

———————

After their father's funeral, Justin and Sacha returned to their own lives; Justin was now a teacher, Sacha a filmmaker. Winter was coming and the weather in Ottawa can be very bleak. The days got shorter and it was dark and grey for much of the time. I have always hated the long dark days, but this bleakness was of another order.

My marriage to Fried did not survive Michel's death. Someone once asked me why I did not fight harder to save it. The answer was that we did fight hard, but not hard enough. Fried bought roses and put them on my pillow and cooked delicious meals; I tried to listen and sympathize with his financial problems. Occasionally, we seemed to be close again and I began to think that all would yet be well; but there were too many cracks between us, too much bitterness. And in any case, everything in me was pushing me to get away, to be alone, to concentrate on my grief. I wanted no one close to me, not even the children, whom I continued to love, but dimly, as if through a haze. When I thought about them it was with a kind of terror, as if something might happen to them as well.

Many things were said that should never have been said and, in due course, Fried left.

In the early days of our prosperity, I had bought a condominium in Ottawa with money from the sale of a lot next to my house.

As it was rented out, Fried moved in for a while with his parents, who were also grieving for Michel and perplexed and deeply unhappy about our separation. When the condo fell vacant, Fried moved in there.

For a while, Kyle and Ally lived with me; I took them to school, shopped, went through the motions of being alive, while living in a cold grey fog that never lifted. In 2000, I sold the house on Victoria Street and moved into a smaller house, not far from Fried. I had told Fried, who found it for me, that the one thing I needed was a lot of light, and in winter, when I had first seen the house, the light had indeed flooded in. But when spring came, and then summer, the trees all around filled in and the house never seemed to get properly lit. I began to feel like a prisoner.

Soon after Michel's death, I bumped into a young friend of ours, a man who had known Michel since childhood. I had been thinking of getting a bicycle and we fell into conversation. He invited me back to his house for a barbecue, and while I was there I smoked a bit of marijuana. I hadn't had any for a while. But marijuana, as I well knew, was my addiction.

If I had any, I wanted not just one joint, or even two, but the whole bag. I wanted to start the day with a joint and end the day with a joint, with few pauses in between. One reason I hadn't been smoking more was because Fried didn't like it. Now I didn't care.

The marijuana allowed me to forget. When I felt so bad I could hardly breathe, I had another joint. I was now able to arrange for a regular supply and just kept smoking. I told myself that I was not really a junkie, in the sense that I never vomited or got the shakes when I didn't have any. But now, looking back, I see that the deep sense of distress and loss I experienced without it was a certain sign of psychological dependency. Many people use food or alcohol as a form of self-medication; for me it was marijuana. This was all part of the denial, thinking that I could cure myself with homemade solutions.

I'm not sure now why those around me did not see that my mental state was deteriorating fast. Knowing my history, why did no one detect the depression that had engulfed me? Perhaps because they mistook depression for grief, fully expecting me to be sad. Or perhaps the acting classes I had taken in New York in my late twenties had taught me how to put up an impenetrable mask. I simply got better at pretending all was well.

I made an effort to plant my deck with bulbs. I went to a bereaved parents' association meeting and listened to the grief they were all suffering but only came home sadder. I did see a good psychiatrist, Dr. Selwyn Smith, but when he left Ottawa not long after, he passed me on to a young woman with a small child and pregnant with a new baby. I knew I couldn't talk to her. I felt too protective, of her as well as of myself. How could I talk to a mother about the death of a child? So I stopped seeing her. People would say to me that they could not begin to imagine how terrible I must be feeling. They were right, and I didn't even want them to try.

But the day came when my fragile sense of myself simply snapped. Justin had come to stay with us. One Saturday morning, I crawled out of bed to make breakfast for him, Kyle and Ally.

They wanted eggs, potatoes, bacon, freshly squeezed juice. When all was ready, I called to them to come and eat, but they were playing video games and paid no attention. I called again: nothing.

And then I exploded, in the most appalling and humiliating way. I yelled and shouted about not being able to bear it any longer, about not being their servant. I told them to get out of the house. And as I ranted and raved, I could see a frightened and sad look in Kyle's eyes. I had held on, behind my mask, for far too long; like a pressure cooker, the steam had been building up, and now, when I could contain it no longer, the release was terrifying in its intensity.

For me this moment spelled ultimate defeat. However depressed or manic I had been in the past, even in my most disturbed states, I had been able to look after and respond to my children. Now I had lost even that capacity.

After this, we decided that Kyle and Ally should move in with Fried. What mother willingly gives up her children? I had indeed failed if I was no longer someone who could give them the security they needed, so I saw surrendering them as an act of true maternal love. For a while, Ally went back and forth between us, and during the summer she was away at a horse camp and with her cousins at the cottage.

I never went back to the house on Newboro Lake where I had been so happy. Fried put my things into black plastic garbage bags and brought them to me.

I kept thinking how Ally simply didn't deserve this. She touched my heart by making huge efforts to cheer me up. She kept telling me to get a dog, so I could take walks. She pressed me to go out, see my friends. Ally was growing up, too fast.

After this, quite slowly, I fell apart. I smoked dope and drank Scotch. I found that the combination dulled the pain and I needed it once the marijuana lost its effectiveness. I ate almost nothing.

Ally had decided that she couldn't bear to live in two places and had opted to make Fried's house her base—where she kept her clothes, her music, her pictures. She had also felt too lonely in my house. The children visited me from time to time and I did my best to provide a home for them, cooking their meals and driving them to school.

That was the best part of my day, driving them to and from school, learning about their lives, talking over their problems. But what a cheerless life for them. Fried put a stop to family dinners after one night in a local restaurant when something was said and I burst into tears and couldn't stop crying. The children stared at me, miserable and bewildered. Christmas that year was bleak. I fed the children pre-stuffed frozen turkey-in-a-box, heated up.

Nothing made much sense to me anymore. I spent the days blaming myself, blaming others. I was extremely lonely. After our breakup, Fried never included me in all the family parties and celebrations that his large family so loved. His sense of hurt and misery took the form of telling me that his family did not want to see me, and telling them that I did not want to see them. His sister, who had become my dearest friend, now avoided me. I would hear from the children about all the fun they had had at the cottage or when they went off skiing together. My isolation had been my choice; but my sense of missing out was acute nonetheless.

Just occasionally, for no reason I could quite fathom, a bout of mania would overcome me. I would suddenly begin to feel stronger, more optimistic, but then too strong, too optimistic, too invincible. Fired by energy and desire, I went shopping, filling my bags with unwanted clothes, expensive sweaters, perfume, cosmetics, handbags, shopping with a kind of ecstatic frenzy.

When I got home and looked at my parcels, the mania would fizzle out and I would wonder what I was doing. Without unpacking them, I would let the parcels pile up in the hall before taking them round to a women's shelter in order to make room for more.

And then the depression would return: I felt myself going down and down into an abyss where the light got fainter and fainter. I thought I would never laugh again. I had been dating a lawyer, and he was concerned and attentive. But he was also very busy. When I was with him and he left early for work, I spent the days pacing up and down his beautiful apartment—more like a museum than a place to live. I would stare at his magnificent pieces of art or out of his plate glass windows at the snowy landscape down below. I preferred to be on my own at home, where no one could see me.

By now I had lost thirty pounds and found it very hard to eat. I couldn't bear for anyone who knew me to speak to me, so I stopped going out. I closed the blinds on my windows. When Justin, Sacha or my mother called, I told them that I was fine, that I couldn't talk for long because I was baking cookies and that I had tickets for the theatre that night. Often I didn't answer the phone and soon, in any case, friends stopped phoning.

Sometimes I felt so lonely in the house that I got into my car and drove round and round the city, stopping, if the weather was fine, to walk by the river. I never visited anyone, for there was no one with whom I wanted to share my misery. Trudging dismally along, I would look into the lighted windows of people's houses, envying the happy faces of the people inside. Who was there who could understand what I was going through?

Everything was spiralling out of control. I was a train on the wrong track and moments from crashing. There was nothing now that could save me. In an old book, I recently discovered, I scrawled incoherent words in the margins and over the print: "How can I survive life without my Miche?" And "I have a broken heart, a damaged soul, an unshakeable sorrow."

Recurring again and again are phrases about how guilty I felt about the other children and how I wanted to die. From the moment I woke up to the moment I went to bed, I lived in a misery-filled limbo where time had stopped and all joy had vanished. Everything that had once been bright and colourful was now flat and grey. In my eyes, I had become dead, unresponsive, incapable, useless.

On December 5, 2000, I made an enormous effort and went to a rock concert in Cranbrook, British Columbia, generously put on by Bryan Adams to raise money for the Avalanche Foundation. No one had ever seen me more cheerful and more alive. I was always able, even if only briefly, to put on a very convincing act, and I did feel genuinely grateful for the $50,000 the evening raised. After that, I shut myself away, stopped eating, and stayed in bed.

But I did have one friend, Michelle Bégin, who was reluctant to take no for an answer. She kept ringing, and when I didn't answer the phone, she rang again, and again, until I did answer. On December 14, having had no answer for several days, Michelle knocked on my door. I didn't answer it. She kept knocking, and then began to ring again. Finally, with extreme reluctance, I opened the door. She found the place in chaos; I was confused, incoherent, my thoughts racing. Getting no sense out of me, Michelle rang the office of Prime Minister Jean Chrétien (he had served under Pierre in three different portfolios) and said that she needed to reach Sacha Trudeau, urgently. Something in her tone must have impressed them, for they found Sacha's number and gave it to her. Sacha rang me and told me to stay put until he could get there.

He arrived next morning to find me leaving the house to attend a meeting at a local school, where a friend's daughter was a pupil. I had promised I would help her with a project. Dimly, with no real idea what I was doing, I felt that this was something I could not duck. Sacha took one look at me, led me back inside, told me that I would only scare the children and put me to bed.

A doctor came, a Dr. Colin Cameron, and he talked to me very calmly, explaining that the depression and mania were now alternating at a frightening rate and that I needed something urgently to slow my mind down. There was nothing for it but to go to hospital. The idea filled me with terror and dread. My memories of psychiatric wards were all too fresh. My one feeling was that I was once again going to be punished and imprisoned.

They insisted. I kept saying that I was fine, that there was nothing wrong with me, that they were all making a mistake.

Through the fog of my mind I knew that I had to escape. Telling Sacha and Dr. Cameron that I needed some clothes in the laundry room and remembering that I had a one-piece ski suit hanging there, I made my way down to the basement, put on the ski suit and let myself out quietly through the back door. Then I ran.

After a while, I found myself back outside my old house on Victoria Street, where I had been so happy. It was snowing and extremely cold. Despite the snowsuit, I couldn't seem to get warm. I hung about for a bit, then rang my former neighbour's bell and asked her young daughter if I could come in and get warm. By now I was shaking all over and making very little sense. The girl looked so alarmed, so appalled by the state I was in, that I left and went on to the house of a good friend, Pauline Bogue.

Finally, Pauline took me home and got hold of Sacha and the police—who had all been out hunting desperately for me. The police now arrived, an ambulance in tow. They trooped upstairs, put me on a stretcher and carried me down before strapping me onto a gurney. I struggled and fought. One of the officers, a tough-looking woman who plainly had little sympathy with such antics, put her hand under the sheet, took hold of my hand and pulled the thumb sharply back towards my wrist. I was in agony; she had dislocated my thumb, whether on purpose or not I never discovered. Clearly, she thought I was drunk.

When we got to the Royal Ottawa Hospital, I kept begging for someone to look at my thumb, which was throbbing. They paid

no attention but began to sedate me. I called for help. What terrified me most was being locked up, and I begged them not to shut
me in. Finally, a psychiatric nurse took pity on me. He fetched a
pillow and helped me into the day room. I was totally exhausted
and fast succumbing to the drugs; I had no more struggle in me.
I took the pillow, put on my coat, crawled over to a corner of the
room and fell asleep on the floor. I had hit rock bottom. There
was nowhere lower for me to go.

CHAPTER 12

CHOOSING SANITY

*A person with a mental illness needs an advocate—someone to
chart the waters, interpret the possible side effects of drugs and provide
reassurance when recovery seems so terribly slow. My oldest sister,
Heather, was that person for me.*

CHRISTMAS 2000

Psychiatrists have long recognized that the process of accepting
an acute mental illness, in much the same way as accepting death,
has five distinct phases. The first phase is denial, a refusal to accept
that what is going on has really anything to do with you: it's the
life you are leading, it's other people, it's the circumstances, it's
extreme bad luck.

Then you start to bargain: Maybe it will all work out if I take
better care of myself, if I find a hobby, join a yoga class, get more
exercise, buy a pet, get up earlier in the morning.

After this comes depression and self-pity: Why me? What
did I do to deserve this? Why isn't this happening to others?

Next comes anger, with oneself and with others: What is wrong with everyone?

And then, but only then, the anger gives way to acceptance: Yes, this is me, this is my life, I am ill, I need help and I will take a hand in my own recovery. I am not an innocent victim; I am a player—*the* player—in this game.

Thirty years in and out of Canada's mental illness services had done me very little lasting good. I had lived the first four stages, again and again, for most of my adult life. I had fallen ill, been treated and gotten better—but I had never really acknowledged what was wrong with me, not deep down. It was now time to embrace the fifth stage: acceptance. And I was lucky in the timing. The public perception of mental illness was finally changing, much helped by new research into brain health and the neurochemistry of moods and disorders. The moment was coming when the stigma was lifting—when the full extent, the sheer number of people affected, was at last beginning to be realized.

Situated on what was then a country road, the Royal Ottawa Hospital had been built in 1910 as a sanatorium for people with tuberculosis. Its last TB ward had been closed in the 1960s, by which time it had become a treatment centre for all kinds of disability, including emotional and psychiatric disorders. The place was grey, dark and extremely gloomy, and I was filled with terror. I arrived on an arctic, snowy day in the middle of a long, cold winter. To help patients and staff navigate the different parts of the hospital, they had built subterranean tunnels and passage-ways—long, dimly lit, echoing corridors lined with air ducts and pipes. I would get to know the tunnels well.

I had been admitted under a seventy-two-hour committal order, which meant that I was not a voluntary patient but incarcerated by social services as a possible danger to myself or to the public. Though there was in fact no likelihood of my harming anyone, not even myself, at that point, the rule was that I was to be observed at all times. When I moved about, I was accompanied; when in my bed, I was watched. This was all part of the horror.

On the first morning, I woke feeling somewhat calmer. The medication given to me the previous night had soothed me. But at the same time, something inside me had been broken by the sheer trauma of my escape through the snow and my treatment at the hands of a police officer. I felt defeated. I had nothing left.

When I looked in the mirror, I could see an elderly hag, my hair dirty and dishevelled, my skin grey, my flesh hanging off me from months of starvation. Normally, I weigh about 147 pounds, but at this point I tipped the scales at 117. Photos of me then are sobering to see.

Sacha's last words to me the night before haunted me: he had said, as they tried to reason with me, that I was possessed. He was right, I was indeed possessed: by fear and sorrow, but mainly by fear. Just how unreasoning, how deranged I had become was clear from the letters I had been writing my mother; she told me later that they were so mad that she had torn them all up.

One of the first things the hospital did was to inform me of my rights. An ombudsman arrived to talk to me, and I told him what the policewoman had done. My thumb was by now hugely swollen and badly bruised. My initial thought was to bring charges against her, for even in my sickened state I felt that such conduct was unacceptable.

But all this was just playing for time. I was prevaricating, denying, blaming others, anything but facing up to the truth. However, I felt somewhat comforted by a visit from our family doctor, Rick Martin, a man who had again and again tried to help me at different stages of my illness. He came to tell me that I was in the best hands, that this was exactly the place for me and that he believed that I would now really get better.

At this point, something really good happened to me. The same doctor who had come to my house, Dr. Cameron, took up my case. Finally, finally, someone from the caring profession who understood what I had been through and how I had suffered, was prepared to take my recovery in hand. He knew that my spirit was broken and he knew how to go about fixing it. Dr. Cameron said that healing would take a long, long time—and he was right about that—but he also assured me that there was, indeed, light at the end of the tunnel. Quite simply, he gave me hope.

Dr. Cameron was young, almost boyish looking, with round glasses and his hair gathered in a ponytail. He had an easy manner about him, as do all who are comfortable in their own shoes.

He was a psychiatrist specializing by training in mood disorders and—this would prove crucial in my case—post-traumatic stress disorder. He also conveyed his absolute determination to make me better. Trusting him, I believed it. In any case, I had very little choice. There was no fight left in me. Something about his manner and his sympathy made me listen and, this time, take it all in. The day had finally arrived when I was able to say, "Please help me. I want to learn how to live with and manage all this."

Dr. Cameron began by talking to me about bipolar illness— the modern term for manic depression—explaining how there was now general agreement that it resulted from a chemical imbalance in the brain. I had barely heard of serotonin or dopamine, but Dr. Cameron gave me lessons in both. Lack of serotonin is believed to depress the brain by failing to conduct positive signals to our emotional cortex, thereby causing depression. Serotonin is a jelly-like chemical in the brain; it's a conductor between neuron transmitters that allows you to feel delight from everyday living. Dopamine is a neurotransmitter and it accounts for the huge surges that come with mania.

Depression starts slowly, and the first victim of diminished serotonin is sleep patterns. You have trouble sleeping—because your thoughts are racing and you have no time for sleep—or you sleep far too much. You stop eating properly and you start loading up on carbohydrates and chocolate and sugar to try to make yourself better because you find yourself slipping. You think these comfort foods will make you feel better, and you start putting on weight. You get sloppy in your appearance and you stop accepting invitations because you're not feeling great and your clothes don't fit. Isolation takes hold, and so does the depression. You've stopped going to the gym or going for that great walk. You're not eating, sleeping or playing well, and those are the things that help you have healthy serotonin levels. That's how we get serotonin—by being alive. With no positive reinforcement, no reminders that anything in life is any good, you start sinking. People around you try to help you out by telling you to get a hobby, and then you start pushing them away, and before you know it you're in the dark. They haven't shunned you; you've just stopped answering their calls and you become more and more alone. Maybe you self-medicate, with alcohol or drugs from the medicine cabinet or the street.

Finally, you do get help. Your doctor sees you and understands by your overwhelming sadness that you're depressed and prescribes a drug to lift your serotonin levels, and you see your doctor once a month to get the drug level adjusted, and people think that's where treatment stops. No, that just got you up on terra firma, where you have the ability, once more, to feel delight, to feel joy. But if you're stuck in a meaningless life, wearing masks and pretending to be someone you're not and not fulfilling your own personal dreams, then nothing has really changed.

My family doctor, who is nearing retirement now, tells me that at least half the patients he sees every day in his office are presenting with problems, often physiological ones, but the root cause is emotional. The lower back, the neck are often places where this referred pain expresses itself, but the pain really starts in the brain.

I remember my family doctor, a very compassionate man, asking me, "Margaret, what's really pinching you?" He knew that my pain had a source. And I wept to realize that he knew.

———————————————

By 2000, science had made considerable breakthroughs in understanding the brain. Though there was still some confusion over the term *bipolar* (some people found the term offensive because they believed it belittled the illness), Dr. Cameron told me he preferred that word to *manic depression* since sufferers must endure both mania and depression. *Bipolar*, on the other hand, seemed to suggest two neat categories at either end of a spectrum. I well knew that the illness was not tidy at all, but had wildly fluctuating highs and lows. Today, however, *bipolar* is the more widely accepted term.

Dr. Cameron seemed to know precisely what I had endured and how much I had suffered. Let no one, he said, make the mistake of thinking that bipolar disorder is not a crippling and destructive illness, with complicated and difficult emotions, with ominous, dark and terrifying lows, with week after week of despair and dread alternating with passionate highs filled with bubbling and brilliant moments of sheer exuberance, and in between every kind of mortifying and embarrassing behaviour, violent outbursts and self-destructive longings. I knew only too well just how seductive my unbridled and manic moods had been, with their explosions of smells and sounds and colours, and how welcome I had found them when faced with Pierre's caution and reason.

Lithium would have been the obvious drug to start me off with, but lithium, as I knew from my earlier hospitalization, did not suit me. There was something in it that I could not tolerate, however small the dose. But Dr. Cameron explained that a whole new generation of mood-stabilizing drugs was now on the market. He began by putting me on something called olanzapine, which had widely been heralded as a miracle drug in schizophrenia and the mood disorders of bipolar illness.

Olanzapine did indeed perform miracles for me. The drug stopped the mania, but the list of potential side effects was long: they included the inability to sit still, dizziness, insomnia, tremor and shaking—of the mouth, tongue, eyelids, arms and legs—which could be irreversible. I was spared all that.

What I got, though, was weight gain. I had lost a great deal of weight in the preceding months, but what happened now took me by surprise. I put on pound after pound after pound. There was also the little matter of cost. When I went to pay for my prescription, I thought the pharmacist had added a zero to the bill—$480. I showed him his mistake: Surely he meant $48? No, he said, the number was right, but there was a program that I could join to help me pay. It made me think again how tough it is for people to afford medicine they desperately need.

The other problem with olanzapine was that, in my case, the drug imposed a ceiling on my feelings, making it very hard to feel despair or elation, or to delight in creativity. After several months of trial and error, Dr. Cameron put me on risperidone, an antipsychotic drug that controlled dopamine in the brain. I easily tolerated the drug and the ceiling lifted.

Risperidone seemed to lessen my oversensitivity to events and situations, and yet left me free to be more proactive, to think of doing something about my situations without collapsing or running away. I had cried my way through the Vietnam War, Biafra and the plight of our aboriginal people in the North; perhaps I would now be able to stop crying and actually do some-

71. At my house on Victoria Street, with the kids.

72. The Kemper clan—Easter celebration.

73. Family picture,
with our dog Sandy,
at 95 Victoria Street.

74. The poster for a 1996
documentary, *Passion before
Reason*, by Canadian
documentary filmmakers
John Curtin and Paul
Carvalho.

75. The Sinclair clan on Grouse Mountain, for my mother's birthday.

76. My family welcomes me home from the hospital.

77. Sophie and I travelled to Ethiopia with the
humanitarian organization WaterCan.

78. Helping women access clean water in Ethiopia is part of
my work with WaterCan.

79. In my sunroom at 95 Victoria with Ally and Michel.

80. Michel playing hacky sack with his friends on the West Coast.

81. Michel in Haida Gwaii
(Queen Charlotte Islands), British Columbia.

82. Justin and Pierre at Kokanee Glacier Lake,
where Michel died.

83. At the Gillespies' house in Vankleek Hill at summer solstice, just before Pierre passed away.

84. Overwhelmed by sadness, just after Pierre's death. This photo was taken only days before I was hospitalized, sick with grief. In the background is a picture of the two of us dancing.

85. With Bryan Adams in 2000. He put on a great concert to raise money for the Canadian Avalanche Foundation in Cranbrook, B.C.

86. A photo of me taken by Bryan Adams for his book on famous women.

87. Sacha and me, opening up Kokanee Glacier Cabin.

88. With Ally and Sophie.

89. At Justin's wedding to Sophie Grégoire in 2005.

90. With Sophie on her wedding day.

91. Ally and me at Justin's wedding.

92. Living in Montreal, my new city. This photo of me and
the boys was taken for *Hello!* magazine at the St. James Hotel.

93. During a speaking engagement at the Bottom Line conference, organized by the Canadian Mental Health Association, Vancouver, 2007.

94. My garden at its best, at Newboro Lake.

95. At Sacha and Zoë's wedding, at the boys' cottage in the Laurentians. From left: Sophie (pregnant with Xavier), Ally, me, Justin, Zoë, Sacha, Kyle.

96. Sacha and me at his wedding reception.

97. Preparing a celebratory feast for my 60th birthday at Betsy's house on the West Coast. From left: niece Jamie, niece Sarah, Betsy, Sacha, niece Chloe, me.

98. With Zoë, at a WaterCan embassy dinner in Ottawa.

99. My niece, Katie Walker.

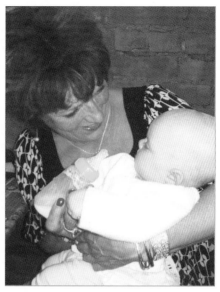

100. Pierre with his uncle Kyle on our fishing boat at Newboro Lake.

101. My first granddaughter, Gala, as in "a very grand celebration."

102. Gala and her beautiful mother, Zoë.

103. Xavier under a portrait of
"Gramma-Yummy" and his dad, baby Justin.

104. Ella-Grace Margaret Trudeau—will she follow
in her grandmother's footsteps?

thing about them. Dr. Cameron took great pains to talk to me about the drugs he was prescribing, urging me to ask him any questions and giving me material to read about the possible side effects.

On the first day, I had been terrified to see the words "anti-psychotic" and asked him in some panic whether he thought that I might be a sociopath. He reassured me that though risperidone was not a drug commonly used for bipolar illness, he had found it extremely helpful in cases like mine; the drug had the great advantage of calming mania while not imposing too heavy a ceiling on thought and creativity.

I was soon feeling immensely better. I settled down to a regime of antidepressants to raise the serotonin, and risperidone to balance my moods. Even so, the precise doses of each remained a matter of endless adjustment, and many months would pass before the combination was exactly right. What Dr. Cameron impressed on me was compliance, the need to trust him and follow his orders carefully.

Dr. Cameron was a psychiatrist in the fullest and best sense, a doctor who believed that there was no simple, magic cure for mental illness, no pill or combination of pills that alone could effect a cure. Real recovery, he said, again and again, was a long journey in which I would have to play my part. I would have to take baby steps, one at a time, and I would have to face the fact that after the mania, after the events of the recent past, there would certainly be a depression, probably a very deep one.

This could not be avoided. I was going to have to learn to face reality, the reality that I had a bipolar illness and must live with certain facts: that I would have this illness my entire life, that Michel was dead and that I must find a way to exist with that knowledge.

I had a choice to make. I could either accept that I would stay on a roller coaster for the rest of my life, ricocheting from high to low, or I would have to engage in the long, slow and painful work that would eventually lead to stability.

Because I had gone without sustained treatment for long periods, the journey to recovery was going to be extremely hard, Dr. Cameron told me, almost impossibly so. The patterns of bipolar illness, the cycles, were by now deeply ingrained in me. I had been diagnosed as manic depressive as a young woman, but even had I understood and acted on that diagnosis, the treatment and drugs were not yet available. So much time had passed, and my behaviours were so entrenched. The good news was that drug and other therapies were available to help me. The bad news? I had to shed many old ways, and learn new ones.

Like a small child, I had to learn new responses to life: not to overreact in the face of criticism, not to wallow in shame and loathing, not to protect myself with delusion, not to blame others for my own inappropriate responses. I listened, I thought, and, at last, I accepted: the fifth stage, acceptance, had begun.

At heart, I knew perfectly well that everything Dr. Cameron said was right; I had known for many years that there was something very wrong with me, but I had stopped believing that I would ever find a cure. I had, quite simply, given up: I believed that I was condemned to a life of unhappiness. I now had to believe that, on the contrary, I could not only accept the hand of life that had been dealt to me but find areas of new happiness.

One of the first steps Dr. Cameron insisted on was that I see a nutritionist. I liked her immediately. I knew that I was in terrible shape and that I had been starving myself for many months, and that whenever moods of depression or mania assailed me the first thing to go had been eating. What I didn't know was the part that malnutrition had played in my eventual collapse.

As the nutritionist explained it, the fuel you put into your body must be like that which goes into supersonic jets—pure and strong. Months of eating beans out of cans, the occasional piece of cheese, with never any fruit or vegetables, had done terrible things to my gastrointestinal system.

Some time in the autumn I had found that I had difficulty swallowing. I would chew interminably but be unable to get the food down and eventually I would spit it out. I remembered how, during the worst times of my life, I had always felt unable either to breathe or to swallow. I now realized that what I had been experiencing was a form of passive suicide. There had been no conscious decision, merely an instinct not to nourish myself.

My stomach had shrunk so much, the nutritionist told me, that I was going to have to start eating properly—but only very slowly or I would not tolerate the food. I told her that I had always liked oatmeal, that it was one of my comfort foods. My mother, heeding an old Scottish tradition, served us this hot cereal from early fall to the end of winter. Every morning, and several times during the day, the nutritionist now appeared at my bedside with small bowls of oatmeal, with salt and sugar and milk.

Though at first I found the oatmeal almost impossible to swallow, and was often sick, I began to look forward to her appearance and realized that I was even quite pleased to eat. The nutritionist put me on a careful diet, with many small meals a day. Though the hospital cafeteria was perfectly adequate, a long time passed before the smell of cooked food stopped making me feel nauseated.

The next doctor I was sent to within the hospital was Dr. Paul Grof, who was born in the former Czechoslovakia, and European doctors have long been interested in vitamins and minerals as supplements. Dr. Grof was also one of the leading psychopharmacologists in the field. He explained in considerable detail what drugs were available, how they worked and what choices were available to me. Dr. Grof underlined that I should think of drugs as a supplement for the brain, where chemicals that for one reason or another were lacking needed replacing in order to restore balance. In much the same way, he told me, I was going to need nutritional supplements, such as the omega-3 fatty acid of fish oil, folic acid, vitamin B. Particularly large doses of that vitamin would not only repair but fine-tune the workings of my neural transmitters.

As important, and more surprising to me, was Dr. Cameron's insistence that I see the hospital's drug addiction specialist—Dr. Allan Wilson. My first reaction was one of irritation and disbelief. What was the point? I wasn't a drug addict, after all; all I had done was to smoke a bit of marijuana over the years.

Or so I told myself at the time. I look back on that thought and I think of what Willie Nelson once told Jay Leno on *The Tonight Show*. Leno noted that Nelson had been picked up by police in Texas and found to be in possession of a little marijuana. "That's a lie!" Nelson countered. "I would never have been in possession of a little marijuana."

I very much liked Dr. Wilson. He was in his early forties, athletic and full of life, with sparkling eyes. He was, and I mean this as a compliment, not too earnest—as some psychiatrists are. *Earnest* is a mean word for me. I have, apparently, freely used sarcasm as a weapon in my life, and for me to call someone "earnest" is one of my unkinder cuts. Earnest people take themselves far too seriously.

Dr. Wilson was no less kind and patient than Dr. Cameron, but he was equally clear. He explained, in great detail, how marijuana had become my own form of self-medication, and how I had used it to fill what was missing in my life. This sense of neediness, of there always being something unfulfilled, was probably caused by my bipolar condition. The need for the drug had been a symptom; I had to learn to feel better without it. I hadn't taken marijuana constantly or even regularly, but when I did use it to try to tame my brain, I binged on it. Marijuana had been an artificial prop, based on delusions, false perceptions, and fuelled by fear. What I now needed to do was find another way to enjoy life without these unreal highs.

More than that, the marijuana had probably been the trigger for many of my bouts of extreme mania. New research was increasingly showing a strong and lasting relationship between the two. Addiction in all its forms—whether to drugs, drink, sex, porn, gambling or food—was beginning to be seen as a form of escape and a symptom of an underlying mental illness.

For so many years, addiction and mental illness were thought to be separate issues; no longer. I listened and took it all in but found it very hard to accept. Marijuana had been a friend that got me through many lonely days. But somewhere inside me I had always suspected that the "friend" had done me harm. Countless times I had reported to doctors that I feared that part of my trouble was taking so much marijuana, only to be told that drugs were unrelated to mental health.

At one point, Dr. Wilson considered whether I might benefit from attending Narcotics Anonymous meetings, but he came to the conclusion that NA might be more than I could take. NA tends to draw the bad boys, men on cool drugs with their motorcycles, and I've always liked the bad boys. On the one hand, Alcoholics Anonymous was an odd choice for I can't drink much before I become ill. On the other hand, I was an addict. All my life, I had self-medicated with marijuana.

So it was decided that AA was a better bet, with fewer bad boys. I gave it a try. Friends in my circle had become addicted to alcohol, had benefited from the AA process and were very committed to it. I was given the location of the closest venue, and it was close, all right, but in another way it was a world apart. I lived in the tony part of town; this AA gathering place was located in one of the poorest parts of Ottawa.

When British rocker Ozzy Osbourne and his band Black Sabbath came to Ottawa in the 1990s, he asked for the AA location in the down-and-out part of the city—I presume where he would feel most at home while he continued to battle his drinking demons. Had our dates coincided, we might have met. In any case, I rubbed shoulders with the poor and the homeless and eventually I found another AA location that had a clientele better suited to my background.

So I went to the meetings, where I chanted and memorized, confessed and held hands. Some knew who I was, some didn't. When my turn came to speak, I talked about the death of my son and the pain of that loss—this was grief work. The famous Big Blue Book embraced by AA didn't really work for me. Most of these men and women repeated their wounds over and over again. The meetings were like theatre, with people reliving the darkest moments of their lives. It was clear to me that they were self-medicating with alcohol, but I also understood that their real ailment was mental illness, something far deeper than dependence on booze. And there was no one there with training in psychiatry. Did a blue book first published in 1939 offer the truth, the secret to beating addiction? All I heard were tired clichés.

But there was this reassuring community, warm company over coffee and an intimacy that came from revealing deep secrets. And while I don't necessarily believe in the AA process, I do believe that I was helped by going to those meetings.

As important as the antipsychotic drugs and antidepressants, however, was the next step Dr. Cameron proposed to me. None of my treatment was likely to have a lasting effect, he explained, without some regular psychotherapy. There was a great deal that I needed to understand about my past behaviour, and many responses that I had to unlearn. The muddled cobweb of my unquiet mind had to be spun anew. As Dr. Cameron put it, psychotherapy would be extremely serious and hard work, no fun at all, and bound to come up were issues that I would prefer not to face. But face them I must. Foremost was my life-long and exceptional sensitivity to pain, guilt and other people's suffering. I had always cried too readily, been too easily obsessed with images of grief and destruction.

Growing up in a world in which I felt I had to please every-one, I had lost my sense of balance—an imbalance only intensi-fied by marriage to an older, very rational man with whom I had little in common beyond our shared love for the children. The huge differences in our ages and characters doomed the marriage in any case. Bipolar disorder was not the straw that broke the camel's back, but more like a huge round bale of straw weighing many hundreds of pounds.

And because I had lived behind a mask, trying to behave in ways that didn't come naturally to me, there were times when I had reacted with self-destructive behaviour and by taking absurd risks. This, in turn, had led to guilt and shame and self-loathing, and to escape them I had turned to anything that made me feel better, namely and most often, marijuana. And that, in turn, had led to hypomania, followed by depression, after which the whole cycle would begin again.

Sometimes these cycles had been slow, taking months or years to unfold; but sometimes the cycles had been extremely rapid, swinging from elation to despair several times in a sin-gle day. I had quite simply lost control of my mind and spent much of my time in a state of "impaired insight." Because I was good at donning masks and acting, I had been able to fool those around me.

Now I needed to learn the real boundaries, the real edges, how to cope with reality and not dwell in fantasy. As for the shame, Dr. Cameron told me that there was no avoiding facing up to the past. But many, many months would have to pass before I broke through to a real glimmer of the better life that lay ahead.

Dr. Cameron had been right in his forecast. There were days when I trudged up and down the hospital's grey, subterranean corridors with nothing but bleakness in my heart. But now I was not only allowed to be sad but encouraged to face the sadness. I was allowed to grieve for Michel and I was helped to do so.

The doctors and psychiatric nurses were wonderful, but one orderly in particular, a gentle man with a goatee and long white hair gathered in a ponytail, was the person who most helped me to face Michel's death and my father's death and to start the painful process of grieving. Discovering that I loved music, he brought tapes into the hospital for me to listen to—the Beatles, George Benson, Sam Cooke, Louis Armstrong, Dave Brubeck and Miles Davis.

We would talk about the songs and the playing, and I found that the music released tears that had been trapped somewhere deep inside me. I would sit listening while tears poured steadily down my cheeks. Until now, I realized, I had been too angry and too frightened to cry properly. Those tears, shed with such anguish, marked a breakthrough in my recovery.

Until then, something inside me had been frozen, as if I had been simply too terrified to let the grief out. With the tears came huge, overwhelming relief. This wasn't like the wailing and keening of the previous years. These were the soft tears of sorrow, the normal and appropriate response to sadness. As Dr. Cameron put it, sorrow does not have to take you into depression. I had to learn to "own my sorrow."

And soon I actually began to enjoy the safe routine of my days. Because I had ranted and raved and screamed the day that I was brought into hospital, the other patients had tended to steer clear of me. The world of a psychiatric ward is a very quiet one. But gradually I was beginning to make friends. One of the secrets of a good ward is to have the patients medicated enough that they remain calm but not so much that they have to be helped out of their chairs. And among the others who haunted the same grim basement corridors that I did, I found friends.

I was still extremely skinny, and had to put socks in my bras and wear jeans suitable for a twelve-year-old. But as soon as I was able to have visitors, a friend came regularly, bringing me little meals of delicious Lebanese food that he knew I loved: hummus, tabouleh, tzatziki, falafel. Every night we had a feast.

I had been given a room of my own, and when the cart with the clean linen came round, we were allowed to choose the colour of our sheets. Since the room itself was so stark, I used pink and yellow sheets to make a skirt for my bed and made an effort to make it all as cozy and homey as I could. Pink is a soothing colour, and yellow is the colour of the sun that brightens my spirit. There was no television in the rooms, and I found concentrating on a book too confusing, but I was happy curled up in my bed.

After a few weeks, I was given a pass to leave the hospital for several hours. My first attempt at negotiating the outside world was not a great success. There was, quite simply, too much stimulation and I was thrown for a loop. I had been feeling guilty about not being at home to shop and bake for Christmas lunch. A friend agreed to drive me down to the local gourmet shop, where he was stocking up on food for his own family Christmas. Standing in the warmth of the shop, surrounded by so many enticing things, so much Christmas food, I became overwhelmed by memories of Christmases with Pierre and the boys, when I had always baked mincemeat tarts and taken them down to the police guards at our gate.

I piled up a basket with mincemeat tarts and cookies and asked my friend to drive me to 24 Sussex. By now it was late and he was reluctant, but we went and the officers were pleased—and very surprised.

I was taught a lesson. I needed to rein things in, and he needed to help me to do so. I wasn't really sorry when he returned me to the hospital. I was beginning to feel very safe there and I knew that I was not ready for more.

Christmas on the psychiatric ward was surprisingly good. We cut red stars out of heavy-stock paper, and hung the decorations on an artificial Christmas tree. When the full Christmas lunch was over, we held hands and sang carols. I could never have imagined being happy in such circumstances, but there was something so secure and safe about the day; I had forgotten that I really could live without constant fear and apprehension.

The holiday was hugely lifted by the presence of my oldest sister, Heather. Unable to bear the thought of me alone on a day that we as a family had always celebrated with such excitement, she abandoned her own family Christmas and came to Ottawa to be at my side. What I vividly remember is her warmth and the tears I shed in her arms, and the feeling that I had an advocate, someone who would help me to navigate the maze around me when I could not do so myself.

I was beginning to discover that a person with a mental illness does not have the ability to understand what is going on. That person needs someone to chart the waters, to read what needs to be read, to talk about the possible side effects of drugs and to provide reassurance when recovery seems so terribly slow. Heather was that person for me. All my life, from my youngest days, she had looked out for me.

And slowly, very slowly, my depression became more manageable. I learned how not to allow depression to suck me down into that grey, bottomless well. Bit by bit, minute increments at a time, the depression ceased to be depression and became mere sadness, which is what it should have been all along.

I knew perfectly well that I had to learn to live with sadness out in the real world, and that there never would, never could, come a time when I would not be sad about Michel's death. Some years later, a woman asked me to write a foreword for a book that she had just finished about palliative care for people who have had to cope with death. She sent me the cover. It was exactly like Edvard Munch's *The Scream,* with graffiti all over the jacket, my name in larger type than the author's, and the words "Get over it."

What I told the author was something that I was busy learn-ing during those first months in the Royal Ottawa Hospital: that her title could not have been more wrong. "Getting over it" was not the issue; "getting on with it" was. There is no alternative to learning how to live with sadness and sorrow. What you need are the tools to help you do that.

There's a postscript to this story. I never did do the foreword for her. Recently, the author sent me an e-mail: she had ditched the old publisher as well as the title and had released the book under a new title. The old one, she now agreed, was inappropriate and even distressing.

In 2000, smoking in hospitals was still permitted: a room was set aside for patients to use. I was a heavy smoker then, and here the smokers met and talked, danced and learned about each other. That room was our safe place. No doctor or nurse ever came in. This was hardly surprising, as the air was so thick with smoke it was hard to see across the room. One of the first things I did was to take down the curtains hanging in the room and wash them; they had originally been white and were now a yellow-grey col-our. In the evenings and at odd moments during the day, we sat and exchanged our experiences and stories, and I learned a lot about the many unhappy forms that mental illness can take and the tragedies that can befall people with depression and mania.

I had been checked into the hospital under another name—Carol Wilson—but I found that almost impossible to remember myself. Soon everyone knew who I was. (A measure of my mania, thought some, was that I believed myself to be Margaret Trudeau!) We also engaged in group therapy, as well as art classes, which I felt gave me some kind of purpose. The days on a mental ward can be very long and tedious. I had railed and ranted against my imprisonment for the first forty-eight hours, but after that I had felt increasingly content to be just where I was. I felt safe.

I stayed in the Royal Ottawa Hospital for two and a half months. I emerged to a new world, one in which there would be no more marijuana, no more delusions, no more self-punishment. I was still in regular therapy, with my kind and imaginative psychiatrist, Dr. Cameron. He was as interested as I was in the possibility of using alternative therapies to work on the particular nature of my mental troubles. Seeing how fearful I still was of eating, and how my breathing was compromised when I was unhappy, he used hypnosis to help me find somewhere that I could feel safe.

He used a certain memory, a beautiful and peaceful memory that captures all that I love in life. When assailed by my fears or when my thoughts begin to race, I can go to this place in my mind and calm down, then reflect and think twice. That place is private, and no one goes there but me. For others, it may be a particular walk or the smile of the grocer that morning—whatever. Find a place that is quiet and reassuring to you, as familiar as an old pair of slippers, a place where you can let your mind rest. But—and this will seem curious—don't think when you're there; just be there and enjoy the beauty. Then, when you've left that place, only then should you reconsider whatever it is that has made you react, perhaps harshly.

Dr. Cameron wanted to disperse the great weight of my sadness. I had to learn to handle the pain of Michel's death, a pain I would have to bear for the rest of my life. I had a wound but the cut was still raw and in need of protective scar tissue. There was nothing wrong with sorrow, but I had to be taught not to wallow in it, not to indulge in self-pity, not to feel so constantly guilty.

With Dr. Cameron's help, I at last fully understood that I had spent many years—probably since childhood—feeling inadequate and unacceptable. Pierre's Catholicism, with its emphasis on guilt and sin, had only increased my load. To cope, I had adopted a mask, but that mask had slipped and was no longer appropriate. The new me had to live without a mask.

Dr. Cameron gave me books by spiritual writers such as Deepak Chopra, who had thought deeply about how to live consciously in the everyday world, and these I found immensely helpful. During my sessions with Dr. Cameron, we talked about the ideas of innocence, experience and redemption, about how one can lose one's soul yet find it again.

One day, when I was going on yet again about the terrible things that I had done to Pierre, Fried and the children, he suddenly said, "You are so incredibly hard on yourself. By the way you talk you would think that you had been an axe murderer and a criminal. Nothing you did was terrible. Yes, you did do some embarrassing things, but never anything seriously harmful. You think that you are the most despicable speck on the planet. You're not. No one is perfect. We're all flawed, full of imperfections. You're you—and you must learn to forgive yourself for your mistakes." This all made sense.

Dr. Cameron also made me realize the impact on the mind of regular and hard exercise of the body. One day, asking me about my daily walks, he wondered whether, as I walked along, I looked up or down. I told him I would check. Next day, in the park, I discovered that I always looked down, at the path in front of me, at the puddles left by the rain, at the concrete and the stones.

"Try looking up," he suggested when I next saw him. And so I did. As I walked, I began to notice the trees and the changing sky and the play of the clouds and then I began to make contact with other walkers, instead of shuffling round in my lonely fashion. Soon after I got out of hospital, Sacha and Justin bought me a puppy. I made good friends as I walked him each morning. Then I found a personal trainer, and over about twenty sessions I got him to teach me exactly how each muscle in the body works and how best to make it function well. Exercise, as Dr. Cameron had explained, raises serotonin in the body.

I let no day pass without some form of exercise—even if it means doing deep-knee bends while I'm stirring the stew. Sometimes I run on Mount Royal, sprinting as if a gun has gone off. Whatever regimen you devise, just know that you'll never get it perfect. Time, travel, circumstance will all invariably cut into your best-laid plans, but the two major components of my stability, I am convinced, are sleeping well and eating well. If I do that, everything else seems to fall into place.

A pup. Looking up. Getting the body moving again. Sometimes very simple things can make a huge difference.

Soon after I got home, Sacha came to talk to me about money. While I was in hospital, he had gathered all my recent bank statements. He discovered that, in my mania, I had squandered most of the money from the original sale of my house on Victoria Street. Since the reason for selling the house had been to create a nest egg, this was extremely depressing. I recalled the uncontrolled shopping sprees in which I had thought nothing of spending thousands of dollars on clothes I neither wanted nor needed—or could even fit into. In those states of manic delusion, I had had no trouble in convincing myself that the clothes and the jewellery and the perfume were investments in myself and in my life, the life of a successful woman with exciting new prospects for a rich and prosperous future. And, as Sacha discovered, I had been ridiculously, inappropriately generous, showering friends and strangers with unworn clothes and unwanted objects.

Some of this behaviour, I knew, was rooted in my childhood, when we had been taught to be generous towards other people. But I was also responding to a deep guilt for having fine things and to the knowledge that my mother would have profoundly disapproved of such extravagance and waste. Driven by guilt, I bestowed the items as fast as I bought them. None of this stuff, perhaps surprisingly, was junk: even in my mania, I shopped carefully, but extremely expensively.

When, many years later, President Obama accused Americans of living recklessly and excessively, his words struck a chord with me. Mania had made me precisely that: reckless and out of control.

Now, with the sober reality of my new life, I became painfully aware that I was running out of money. Sacha pointed to the
receipts from the department stores, the huge amounts taken out
in cash, the dozens of still unpaid bills. Between us, we decided
that he would now take charge of my finances, that he would
have power of attorney for my affairs and that he would give me
a monthly allowance for my expenses.

What he didn't tell me was that he and Justin had decided
that from now on, the two of them would make sure I was financially solvent. Unbeknown to me, they had told Fried that he
should stop his small allowance to me and simply continue to
pay for Alicia and Kyle. The boys did this to spare Fried financial hardship and to let him focus on his children. Unfortunately,
Sacha forgot to mention this detail to me, with the result that
when I saw from my next bank statements that Fried's cheques
had stopped coming, I was immensely hurt. I took this to be
punishment, and heartless punishment, for what I had put him
through. Only many years later did I learn the truth.

Unable even to pay my cleaning lady, aware that my sons
were making financial decisions for me and providing for me
(though even with their allowance, I was still short), I found my
poverty humiliating. Most demeaning of all was that I had to
report to a social services office that dealt with money management. "Guardianship," it was called, with my doctor and Sacha
insisting on it.

I had to visit an office in Ottawa's equivalent of skid row,
where a young woman my daughter's age told me exactly what
I could spend money on and what not, and how much it should

all cost. I had to show her my bills, which she then paid from my account, before lecturing me on what funds remained. This process was perhaps necessary; it was certainly painful. The strict monitoring of personal finances went on for some three or four months. It was humiliating, like being married to Pierre Trudeau.

I came home as spring 2001 began. My medication had been carefully regulated, I was seeing Dr. Cameron once a week for therapy, I was embarked on an exercise program and I was full of plans. One of the first things I did was to go to the grocery store and stock up on food. I began cooking again.

I felt clean, shorn, coached in new ways of looking at life, not avoiding pain but confronting it, not overreacting but listening, not closing myself away but examining why I found certain things so hard and hurtful. The healing process had begun.

Laughter, which I had lost from my life, was coming back to me. And I knew from Dr. Cameron that a normal, healthy person produces serotonin from laughing as well as from exercise. I had discovered that the fifth step—that of acceptance—was possible. The question was, could I maintain it?

CHAPTER 13

ME, AT LAST

I remember Barbara, frail and standing in the cold and the rain with a glass
of dirty water in her hand—a prop as she talked to reporters about
the dearth of good water in the world.
"You should be a pot of honey to these bees," she said in an aside to me.
"But give them real nourishment." Barbara was saying: use your name
and celebrity to spread the word on water.

VANCOUVER, 1976

Emerging from the cocoon of the Royal Ottawa Hospital was extremely hard. Like all patients who spend several months in hospital, I had grown dependent on the care, the familiarity of my surroundings and the sameness of my days. Sometimes I felt like a small child, navigating my way through an alien world. But something very fundamental had changed in me. I had at last accepted my illness and was no longer fighting it. I knew that in the end only I could take hold of my life, and there was too much at stake for me to duck the challenge. I had made my choice: I was going to be sane, and this time I would see it through.

I was determined, in a way I had never been before, to stay well, to remake my life, to become once more a reliable mother to my children. I would be neither victim nor casualty. The two years leading up to my breakdown and the months I had been a mental patient had been extremely tough on the children, particularly the younger ones.

Ally turned twelve as I came out of hospital, and Kyle would be seventeen in the autumn of 2001. That they had remained so steady was a credit to Fried's care and their own resilient natures. But I had a lot of building—of trust more than anything else— to do.

Kyle had left Fried's home across the street and returned to live with me. His unconditional love for me kept me alive. He has always shown compassion and empathy for others, and my gratitude to him will last forever. I was so alone, separated from all the Kemper family, whom I dearly loved and missed, distanced by geography from Justin and Sacha.

I wasn't the best mother to Kyle then, but I tried my best. After all, I was the only mother he had. I drove him to and from school each day so that I had time with him, as I did with Ally all her school days. The love of my children always trumped my longing to end my miserable life.

My darling daughter continually encouraged me to get better and applauded every baby step I took in my recovery. Every little thing that came my way we'd analyze together: Was

Mommy ready to take this on, or not? Ally's loyalty and maturity, well beyond her years, helped heal my broken heart.

I was very pleased one day when she asked me to come to her school to listen to a presentation she was to give. She had chosen, she told me, to speak on the subject of mental illness. As I listened to her talk, I felt both pride and regret: pride in how well she had mastered and presented the subject, terrible regret that she had had to learn so much in such a personal and painful way.

I was particularly happy to hear her talk so passionately about how mentally ill people suffer from stigma. She told her classmates that mental illness was not a character flaw but a disease like any other. To my surprise and, initially, my amusement, she ended her talk with the words, "Today, we have a guest speaker. It's my mother, and she has been in a mental hospital."

I realized how important this moment of recognition was— for her as well as for me. I was my daughter's show-and-tell. My message to the class was the one that I believe most passionately: people who have a mental illness need to get help. I found that my audience of young teenagers were very open when talking about their emotions, and several mentioned relations who suffered from depression.

They asked me whether it was worrying and a sign of depression that they liked to sleep for so long and found getting up so hard. I assured them that this was entirely normal behaviour for teenagers. The classroom experience made me wonder whether the fact that so many of this generation's lyrics and songs are about emotions hasn't made young people more compassionate, and made me hope that this may indeed be one way of breaking the stigma about mental illness.

I owe my recovery, my mental health, to Alicia. She is so much a mixture of her northern Germanic father and me. She has my body, my quicksilver nature; she's always busy, flutters about. And yet she has that German side—sensible, organized, tentative, careful and smart.

I felt sad when I could not be her mother; Fried was her mother for a time. But Ally understood and she encouraged me to take small steps. When she was in first year at Concordia University, studying political science, we were both lonely. We had left behind friends and roots in Ottawa to come to Montreal, so we'd watch movies and have dinner together, and shop 'til we dropped. As I write this, Alicia is in her third year, she's twenty-one and she has a very nice young man in her life—a pre-med student at McGill—so I see less of her. But we still talk a lot on the phone. She is my sunshine on a rainy day.

Kyle, too, played a critical role in my recovery. Everybody who knows Kyle loves him; he's special. Bright, bright, bright. Like his brother Michel, he went to Dalhousie University in Halifax. After Michel died and I was breaking down, he came and lived with me at my house in Ottawa and would buy groceries for me, and he became my gentle protector. He would cook for me and do all the ordinary chores that I then found extraordinarily challenging. In depression, it's hard to think even one step beyond right where you are.

Kyle is the most wonderful boy—what I call a "metro hippie." He's a hippie in his soul, a loving and easy and gentle person with beautiful values, and he loves music. There's a softness and gentleness in him. Oh, I love my Kylie; there's a lot of me in him. But with his degree in economics, he's also modern and relevant; he's a huge hockey fan and an avid fisherman, and he works in the high-tech software industry developing and marketing a software application for the BlackBerry.

At the time of Pierre's death, my niece answered the door. A reporter was looking to speak with Justin. Not here. What about Sacha? Not here either. What about "the other brother," the reporter asked, referring to Kyle. All the siblings had a good laugh when they heard that phrase, and for a while that's what they all called him. Justin and Sacha are jealous that Kyle has had the most wonderful anonymity.

Whenever I speak about my children, all five of them, I feel a great pride. I find myself smiling and talking a little faster; I can't help it. I brag about them.

Friends, too, help keep me afloat. When I was living in Ottawa with Pierre, the Gang of Five (Nancy Pitfield, Jane Faulkner, Gro Southam, Rosemary Shepherd and me) was a source of both fun and strength. We would have lunches and play groups and paint each other's nurseries and support one another. Later, when I had Kyle, I joined the local parent preschool resource centre and we would go to each other's homes; we had a book club and a mothers' group. Now I'm in a later stage, and I have girlfriends all over the country, all over the world. Often they have very nice families and, in essence, I "borrow" these families—for sharing Sunday dinner and helping kids with homework. Friendship comes and goes in waves and tides.

I was reading in *Maclean's* magazine a few years ago about the epidemic of Canadian women leaving their husbands after twenty-five and thirty years of marriage and after the children have gone. They're saying, "Red, I'm not washing your socks one more day. We're selling this big family home, I'm going to get half the money. I'm going to buy a little townhouse and I'm going to go on cruises with my girlfriends. Goodbye." And why not?

I look back on my life with men, and sometimes my judgment is harsh. I think of the moment that Pierre had his former girlfriend counsel me during one of my periods of mental anguish. What was he thinking? Many men just don't get it. They're ruled by testosterone, and women are ruled by estrogen. I do take heart when I see young husbands who are emotionally intelligent, doing dishes, in touch with their wives, and it makes me think that mothers are doing a better job of raising their sons. Pierre did change diapers and get up in the night for our babies; I'll give him that—but he was not a husband in touch with his wife.

I am always aware that just as blaming others for my sadness is inappropriate, so is depending on others. For all the help that family and friends can offer—and I would not have the life I have without the support of my family—it's also true that ultimately those of us with mental illness must battle alone.

One afternoon, in 2007, many years after I left the hospital, I was living in Montreal and felt like going to the movies. Sean Penn, one of my favourite directors, had a film showing called *Into the Wild*.

Soon, sitting in the darkened and largely empty cinema, I found myself drawn with growing unease into the story—the story was that of a young man, the son of an abusive, controlling father.

The film opens on the day of his graduation, with a celebratory lunch. The young man has done extremely well in his studies and his father presents him with a cheque for his tuition at Harvard Medical School. Leaving the restaurant, the young man hands the signed cheque to the first person he sees with a hand out, burns his identity papers and heads out into the world to discover himself. The resemblance between the young actor (played by then twenty-two-year-old Emile Hirsch) and Michel, between the film's story and Michel's quest for the wild, his determination to challenge nature—are uncanny. For the rest of the movie, I could see only Michel's face before me.

The young man in the film is delighted by the people and places he sees on his travels and he ends up in Alaska. But here, not anticipating the dangers of winter and isolation, he dies of starvation, just as Michel, heedless of the danger, had been drawn to his own death.

I found myself sucked back into a web of mourning: Michel, too, had not anticipated the dangers, and he, too, had died. I began to cry and could not stop. I came out of the cinema weeping, terrified that once I got home I would collapse on the floor and never get up again. That was always my great fear: falling to the floor and being unable to get up. For those who have never suffered from severe depression, there is an image to ponder: you are on the floor and you lack the energy to lift even a finger. You are dead weight.

But I did not fall to the floor. I went straight home and began to cook. I cooked pies and cakes and sauces, and when they were done I froze them. I made a huge dish of osso bucco. I cooked the veal slowly in its sauce, and then froze that too. And when, two weeks later, my daughter-in-law Sophie gave birth to little Xavier James Trudeau and asked me if I had anything in the freezer I could bring to the hospital for her and Justin to eat, the osso bucco was there, ready for them.

I was reminded all over again of the pleasure of giving something to others. And even as I was cooking, I thought to myself: I have to be able to change my thoughts, to distract myself, not by drugs or drink but by positive actions. I had been given the tools to do so. I have a choice—to switch from negative thoughts to positive ones, to make the light reappear and the darkness recede.

Each victory over myself, however small, marked another minute step towards health. I was continuing with my therapy, going to see Dr. Cameron once a week. In cognitive therapy sessions, I was learning not to suppress or ignore negative feelings but to "own them" and thus acquire new purchase over my life. Slowly, very slowly, I was learning not to dramatically exit a room and slam the door when angry or frustrated, but to stop, consider, actually listen to what was being said, then deal with it. Mishearing things and overreacting, hearing the bad things and never the good, had been so much a part of me for so long that I found this new approach hard. Dr. Cameron taught me not to panic and hide myself away, not to shut people out and punish those I thought were hurting me, but to air these great waves of emotions without fear.

One of Dr. Cameron's great strengths is his willingness to try anything and everything that might help. Unlike my first experiences, with the psychiatrist who had tried to turn me into Pierre's perfect wife and a fine first lady of Canada, he was interested only in steering me towards a lasting sanity in which I could be myself. Just coming into fashion was the term "emotional intelligence," which summed up for me everything I felt about my own long lack of it.

Anyone can become angry, Aristotle once wrote; there was nothing strange or inappropriate about that, "but to be angry with the right person, to the right degree, at the right time, for the right purpose and in the right way—that is not easy." As the Greek philosopher defined it, in his *Nicomachean Ethics,* our passions— if properly understood and controlled—have wisdom, and can guide our thinking and our survival. But those passions can easily go awry and often do so. The problem, as Aristotle saw it, was not the emotions but their appropriateness and how to bring intelligence to bear on them. For most of my life, my emotions had led wild lives of their own, far beyond the control of my intellect.

Under Dr. Cameron's guidance, I also branched out, talked to other people about mental illness, researched the terms and the cures, and started doing yoga.

"You must realize the power of the mind," he told me. "Never underestimate the tricks that the brain can play on you and how quickly it can malfunction. Fear, guilt, loathing are very seductive.

You have to hang on to the fact that you have the right to happiness, that you are not condemned to the dark world of recrimination and regrets. You are not alone in this, and you will need help to manage, but in the end it is up to you to find out how your mind works and to learn the skills to cope with whatever comes your way. No one is perfect. We are all filled with flaws—but that is the joy of life."

He explained that healthy brains, equipped with the right kind of "emotional intelligence," can absorb new information, withstand stresses and challenges, and work with them. I was finally understanding what the Buddhists say: the only constant in life is change.

For the most part, I heeded Dr. Cameron's words and worked on getting better. I revived old friendships and I grew close to the children again. When I felt restless and unable to concentrate, I put on earphones and listened to classical music for hour after hour, soothed and grounded by the sounds. What I really liked was CBC Radio 2's continuous classical music program, and I found the randomness of the pieces exciting—Bach one minute, Mozart the next. It was really nice to have the time to lie still and just listen. I learned something that I could never have imagined: that joy sometimes lives in the pauses. When I had trouble breathing, I did my yoga exercises.

Dr. Cameron was such a great gift for me. He just guided me through this long, long process: three years of cognitive therapy, hypnosis, deep meditation and changing the way I think. If you repeat the same behaviour and thinking over and over again, you get more than stuck; you become paralyzed. Changing my guilt and my fear, finding the things I had been searching for so much in my twenties—day-to-day happiness, peace of mind, waking up in anticipation of a good day. Changing my whole approach: this was my task. Instead of waking up every morning with dread— how am I going to get through this day?

Dr. Cameron was a man with a plan—one that was not about controlling me but about setting me free. Once the medication was right (and it took a long time to adjust the delicate chemistry of my brain), I acquired other tools. I learned to reflect with intelligence, not emotion. And I learned tricks: imaging to regain control, leaving the room (I'm a great one for leaving the room when something or someone has angered or upset me), taking a deep breath.

Something unfortunate happened then that could have set me back, something that in the old days would have proved devastating but that now merely served to strengthen me.

One summer night near the end of May in 2004, I was driving home late from a barbecue dinner when I was pulled over by a policeman on the Vanier Parkway in Ottawa. He said he was checking the ownership of vehicles on his computer, and he asked me whether I had had anything to drink. I told him that I had.

Since he had no Breathalyzer with him, he told me to sit in the police car while one was brought. It arrived and my breath sample showed that I was slightly over the limit, so he told me that they would have to take me to the police station—in handcuffs.

There, he took away my running shoes and told me that I could phone a lawyer. My one thought at that point was for my new puppy, which needed to be let out and exercised. I rang Kyle, who said that he would take him out. My enduring memory is of seeing the officer who had arrested me punch the air in front of his colleagues in what looked like a victory signal.

I was put into a booth, handed a list of criminal lawyers, and at my request a policeman dialled the first lawyer on the list. When there was no answer, we moved on to the next. By now I had calmed down a bit. The next lawyer on the list was also not answering, but then I saw the name of a lawyer I knew. The policeman phoned for me and I spoke to that lawyer, but no one at the police station told me that under the law I was free to talk to my lawyer for up to two hours—before giving a breath sample.

Clear to me was the officers' desire to hurry the whole process along while I was still over the limit. A policewoman then informed me that I would be held until I "sobered up," and I was put into a cell—an open cell with only bars between prisoners and police officers. Next to me was a woman, dishevelled and drunk, screaming like a banshee. When I used the toilet, a policeman walked past and stared at me. I was finally released at 5:30 the next morning.

In a funny way, the whole humiliating event marked a true turning point in my life. I emerged into a misty dawn with an icy cold determination that I would not go down in history as a drunk driver and a mental patient. I would find a role, a job, an activity, something that really mattered.

In the event, over the course of four years, there were one

trial and two appeals—to determine whether my rights had been violated. The trial judge ruled they had. Then the Crown appealed and the judge in that case overturned the first verdict. Then I won before the Ontario Court of Appeal.

After a small fortune in lawyers' fees, the case was finally thrown out. There had been no reason to stop me, the police officer at trial agreed I had been polite and co-operative, and the case against me was deemed full of errors. I can only believe that when he saw the name Kemper, the officer thought he had nabbed a very big fish. This outcome was just as well, for a guilty verdict would have left me with a criminal record and I would not have been able to travel to the United States. The police were found to have violated my rights—the very rights that Pierre, as prime minister, had fought so hard to introduce.

I was acquitted. The press, however, had a field day and once more I began to hate them, their power, their intrusiveness. The *Ottawa Citizen* ran the story on the front page—even though there was no accident and no one hurt. For the first time, I felt that I really understood the power of the press in ruining people's lives. But the rage I felt was good. My anger served to strengthen my determination that I would take responsibility for every corner of my life. I am a mother who is against drunk driving. I warn everyone I know not to drink and drive.

What I did was irresponsible. I was over the limit but didn't know that. What happened to me was humiliating and horrible, and a very expensive life lesson.

Back in 2004, one thing was clear: I needed to work. A very good friend, Christine Shaikin, who owns one of the best stores for designer clothes in Ottawa (Justine's, on Sussex Drive) suggested that I go to work there on Saturdays. Given my focus at the time—that what really mattered was on the inside, not the outside—the choice of work was peculiar. But Christine was kind and patient and didn't seem to mind my turning up wearing unfashionable clothes or even discouraging the customers from buying very expensive clothes when I didn't think such choices suited them.

Soon after that job came along, so did another. I met a woman, Sandra Cairns, at a dinner party given by Christine. When Sandra asked me what I did, I told her I was looking for work.

"Come work for me," she said. Sandra operates a small business organizing the relocation of employees transferred to new jobs in different cities, and she wanted someone who could drive and was computer savvy. I had to tell Sandra that I had lost my licence for three months (from the drunk-driving charge) and had never used the Internet.

But something about my story must have intrigued her, and soon I found myself—neatly dressed in new clothes given to me by Justin and Sacha—sharing an office with five other women upstairs in an old house in downtown Ottawa. This was not just a generous birthday present but one more step on the road to recovery. I now started caring about my appearance again, after years of not really minding how I looked.

Here I was, arranging the lives of other people when I could barely arrange my own. There was something decidedly comic about that. But I soon found that I had a knack for matching people's requests to reality, getting children into new schools, finding ballet classes in Ottawa, taking the wives of senior executives on tours of the city and showing them where to shop. I now had a reason for getting up in the morning. I learned to use the computer and the Internet, I met interesting people and I loved the coffee breaks with my fellow workers. I was particularly grateful for the kindness of all who worked with me at Dada Destination Services.

Sacha, who was still watching over my finances, had assured me that the children's allowance to me—for Sacha and Justin had inherited all of Pierre's money—would not be altered by anything I earned. The wages would simply be icing on the cake.

I was so grateful for the freedom my wages gave me. Finally, I had enough money to go to the theatre and to travel. I had my life back, though I did discover that skin-deep tolerance of mental disorders remained. When I applied for general insurance, I was obliged to reveal that I suffered from bipolar illness; this was enough to ensure that I would be rejected for any long-term disability coverage.

My road to recovery was also marked by volunteering, and I would begin to see and understand the value of setting my own problems aside and helping to solve the problems of others. Fresh, clean water is a precious resource that we take for granted in this country. Some of the happiest times in my life—at Harrington Lake, Newboro Lake, at my grandmother's place by the ocean—have been by water. But clean water is in short supply around the world, and it made perfect sense that access to water would be my next mission.

My interest in water goes back to the time of the 1976 United Nations Conference on Human Settlements at Jericho Park in Vancouver, which I, as the prime minister's wife, helped to convene. Pierre was hosting world government leaders; I was hosting on the non-governmental side. Of all the duties I performed during my seven years as the prime minister's wife, this was one of the most important.

I was already interested in water and the crucial role it plays in people's lives. I had travelled widely at Pierre's side and I had seen with my own eyes that often the difference between a community that thrived and one that didn't was the quality of the water—and access to it. Margaret Mead, the celebrated American cultural anthropologist, was there at that conference (she would die, sadly, two years later), and I was thrilled to meet her, for I had studied her work at university. So was Barbara Ward, the British writer and economist who believed that wealthy countries had a moral obligation to help poor countries. For her, redistributing wealth and conserving resources were linked, and she argued that the future of the planet depended on it.

I remember Barbara, frail and standing in the cold and the rain with a glass of dirty water in her hand—a prop as she talked to reporters about the dearth of good water in the world. Barbara said something most important as the paparazzi milled all around me.

"You should be like a pot of honey to these bees," she said in an aside to me. "But give them real nourishment." Barbara was saying: use your name and celebrity to spread the word on water. It took some time, but I finally did take her advice. Over the years, I had read articles about droughts and water shortages, about the parts of the world in which women have to walk many miles each day in search of clean water for their children. Then one day, many years later, when I was a field-trip mom accompanying Ally and her class on a visit to the Canadian Museum of Nature in Ottawa, I saw a stall with photographs describing the work done by WaterCan. I was told that this Canadian charity, which got its start in 1987, partners with local organizations in Uganda, Tanzania, Ethiopia and Kenya, bringing to villages clean water, basic sanitation and education about hygiene.

In these parts of the world, water is women's work, and women are also expected to ration the supply and take turns keeping away animals that might spoil the source. Some of these women must walk many miles to get clean water, which they then carry back home in containers perched on their heads. All this time devoted to fetching water eats up time, time that would be better spent educating their children, cooking, running a business, educating themselves or in well-deserved rest. Alone and vulnerable to rape on these water-related sorties, these women are prime targets for men with guns and Jeeps. Digging a new well in a village, as WaterCan does, transforms that village and empowers the women in it, helping them out of poverty.

Here, at last, was the "nourishment" that Barbara Ward had had in mind for me. Joining forces with WaterCan appealed to me greatly, and in 1996 I did just that—I started giving interviews and making speeches about the plight of the world's one billion people who lack access to clean water.

When Michel died, then executive director Nicole Bosley helped me to answer some of the many letters of sympathy that came to me. And in 2002, WaterCan invited me to become their honorary president, an offer I was proud to accept.

I have taken three trips to Africa to see for myself the work that WaterCan does. Several years ago, I took my daughter-in-law Sophie with me, a CTV camera crew in tow. We saw children with the distended bellies of protein deficiency, and women rising before dawn each day for the long trudge to collect water. I saw wells surrounded by animals defecating into the water, which was then borne back on women's heads in cans. Grandmothers, I was told, dipped a finger into the water when a baby was born and gave it to the infant to suck; if the infant tolerated the water, then that child would survive. I have been struck by the incredible drudgery of these women and the uncomplaining way in which they lived their lives.

I now redoubled my efforts for WaterCan, exploring with them ways of raising money for hand pumps (so basic that their upkeep requires no sophisticated technology), for concrete latrines and for containers to catch and store water in the rainy season. On a second visit to Uganda, I found that a woman in a remote village had been much affected by the well we had installed there. She had been to Kampala to learn to read and write, and had become the village secretary.

"What difference," I asked her, "is water making to the people?"

"The children are no longer dying," she replied, adding that since many more boys and girls thrived, they now needed books and pencils and soccer balls. (Though WaterCan reserves its funds exclusively for water and sanitation, we passed on their request to other organizations.)

Another woman, now spared daily walks to distant water holes, had begun to grow and sell vegetables. With the money she made, she bought herself a sewing machine and was making clothes for other villagers. Clean water not only improved the health of villages, it empowered the women.

For the first time in my life, I was using my name and my curious status as a celebrity to some important end. I continue to raise money for WaterCan, to host fundraising dinners, to speak in schools to raise awareness of water, and to speak out on Water-Can's behalf.

The second time I went to Uganda, I decided to open a well in Michel's memory. When the moment came, I was overcome by tears, but every woman present came to hug me when it was explained that my son had died. So many of their own children had died of disease caused by waterborne illness, and I felt we shared a common grief. From African women I learned many new lessons on my road to recovery.

We went to another village in northern Uganda, at the border with Sudan. WaterCan had provided a well the previous year and we were there to check on its success. But unlike other villages we visited, this one had a forlorn and desperate air. The villagers were duly grateful and welcomed us, but they never smiled. We discovered that two weeks earlier, raiders had come in the middle of the night, pulled eight young boys out of their beds, roped them together and led them away into the darkness crying and struggling. They had been conscripted as child soldiers and had not been seen since.

I believe deeply, passionately, that access to clean drinking water is a God-given, universal right, one that should be protected. And I was embarrassed to observe what happened in 2002, when the United Nations Commission on Human Rights considered whether water, along with the right to food and shelter, was indeed a basic human right. Fifty-three countries voted on the resolution, with thirty-seven voting yes, fifteen countries abstaining, and one voting no. The lone naysayer was Canada.

Christina Lubbock, then executive director of WaterCan, was as appalled as I was. "I can't begin to think who would turn down the idea of water being a right, especially from Canada, where we have such an abundance of it," she said. Canada is home to 0.5 per cent of the world's population and 20 per cent of the world's freshwater supply. "All of us who work for WaterCan," Christina said at the time, "would believe this is a human right to have safe water to drink, just as it's a human right to have safe air to breathe."

Maude Barlow of the Council of Canadians calls water "blue gold," and she's absolutely right. Multinational corporations such as Monsanto and Bechtel know that global consumption of water is doubling every twenty years and they want to control the supply, of course. Greed has already diverted and polluted so much water. Imagine the huge economic ripples if water became a commodity, to be bought and sold to the highest bidder.

In Ethiopia, on a visit with WaterCan, I made a point of visiting a psychiatric hospital begun in Addis Ababa by Dr. Clare Pain, assistant professor of psychiatry at the University of Toronto. Until she came along, there had been almost no psychiatric medicine in the country. Even though the three newly trained resident psychiatrists were making huge improvements in the capital, I saw a vision of mental illness that haunts me yet. I realized how unbelievably fortunate I was to have been born in Canada.

I was taken to see what they called an "asylum for the insane," and there I found men and women in black-and-white striped pyjamas, numbers painted on the back, some wearing shackles and shuffling around. What few drugs were available tended to be those no longer used in the West, dumped as part of aid programs. Because there was no money for modern drugs, the patients were kept in a semi-comatose state. I asked the one nurse in a woman's ward of forty beds how she managed to look after them all.

"The only difficult time," the nurse told me, "is in the morning when they wake up, before the medication calms them." Near the ward was the room for electroshock treatment. Until the new director stopped the practice, electroconvulsive therapy (ECT) was used to discipline unruly patients. I was reminded, with horror, of the film *One Flew over the Cuckoo's Nest*.

During all my stays in hospital, I had never been given electroconvulsive therapy. I had discussed it with Dr. Cameron, but I had been reluctant to submit to what is usually still regarded as a last resort, a genuine shock to the system. I did not fear ECT, since I knew that modern methods are humane and many people have been vastly helped by it. But I was worried about the memory loss that ECT can cause, and painful as many of my memories are, I still didn't want to lose a single one of them. In any case, I felt that I had already been shocked by all that had happened to me; I needed balance, not further shocks. What stuck in my mind, however, was this fact: some psychiatrists claim that were they to find themselves in a deep depression, their first choice of treatment would be ECT.

Though no one ever pressed me to try ECT, I had witnessed good results for myself while I was in hospital. A young girl who was very severely depressed had been taken away for electroshock treatment, and I talked to the nurse about how it worried me. The girl came back sleepy and disoriented from the sedation, but in the days that followed, her depression lifted.

Not long before Michel's death, Speakers' Spotlight, an agency that books lecturers, had invited me to join their bureau. My first booking had been at a street event in Toronto, a fundraising gathering for a battered women's shelter, and I had decided to talk to them about water. There were about a thousand people present. I had written it all out, drawn up my bullet points and was not unduly nervous about the event. A combination of my years with Pierre and my short training as an actress had, I thought, taught me to handle such things. But my talk was not altogether successful, and I found the careful preparation and the bullet points hindered me. I was stilted and lost my place. A poor performance, I thought.

Early in 2006, I was asked to a cocktail party for volunteers and fundraisers to help launch a new Royal Ottawa Mental Health Centre to replace the shabby and old-fashioned complex of Victorian buildings. I felt so grateful for what the hospital and its staff had done for me. Before I left that evening, I asked the chief executive, Bruce Swan, whether there was anything I could do to help. He said he would think it over and get in touch with me; I imagined he would come back and suggest that I join a fundraising gala committee.

A week later, he invited me to his office. With him was a colleague, Kathy Hendrick, who was the director of communications for the hospital. They wanted me to become a champion for mental health. I had the profile, I was articulate, people would listen, and had I not offered to help? What was more, this was to be paid work—I could charge for any talks and lectures I was invited to give.

But I should not fool myself, Bruce and Kathy warned me: the work would be hard and demanding. This was a daunting prospect—actually coming out and telling the world what I had been through went far beyond anything I had contemplated. I went home and considered it carefully. Told about the offer, Sacha worried that the strain of such work might lead to a relapse, and he had my doctor talk to me about his fears. But the doctor agreed with me: work would make me feel needed, and not since mothering small children had I felt that.

I rang Bruce to tell him I would give it a go. The whole idea suddenly filled me with a feeling of purpose I had never experienced before. This was scary, but exciting. As a first assignment, I agreed to hold a press conference.

This next step could well have turned me off the whole idea forever. The press had been invited to gather in the gymnasium of the hospital, and when I walked onto the platform, I faced a sea of skeptical and not altogether friendly faces. Many belonged to political journalists I had known during my years with Pierre and who had seldom been well disposed towards me. However, I knew that I was well on the way to recovery myself, and better than anyone I understood how tough recovery could be.

All the same, I had not quite bargained for this. As it happened, the press conference went well and I had less difficulty than I had expected in standing up and declaring, "All my adult life, I have suffered from a mental illness." Just saying those words offered me an overwhelming sense of relief. I had said the unsayable and survived. The reaction of the press was warm. Several journalists I considered my foes later came up to me with words of encouragement.

What happened afterwards is what I found so disturbing. A reporter with CBC-TV had managed to persuade the organizers that I would do a special personal interview with her. She had decided that the best place for it would be in the dark tunnels connecting the different parts of the hospital, and because I so wanted a new building—light, airy and friendly—I agreed that this grim backdrop would make the point perfectly that the hospital needed replacing.

However, I wasn't prepared for her questions. Before the interview, she asked, "This is where you live? Where you spend your time?" She clearly hadn't bothered to find out that I had left the hospital five years before; nor had she listened at the press conference. I cut off the interview. Her producer, who had done her homework, was deeply embarrassed and apologized profusely later.

As we were leaving the tunnels and about to get into the elevator, the reporter said seriously, "I'm as nuts as you are, I have to use the stairs." She was claustrophobic and wouldn't enter an elevator. This exchange could have put an end to my work for mental health. On the contrary, the episode—and the reporter's slur against people with mental illness—had an electrifying effect on me. Absolutely clear to me now was my obligation to break through the prejudice and myths, the lack of sympathy and understanding that surround people who suffer from mental illnesses. Mental disease is a frightening and lonely place. Not needed, at all, are jokes about mental retards and misperceptions about insanity.

So the thoughtless reporter actually did me a huge service. She taught me that most people do not understand mental illness and find it easy to ridicule. That journalist propelled me into a job, a campaign and a cause.

The most surprising thing for me was that I turned out to be a natural public speaker. I had none of the terrors that I had expected, and once I got into my stride, I found that I had much to say and a great passion to deliver it. Some time before, Speakers' Spotlight had booked me to talk at a Women of Courage event. I decided to use the occasion to launch my new crusade. The venue was the dining room of a conference centre in Mississauga, west of Toronto, and when I rose to my feet, no one knew what I was about to say. I had spoken often in the past, but this was something different. I had my notes, a few quotes from people who had written on courage, but that was all. The hall fell silent; the vast audience of women looked at me.

And then I started speaking about courage and about myself, about my life, about Michel's death, about my breakdowns and the many weeks I had spent in mental hospitals; I told them what it felt like to be so depressed that the whole world looks bleached of life and you dread the day. I told them about mania, and how I used to believe myself the most clever and most interesting woman in the world and how there was nothing, no feat, that I did not assume I could do. I told them about being frightened and miserable and confused and how there had been many, many days when I had wished I was dead. I told them what my illness had done to my family and how my children had suffered. I spoke for forty-five minutes without pausing or looking at my notes, and as I spoke I realized what an incredible relief it was not to have to pretend any longer. And when I stopped, the audience rose to their feet and clapped and clapped.

After that, invitations began to pour in. From the 165 local branches of the Canadian Mental Health Association, from women's lecture series and from insurance companies. They seemed especially keen to hear my message that if caught early, mental illness does not have to be crippling. I accepted all the invitations that I could. I talked to groups of a few hundred people in small church halls and audiences of several thousand in conference centres. The lectures brought in some money, which I desperately needed, but more than that, the work gave me a sense that I was, at last, doing something important. In my audiences were people who had felt just the way I had, and they were immensely reassured to hear someone saying the things that they had never dared to say. And there were families who had watched people they loved suffer without knowing what they were going through.

I knew exactly what I wanted to say and how I wanted to say it. I wanted to convey the message that mental illness attacks people of all ages and at all stages of life; that bipolar disorder stems from a chemical imbalance that can be treated; that bipolar illness has to be diagnosed before it gets too ingrained and before the cycles of mania and depression are too firmly entrenched—in fact, before the cycle has a chance to become a pattern in the brain; that mood-stabilizing drugs can not only maintain a balance but also slow down the progress of the illness.

I wanted to warn women that in the world of patients, women who are mentally ill lie at the very bottom of the pile, frequently not treated for their physical ailments. In 2010, the Standing Senate Committee on Social Affairs, Science and Technology conducted cross-country hearings as part of a broader examination by the federal government of the status of mental health care in Canada. During 130 hours of hearings with more than 300 witnesses testifying, what the committee heard over and over again was that patients with mental illness continue to be dismissed—especially if they are women. A man with a heart condition consistently gets more and better medical care than a woman with debilitating depression. Both patients have been put out of commission by their illness, but the physical problem gets the attention; the mental one gets short shrift.

I wanted to convey how painful, terrifying, lonely and confusing mental illness is and how easily it can be made worse by addiction—to alcohol, to drugs, even to food. When life ceases to have meaning, I told my audiences, then you have to change it.

I could not speak about other forms of mental illness, I told them, only about the one I had suffered from myself. I wanted to urge people not to live in a state of denial but to seek help, to face reality, not to lock themselves away and shut others out. I soon understood that the way to interest and draw in my audience was to tell it all like a story—my story—as if I were talking to them over the kitchen table, not preaching but having a conversation.

The fact that I had lost many valuable years through not being diagnosed, that by the time I finally received the right treatment I had been deep into the pattern—this carried weight. People who are ill must not let this happen, I would say: too many bipolar sufferers are picked up and identified only once the police are called in. The highest rate of suicide among people with mental illnesses is for those who are bipolar. And to break the intensity of what I was saying, I learned to intersperse my talk with some lighter stories, even some jokes.

A sample: There's a joke I tell about denial. The husband in an elderly couple goes to his audiologist, complaining that his wife is losing her hearing and won't see a doctor. "Well, why not figure out the range of her hearing?" the audiologist suggests. So the husband goes to the farthest room in the house and calls out, "Honey, what's for dinner?" No response. The husband tries again and again, moving from room to room, a little closer each time and posing the same question. Finally, he gets right up to his wife's ear and shouts, "Honey, what's for dinner?" She replies, "For the fifth time, chicken!"

I like to have the whole room shaking with laughter—and this joke always accomplishes that. Laughter is so important and it's such a relief. Like we are after a rainstorm, everyone is happier.

The shame, I tell my audience, is not in having a mental illness but in doing nothing about it. Looking out across the lecture room, I would see people nodding. Often, people in the audience cry.

I know from the research that 90 per cent of marriages fail when one partner suffers from bipolar disorder. This may seem odd, but marriages involving two bipolar sufferers often endure— both individuals are on the same page.

One controversial aspect of my talks is my mention of fibro-myalgia. I will give these talks and later meet with members of the audience, and some dispute the fact that fibromyalgia is related to mental illness—but it often is. This is mental pain manifesting as physical pain. I had been put in a gilded cage, and this was the price I paid.

I talk about the need for change, and how debilitating it

is to live in your grief and be defined by it. I call it "wound-ology"—letting our pasts define our futures. These prisons of our own construction, these labels, are crippling. I talk about the importance of compassion and warm-heartedness, two values I prize highly, and forgiveness. You have to forgive yourself and what happened to you.

So many women, women especially, are in denial. They blame life or their families or their husbands or their upbringing or sexual abuse. I know women who have been divorced twenty and thirty years, and they're still angry. You can get enormously self-absorbed—like an injured animal crawling into a cave. You know when you've hit bottom; it's the last stage before suicide.

Eventually, you do get bored of your own issues, and sometimes the first job is getting a job and crawling out of that cave. Low self-esteem is the biggest disabler of people with mental illness, so volunteer work or paid work can help a person both gain confidence and get started. You need obligations and responsibilities.

You need to be busy. If volunteer or paid work doesn't suit you, enrol, enrol. Take yoga classes, cooking classes, tennis lessons. Get the ball rolling. I especially love to cook. Cooking is tactile; it involves mixing tastes and colours, it has a beginning and a middle and an end, and it involves nurturing others.

The other thing I advise those who have suffered mental illness is to have an advocate. When you are mentally unbalanced, you don't have the words; you need the questions to get the answers. Why this pill and not another? What are the side effects? Will I gain weight? The best advocate is someone who loves you but who has no personal stake in your outcome, someone who can access information for you, do research for you, speak up for you. Across Canada, the almost two hundred offices of the Canadian Mental Health Association offer an enormous wealth of information.

I'm on the board of the new Institute for Mental Health, the beneficiary of a $20 million donation that was used to create the Centre for Brain Health at the University of British Columbia, where important research is underway into the diagnosis and treatment of Alzheimer's disease, Parkinson's disease and psychiatric disorders. For me, the name of the centre is all important; it's not a mental health facility, it's a brain health centre.

In the end, my message is perfectly simple: people get stuck in lives of quiet desperation. They lose the courage to reach out for help. The stigma that surrounds mental illness means that no one likes to think that his or her mind is not functioning as it should. We accept that our lungs or livers may not be perfect—why not our brains? There is no quick fix, no one solution for everyone. Try everything, I say in my talks; never say no to anything that might help; be your own advocate if you can, but follow the advice of a doctor you trust. Intervene, I tell my listeners, for gentle intervention can be a lifeline for people who are unable to choose sanity unless they are helped to do so.

Finally, anyone who has suffered mental illness should consider the simple pleasures of silence and space. Noise can be a huge distraction; at least it is for me. And sometimes noise can be the company of toxic friends whose useless chatter does you no good and possibly harm. Pierre never liked noise, and on that we could agree.

Slowly, I learned to laugh again. I had forgotten the sheer pleasure of being able to laugh, to find things so funny that they lit up my day. The moment that I realized that my sense of laughter had really returned was in the spring of 2005, when I went with Sacha, Ally and Justin's fiancée, Sophie Grégoire, to Cuba with a study group Sacha had organized. For some years, Sacha had been head of Canada World Youth, an organization that is partnered with twenty-five countries and that sends Canadians to other parts of the world, where they are billeted with families and can experience lives very different from their own.

Sacha had been asked to visit Canadian youth on their Cuban visit, and our study group drove around the country—finding one Canadian in a bakery making cakes, another working in a medical centre, a third in a school. One evening I walked along the beach talking to a girl whose father had died shortly before. I reflected on the nature of grieving, and how I had never really grieved for my father. Now I was able to face it calmly.

That night, there was a party. Sacha used his computer to play music and we all danced; I love dancing and I had not danced that way for many years. I felt so incredibly happy that I began to laugh. The laughter bubbling out of me was not because I had remembered something but simply because it was there in me, waiting to come out. I went behind one of the huts and shook and rocked and giggled until I was too weak to go on. Next morning, I woke up with the certain knowledge that I had at last put unmanageable grief behind me, that life was going to be possible.

Real laughter has always done this for me. At Sacha's wedding to Zoë Bedos on September 1, 2008, I slipped away from the table to let out the laughter rising in me. My teenage niece, sitting not far away, observed me leaving and followed me out. Watching me heave and shake, she hastened back to find Sacha.

"We have a problem," she said. "It's your mom. I think she's going crazy again."

Sacha knows me well. "Is she laughing or crying?" he asked his cousin.

"She's laughing."

"Oh, that's fine then," Sacha told her. "She's just too happy."

For a very long time, I had thought that the rest of my life would be spent weeping. Now I knew that while I would always carry grief in my heart, I would also have joy and delight. As I had so painfully learned, life is a question of balance. For laughter and contentment, as for other things, there are tricks and rules to help.

As Dr. Cameron had suggested, I made a practice of not watching disturbing programs on television at night. I did that for years, but I no longer feel the restriction is warranted. Not long ago, in the spring of 2010, I went out and saw a very scary Martin Scorsese film, a cross between a psychological thriller and a mystery, called *Shutter Island*. Violence on the screen still bothers me, so I simply look down.

By day I would absorb the serious news, leaving night for comedy and laughter, to give the mind a rest and let it be still.

On television, I like *The Office,* I like Bill Maher and Jon Stewart and *The Colbert Report,* and I especially like *Weeds*—starring Mary-Louise Parker and about a newly widowed young suburban mother who makes ends meet by selling marijuana. And one movie that really makes me laugh is *Planes, Trains & Automobiles,* a comedy from 1987, starring Steve Martin and John Candy, about two badly matched strangers who become travelling companions and try to get home for Thanksgiving.

I'm wondering now if I will grow sunnier with age. Once my estrogen levels dropped, a window opened. Maybe I'll smile 'til the end of my days. Is it wisdom? Is it knowing that I have survived so many blows and have seen that I can take what life brings? I am surprised by my own resilience, but maybe I shouldn't be. I remember telling a friend about things from my past, then adding, "I will not be crushed. I come from a long line of fighters." I now know that it's possible to be knocked down hard and bounce back, with new projects and a sense of wonder.

Gardening continues to bring me joy. I can get emotional thinking of all the gardens I have created, and lost, in my lifetime. Twenty-four Sussex, Harrington Lake, Newboro Lake: those gardens were the victims of moves and lost marriages. But I keep on creating new gardens. The deck on my Montreal condominium is small, but there's ample space to grow tomatoes and herbs in Mexican clay pots. I have so many pairs of garden gloves, but I never use them. I like to get my nails into the dirt, to feel the roots and the tendrils. I love gardening, and I get that from my grandmother, who gardened to live. Placing a seed in soil is such a simple act of faith, but simplicity—I now know—is where the joy is.

Painting is another source of joy for me. For my sixtieth birthday, Justin and Sacha gave me a set of watercolours and an easel, and I took a course at a fabulous visual-arts centre close to where I live. I am not a good painter; I'm terrible, in fact. But I do have a good eye, so I'll just keep at it. Other than yoga, painting is the only activity that puts me into a state of nothingness, where I lose all sense of time and space. I so love the process of applying colour to canvas, and I love art and I always have. I can get swept away by beautiful pieces of art. One of my most precious pieces (to me, anyway) is a painting I have of a girl alone in a field—a gift from a celebrated French-Canadian painter at the time I married Pierre. It's starkly beautiful.

And I continue to take photographs—too many. One more creative outlet.

In the ten years since I left the Royal Ottawa Hospital, many good things have happened to me. Justin and Sacha are both married to wonderful partners, and they have children of their own, who bring me unfailing pleasure. I have fallen in love with my grandchildren, and our family is growing in a delightful way. I am included once again in Fried's family gatherings, though for my first visit to the house on the lake in many years I decided to sleep not in the house but in my own tent, perched by the water's edge. I have travelled and campaigned for WaterCan and given countless talks on bipolar illness. Over time, my ambition has only grown to talk to, and on behalf of, all those who suffer from bipolar disorder and those who have to live with them.

I remember acting as a child of ten in a skit at school. I played the role of an old man whose wife had died and he had scorched his shirt with an iron and burned his dinner and he was very much alone and depressed. I just sat in a rocking chair and whittled. News of the skit reached the local chapter of the Canadian Mental Health Association; the mini-drama was entered into a competition they were running, and I got the prize.

I had seen, first-hand, depression in the elderly. When Grandma Sinclair died, Grandpa came and lived with us for a while and he was so sad, having lost the love of his life. He didn't want to live; she was his east, his north, his west and his south. This happens so often when a marriage has been solid. One partner dies, and the other soon follows. And, sure enough, in six months Grandpa Sinclair was dead.

So, at the age of ten, I was on stage delivering a message about depression. Fifty-two years later, I was back on the job— delivering a message about depression.

Looking back, I would say I had great teachers—at school, at university, from my family, Pierre Trudeau and Yves Lewis, and at dinners sitting next to Indira Gandhi and Chou En-lai, Fidel Castro, Jimmy and Rosalynn Carter. It was Rosalynn Carter who gave me my marching orders and later got me thinking about mental health issues. She knew how I had suffered.

In 2007, I decided to follow Justin, Sacha and Ally to Montreal, where the boys had made their lives and where Ally had been accepted to Concordia University. When my first grandson was born, on December 22, 2006, my heart had exploded: I was head-over-heels in love with little Pierre Trudeau. With a speed and ease that would never have been conceivable in my earlier days, I sold my house, packed my boxes and found a condominium from the 1920s in downtown Montreal.

I had told Dr. Cameron that I would never be able to move house because of the boxes—dozens and dozens of boxes full of things in my basement, things that made me cry every time I thought of them. The day will come, he said, when you'll be able to do it. And he was right.

Soon enough I would have proof of my healing. In March of 2009, a dear, dear friend of mine died in hospital, and I was there for him. I helped him die. Grief did not overwhelm me as it had in the past. This time I had the tools.

My friend's name was Guy Rivet, and I had met him in Ottawa some thirty years beforehand, when he ran a New Age store in the ByWard Market. Later, he became a chef and taught courses in cooking at Lester B. Pearson College in Montreal. When I moved to that city, he was the only person I knew, and of course we reconnected. When I first arrived we would "date" every Saturday night (he was a gay man, and thus the quotation marks), and sometimes we'd go to refined restaurants where his students had found work.

Guy was a tall, thin man who moved with such grace. A Franco-Ontarian in his mid-fifties, he had intense, yet curious eyes. Guy loved music and art, but his greatest passion was the world of the spirit, the creative consciousness. He was so sad to die because he was convinced that he was to be one of the guides to take us into the new world of enlightenment and peace, which the Mayans had predicted would happen in 2012. Guy and I were born on the same day, and we shared the same interest in mysticism. Every time he chanced across a book he thought I'd like on that subject, he would send it to me.

He was very much a part of my inner circle, and a great gift to me. Guy taught me a lot about cooking, and we made elaborate travel plans together. Then all those dreams were stolen away.

Guy was diagnosed with colon cancer. When I'd got my sanity back, I always questioned whether I would be able to withstand another hard blow, such as the death of a cherished friend.

"Of course you will," Guy assured me. And he, like Dr. Cameron, was right about that.

Guy was admitted to hospital, and I and several others formed a palliative care team that stayed with him around the clock, our shifts running four to six hours long. Sometimes I had to advocate strenuously for him when medical staff refused him morphine; they argued that he was in a position to make that request himself. But of course he wasn't. All Guy wanted was peace and silence. He loathed and feared doctors and hospitals, and when he said to their questions "No!" he really meant this: leave me be with the friends I trust.

Guy's death was a terrible loss for me. He said that he'd never leave me, that his spirit would continue to support me long after he died. I remember asking his aunt if she had any thoughts on what his totemic bird might be. A hawk, perhaps? A raven?

"Oh no," she replied. "In our family, we drop pennies from heaven."

And sure enough, I did find pennies after Guy died, and in the most improbable places.

Guy Rivet was a true friend, loyal and fierce in his love. He would constantly scold me for unnecessarily worrying about money. He always assured me that since my intentions were good, I would always have what I needed. I try to heed his advice and I am reminded often that the promise of pennies has been delivered: I have steady work and income and all that I need.

I miss Guy every day. He was the first of my friends I was ever there for, really there for, when that friend needed me most.

A few years ago, Justin and I were giving a speech before a huge crowd, the Board of Trade in Toronto. I laugh out loud, I hoot, to recall it. Justin was to introduce me in front of all these bigwigs.

"I want you to know something about my mother," he began. "Few in this audience and few in this country know it. She was, and is, way, way, way smarter than my father." I just about fell off my chair.

Perhaps what Justin meant was this: Pierre was trapped in his Jesuit prison. He was a far greater human being in terms of his substantive contribution than someone who's got a quick wit. It's not true what Justin said of me, but that is a measure of his adoration. Boys do love their mothers. Justin had every reason to understand that the kind of intelligence that I apply to life is different from the one deployed by Pierre, who had in him a little of the Jesuit scholar and a little of *Star Trek*'s Mr. Spock. Justin's father was totally the man of reason and quiet dignity. And then there was Mom . . .

Justin and I have done a few of these Mom & Son presentations. Another time, we spoke to a large gathering of Jewish ladies in Montreal, and once again, Justin spoke in praise of his mother. It was very funny. Afterwards, some of the ladies came up to me. "What did you do? My son, he never calls . . ."

Over time, I have changed medicines and dosages and learned how to monitor myself and my moods, so I am vigilant for telltale signs of instability. I have accepted that there is a trade-off between feeling calm and able to handle the world and a tranquility that I sometimes find hard to adjust to.

I have learned to avoid too much alcohol and to try to keep away from marijuana. The scientific jury is still out on that drug. My current psychiatrist does not oppose the controlled use of marijuana because the drug can bring a patient into focus, and marijuana can also lift depression. Yet marijuana can also trigger mania—as it so often did with me. I may remember its highs with nostalgia and I can recall the excitement of mania, its all-enveloping sense of optimism and achievement, but I do not wish for the depression that inevitably followed, nor for the falsity of moods that are not grounded in reality. Marijuana is my addiction. I love it, and I occasionally take a puff with friends, but I cannot and must not use that psychotropic drug as I once did. How marijuana provokes mania is still a matter of scientific debate, but that it does is no longer being questioned.

For thirty years, I told myself that the doors of perception—that moment when the mind seems to go beyond the everyday and the commonplace—were all about pushing constantly at the edges. I have since discovered the far greater satisfaction in balance, in knowing my limits, in knowing when to exit, when to be alone, when to go to sleep. But I will never be anything but mercurial and I am instinctively wary of a world that is too flat, too unbuffeted by strong emotions or moments of profound feeling and even restlessness. In the past, I enjoyed brief moments of elation, often tinged with madness. I prefer what I have now: listening to other people, not letting them down, and the peace and calm of an ordered world.

One day not long ago, when I was talking to a large audience about bipolar illness, a psychiatrist put up her hand.

"But don't you realize," she said, "that there is no cure from being bipolar, no total recovery?"

"Yes," I replied, "I do indeed know that. But what I have recovered from is fear—the constant fear of my bipolar condition."

AFTERWORD

Time has helped to heal my broken heart, and my faith has been restored. With every new addition to our family, the circle of life, loss and redemption has been shown to me. My sons, Justin and Sacha, chose strong, loving women to be their life partners, and the love I feel for them is the same as I feel for my own children.

After Michel's and Pierre's deaths, I felt our family had been so depleted. In the last few years, Pierre's and my boys have given to me the finest gift a mother could have—four healthy, beautiful grandchildren, Pierre, Xavier, Gala and Ella-Grace (in order of their appearance). My role as grandmother is the best one I have ever had.

Not long ago, Alicia turned twenty-one and there was a big party at Grandma's house, as the grandchildren call my fifth-floor condominium. Let me paint the scene. The orders have come in: there's osso bucco cooking on the stove, there are mashed potatoes and Sacha has asked for some special noodles that I bought at a German store in Ottawa. We have two cakes, a lemon-glazed cake that is Ally's favourite and the banana cake with brown sugar icing that is Sacha and Sophie's favourite. There are nineteen people— Ally's boyfriend, the children, the grandchildren.

At one point, little Xavier—who is big for his age—has little Pierre pinned under him. "Gwamma, pweese help me!" the toddler calls out. There is so much fun, so much laughter. And there are so many cozy places in this condominium. Sacha and Justin will be in one corner having a heated discussion, and the girls always help me before and after with the cleaning and the cooking and the dishes—otherwise I couldn't do it.

And, of course, there is the ritual of the "dwarf-tossing," as we call it. Justin and Sacha literally toss their babies across the room, as the babies scream their delight and their mothers and aunts and uncles—not to mention their grandmother—scream theirs. The custom started years ago when one of us saw a painting of Queen Victoria on a beach in Jamaica watching as these huge men tossed their tiny counterparts. We are a nutty family, after all.

The boys have use of Pierre's cottage deep in the woods at Morin-Heights in the Laurentians, and one time several years ago I went up there in midwinter with two girlfriends. The plan was to cross-country ski, snowshoe and hike outside, and inside play double dominoes, drink wine and eat delicious food. I had brought with me my year-old black Lab.

The phone rang. A woman who identified herself as Caroline St. Ange told me in a very thick Québécois accent that she was in charge of wildlife and the environment for that area. She said she was calling cabins and cottages to alert people that a bear had come out of hibernation and was wreaking havoc. The creature had already broken into cabins close by and killed a dog.

"Oh gosh," I told her, "what should I do?"

"Do you have curtains on the cabin windows?" Madame St. Ange asked me by way of reply.

"No," I said.

"Oh," came the replay. She sounded disappointed. "This is too bad."

Then came her advice. If we spotted the bear, we were to retreat upstairs in the cabin. Told about the dog, the woman warned us to keep her inside and always on a leash when outside.

I called Justin and told him that some sort of forest ranger had just called to say there was a rampaging bear, an angry, hungry bear, on the loose.

"Oh Mommy," my eldest said. "Look, find Dad's gun—you know where it is." Pierre had taught the boys to shoot a rifle, using targets. Well, I don't shoot guns, but a little light went on. One of my friends at the cottage, who at that moment was heartily knocking back wine, is a sharpshooter. Now the plan, should the bear crash inside, was to have this riflewoman shoot down the stairs.

Four hours passed. We were all on bear watch, but the wine continued to be poured. The phone rang again. It was Madame St. Ange with more advice: when we went outside, we were to wear no bright colours but camouflage colours that would blend in with the forest. And where I could purchase these clothes, she further advised, was at Holt Renfrew with a personal shopper named Sophie Grégoire—then Justin's girlfriend.

"Oh &%#*@!" I said. It was all an elaborate prank. I immediately called Justin and bawled him out. You went too far, I told him. "Do not give three old ladies who have been drinking wine access to a loaded shotgun!"

Welcome to the Trudeau clan.

A friend once told me that when her first grandchild was born, she became determined to do her part to make all humanity better. I share her desire to make as good a world as I can, in my own small way, for the sake of my darling grandchildren. While they may, like me, not be proud of some of the things I have done in the past, I hope that they will learn from me to reach out with courage when they falter, to ask for help when they cannot walk alone.

"Friends will come and go," my father used to say, "but your family will always be there for you." I have been blessed with a fine family. For that, and that alone, I will be eternally grateful.

On a final note, I consider my bipolar condition a gift to me. I have almost touched heaven in my mania, I have been plunged into the depths of despair in my depressions, but with the love and compassion that have been shown to me, I have weathered all the storms, and I believe I am equipped now to face any new challenges that life will inevitably put before me. My hope is that by sharing my journey with others, some readers—whether themselves afflicted with mental illness or close to one who is—will acquire a clearer idea of what it is to suffer from a brain chemistry disorder. May you find the courage to face your own realities and find the words to call for help.

Lessons from *Changing My Mind*

by Dr. Colin Cameron

In December 2000, I received an urgent call from a very concerned friend of Margaret's. She agreed to an assessment but not at the Royal Ottawa Hospital, where I worked. Could I go to her Rockcliffe home? I had never seen her before, so this was an unusual request, but her family was desperate so off I went, uncertain about what to expect.

When I arrived, Sacha answered the door and introduced me to his mother. Margaret was in her nightgown, quite emaciated and with her hair unkempt. She seemed amused by my presence, and with a laugh invited me in. She did not seem to understand why her family had concerns.

We went to the living room, where I noted dried pine needles strewn across the floor leading to the fireplace. Sacha told me that she had had a fire going that morning when he got there from Montreal. Margaret spoke loudly and rapidly, alternating between tears and bursting into song. Elation, fear and sadness—her mood was all over the place. She made numerous phone calls between my questions, and went on about all the important things she had to do, including a trip to Africa. Margaret shared with me family photos and her grief at losing Michel and Pierre. She then became more irritated by my inquiries, and let me know I was intruding. Could I please keep my visit brief? When I expressed concern for her safety, she shifted to indignation and retreated promptly to take a bath, stumbling on her way up the stairs.

I conferred with Sacha, who very much wanted his mother to get help, but he feared that hospitalization might antagonize her and only make things worse. He offered to stay with her, but I convinced him that his love was no match for her illness. She already believed that her own son wanted to kill her, and there was no way Sacha could stand guard twenty-four hours a day to keep her safe.

With Sacha's approval, I filled out a seventy-two-hour assessment order to force her into hospital, a form I intended to present to her when she finished her bath. Margaret's intuition, however, had led her to catch wind of our intentions, and she quietly escaped into the dark of the late winter afternoon. After hours of searching, the police finally found Margaret and brought her to hospital. All this was decidedly against her will. She was enraged and very, very frightened. And so began our five years of work together.

Margaret's initial resistance to accepting psychiatric help is an all too common story. Mental illness itself sometimes plays a role in such resistance by impairing insight into what's actually going on. Stigma, however, is the key impediment for most patients, perhaps even more so for people in the public eye such as Margaret. Previous negative experiences with treatment also often contribute, as they did in her case.

Such negative experiences can include barriers to getting help when it's asked for. (Canada ranks near the bottom of the pack in funding mental health services compared to other developed countries, according to a May 2008 article in *The Canadian Journal of Psychiatry*.) For many patients, help arrives only when danger is imminent to the person or to others and the issue gets forced. The courageous intervention of friends and family is often instrumental in making this happen. The import of such intervention is exemplified by Margaret's case. Who knows what catastrophe loomed had her friends and family not taken action as they did?

Things were touch and go between Margaret and me for the first several weeks, and her trust in me was tenuous. Soon after hospitalization, she was found incapable of making treatment decisions, and Sacha provided substitute consent. That Margaret did not legally challenge either this or her involuntary status, as was her right, indicated that part of her was now accepting help.

Initially reluctant to take the pills prescribed (an antipsychotic and mood stabilizer), she did comply, knowing that she would be forced to take the medicine by injection if she did not. In time, however, she began to feel better and her insight improved. As is typical, within a short time (about two weeks), trust started to develop and she chose to stay voluntarily. With her insight improved, she took over her own treatment decisions. Forced treatment was over, and real collaboration began.

The meds were adjusted gradually, and the hard slog of therapy commenced. After ten weeks, Margaret was discharged, not yet quite sure of her new life. Like so many patients with mental illness, avoidance had become a deeply ingrained habit. Avoidance seems so appealing when the alternative is pain.

But pain is not the enemy; it's avoidance of it that can kill (through addiction, recklessness, suicide or self-neglect). What gets lost is this hard truth: attempting to wall pain out tends simply to seal it in. It takes guts to make the shift towards dealing directly with our difficulties rather than simply wishing them away, and Margaret showed plenty of guts.

Cognitive behavioural therapy is focused on challenging the logic of our automatic thoughts and differentiating between what is and what is not in our control. This paradigm posits that it is our faulty thinking that disturbs our emotions, and that by having more balanced thoughts we can have more balanced emotions. Emotion focused therapy, on the other hand, contends that it is emotional suffering that leads to disturbed thoughts, and that by working directly with the emotions we can reframe them to allow for healthier cognition and the ability to find new meaning. Although these two therapies approach emotional upset from different directions, they actually complement each other well, and both were helpful in Margaret's treatment.

"The Serenity Prayer," associated with the theologian Reinhold Niebuhr, sums up the early task of therapy:

God, grant me serenity
To accept the things I cannot change;
Courage to change the things I can;
And wisdom to know the difference.

With knowing the difference comes a realistic action plan and opportunity for a new direction. Life may never be the same as it was before illness set in, but wisdom can grow in unforeseen ways. The late Viktor Frankl, an Austrian neurologist, psychiatrist and Holocaust survivor, put it well in his book *Man's Search for Meaning*: "When we are no longer able to change a situation . . . we are challenged to change ourselves." And change Margaret did. As a psychiatrist, I have the privilege almost daily of witnessing people change themselves in truly inspirational ways. Margaret's example is an excellent illustration.

She set out to change her entire approach to life, including diet, exercise and giving up marijuana. To protect private time and space, she had to prioritize certain important relationships and let go of others. It was essential for Margaret to grasp and accept all aspects of herself, including making peace with her twin demons: bipolar illness and pain. To honour and respect these demons took courage and opened doors to her new sense of purpose. It is the skilled canoeist who paddles through rapids to find calmer water downstream and the novice who tries to avoid the whitewater and backpaddles en route to exhaustion and trouble. Scary as it was, Margaret paddled with determination.

Emotion focused therapy is often like composting life's garbage with the goal of creating fertile soil for wisdom and meaning to grow. As for many patients grappling with mental illness, meditation and hypnosis played a valuable role in helping Margaret to navigate her emotions and to find meaning in her pain. In a state of deep relaxation, imagining Michel and honouring her grief allowed her to accept suggestions about reframing that grief.

Her pain, after all, was a testament to her profound love for Michel and the depth of their connection, and honouring that pain became a way to honour Michel and the relationship they had. In time, this work yielded room for feelings of gratitude for their precious time together and opened space to honour his life by raising awareness and funds for avalanche prevention and relief. Pain transformed for the betterment of others: what higher purpose and meaning can there be?

Painstakingly over the years, Margaret did similar work to grieve the death of Pierre, the breakup of her second marriage, and the impact of bipolar disorder on her life. She paid particular significance to honouring her shame and guilt over things done and not done, especially involving her children. Shame and guilt taught her not about being shameful or guilty but about love, being human and her wish that so many things could have been different. And it was out of these feelings that Margaret began to be different, as was suggested by the words of Mahatma Gandhi. "Be the change you want to see in the world," he counselled.

Psychiatry and neuroscience have brought great progress and promise, yet there is still so much to learn about mental illness and so much work to be done. Not everyone fully benefits from the treatments available today, and stigma and inadequate resources remain barriers for many people. The ability to achieve acceptance, stability and meaning cannot be reduced to simple answers or any one thing. No one medication or therapy helps everyone. Medication treatment is no doubt frequently central in the acute phase of illness, but over time other approaches tend to come into play and complement one another. These may include diet, exercise, addiction treatment, stress management, meditation, psychotherapy and family therapy, to name but a few. Spiritual pursuits also help many people.

Margaret's openness to all these aspects served her well, as did becoming proactively engaged and informed. Changing her mind changed not only her life for the better but the lives of her family and friends. The hope of this book is that others, too, will be changed. *Changing My Mind* reminds us all that where there is desperation there is hope, and where there is pain there is an opportunity for wisdom and growth. This book also reminds us that much work remains to be done: to end stigma and to expand mental health services, education and research. The challenge for us all is to change our minds about mental illness, to be the change the world requires. Thank you, Margaret, for your work, which is an inspiration to us all.

Colin Cameron, MDCM, FRCPC
Clinical Director
Integrated Forensic Program–Secure Treatment Unit
Royal Ottawa Health Care Group
Brockville, ON

THE IMPORTANCE OF MARGARET'S MESSAGE

by Dr. Paul Grof

The suffering that comes with depressions and manias has been afflicting people for millennia, but it is only during the past four decades that our knowledge about the brain and bipolar illness has expanded exponentially. There has been much to learn: the human brain is a very intricate organ with a large number of neurochemical, hormonal, metabolic, genetic, electrical and energetic processes running parallel to one another, both in health and in bipolar illness.

What's wrong? During the attacks of mania or depression neuroscientists have thus far studied extensively the neurochemical changes that take place, for example, in neurotransmitters to which Margaret has referred. However, the origin of mood dysregulation can also involve genetic factors, difficult experiences from childhood, psychological traumas such as a severe loss, or abuse of chemicals such as alcohol or street drugs.

Although much evidence points to the brain as the main culprit, when a person becomes ill with depression or mania the whole body suffers. When someone becomes as markedly depressed as Margaret did on several occasions, not just the mind but the whole being transforms; eating habits change, nutrition suffers, the management of electrolytes in the body and hydration are altered and the person often starts looking older and run down.

Important ingredients of effective help include correct diagnosis, effective treatment, acceptance of the predicament and a good support system.

The "bipolar label." To correctly identify the illness, the physician needs to gets to know the patient well. This knowledge includes, in particular, the individual manifestation of depressions and manias, any other psychiatric or medical symptoms, childhood development, the course of problems over time and family background. The more one understands the patient's situation the more one can help. No small task in health care dominated by rush and waiting lists, this process is an essential one. Unfortunately, a correct diagnosis is too often established only after an unacceptable delay

To be practically useful, a diagnosis has to consider several types of bipolar disorder. Each manifests with a different clinical profile and benefits from a different treatment strategy. The relevant aspects of the profile are the same as the elements of comprehensive diagnosis mentioned above, in particular the symptoms, clinical course and family history. Each type of bipolar illness can be identified by a careful, comprehensive assessment. These types appear to be widespread: I found the same patterns while examining several hundred patients in seven countries outside North America.

Action. Effective treatment of bipolar disorder should include both the mind and the body, and mood regulation can be effectively influenced from several directions. The choice of a primary mood stabilizer carefully tailored to the patient's clinical profile is essential; otherwise, the patient ends up on a large cocktail of drugs—polypharmacy. Each type of bipolar illness has its effective primary mood stabilizer and helpful ways of treating low moods. There is, for example, a characteristic clinical profile that responds best to lithium. Thus, for some patients lithium is the best solution, while others such as Margaret fare much better on neuroleptics (e.g., olanzapine, risperidone and quetiapine) or require lamotrigine.

The desired response to psychotropic drugs depends also on the general medical health and metabolic situation of the patient. Otherwise the drugs may not work properly. Medication can be augmented with supplements such as hormones, vitamins, amino acids and omega-3 fatty acids. These additions are particularly crucial in situations such as Margaret's, when the depression is severe and the metabolism in the body is compromised.

Explanation. However helpful the chosen treatment could be, it will work only if the patient follows advice and adheres to it for the long run. Margaret gets this point across very well. Thus, individuals who suffer from bipolar illness should be offered a sufficient explanation of the roots of the illness and of the way the treatment may help. Understanding supports acceptance of the illness.

The brain, like most complex systems, maintains its stability by markedly oscillating its levels of activity. One can see that in bipolar disorder these oscillations are not fine tuned and at times jump out of the person's normal range. At that level of abnormal biological arousal, the mind cannot function normally and the patient starts experiencing abnormal moods and distorted thinking. Effective interventions help bring arousal back to normal range and keep it there. In a complex system, the desired change can be achieved from different directions and by several mechanisms.

Having treated and researched bipolar disorders for several decades through observations and systematic studies, my colleagues and I have come to understand that, as with most complex systems, the human brain fortunately has an amazing ability to self-regulate, as long as the conditions are favourable. Under the right circumstances, patients in fact heal their own depression or mania. From this angle, my task is helping to protect the patient against self-harm and to create conditions for the patient's self-healing. Treatment must be tailored to the individual's situation. Thus, in addition to the options already mentioned, self-healing can be achieved through physical exercise, alternative approaches and psychological support focused on reducing excessive stress, removing strangulated emotions and ensuring the patient's understanding.

The central legacy I have taken from Margaret's book is that for healing bipolar illness it is very important that the patient recognize and accept the illness, seek help and follow the correct advice. Such a message is very timely and has prophetic value. The research of Dr. Anne Duffy and others (see, for example, *The Canadian Journal of Psychiatry*, August 2010 issue) suggests strongly that, for reasons that are still unclear, emerging generations suffer from the manifestations of bipolar illness earlier and more than their parents and grandparents did. Yet they struggle to accept their predicament and available treatments and urgently need to heed Margaret's words.

Paul Grof, MD, PhD, FRCP
Mood Disorders Centre of Ottawa and
Department of Psychiatry, University of Toronto

PERINATAL PSYCHIATRIC MOOD DISORDERS

by Dr. Shaila Misri

In 1858, French physician Louis-Victor Marcé published *Traité de la Folie des Femmes Enceintes,* a treatise on psychiatric disorders during pregnancy and after delivery. More than 150 years later, doctors are still puzzled by the phenomenon of mental illness related to the perinatal period—which is a time of joy and happiness for most women. The unexpected onset of these conditions has a devastating effect on the mother, her newborn and the family.

Postpartum psychiatric disorders can present as postpartum blues (up to 70 per cent), postpartum depression (about 12 per cent) or postpartum psychosis (1 to 2 in 1,000). The blues are transient, peak on day three or five and usually disappear without treatment. Postpartum depression is characterized by lack of interest in the baby, insomnia, appetite disturbance, low motivation, difficulty making decisions, crying spells, a feeling of being overwhelmed and, finally, *lack of joy*. Frequently, these symptoms are associated with moderate to severe anxiety, manifested as panic attacks, constant preoccupation with worry or obsessive compulsive behaviours. Unless these conditions are identified and treated, a mother can become paralyzed/dysfunctional and experience chronic relapsing symptoms that affect maternal–infant bonding. The possibility of suicide can never be ruled out in untreated depression.

Postpartum psychosis has maximum morbidity and mortality associated with it and is now believed to be closely linked to, if not a variant of, bipolar disorder type I. Some 40 to 80 per cent of women who experience their first psychotic episode in the postpartum period will have subsequent episodes that are not linked to childbirth and will eventually meet the criteria for bipolar disorder. Approximately 50 per cent of women with a history of bipolar disease experience an exacerbation of the illness during pregnancy. Generally, pregnancy does not protect women from the occurrence of mental illness. Therefore, close monitoring of the course of the illness is necessary in each trimester of pregnancy. Postpartum psychosis has a sudden, dramatic onset with rapid escalation of symptoms that shock and disrupt the family. Hypomanic episodes are characterized by elevated mood, rapid speech, hyperactivity, hypersexuality, excessive spending, insomnia, impaired judgment, heightened irritability and labile mood. Hallucinations and/or delusions of harming the baby need immediate management as infanticide (2 to 4 per cent) is not an uncommon consequence. This is a medical emergency for which intervention is warranted, with hospitalization.

Ideally, treatment of perinatal mental illness requires a comprehensive biopsychosocial approach. Biological management includes medications and electroconvulsive therapy (ECT); psychological treatment involves psychotherapies; social interventions consist of family support, self-care and healthy lifestyle choices such as proper diet and regular exercise.

Pharmacotherapy during pregnancy and breastfeeding is a dilemma for the patient and the treating physician alike due to the contradictory nature of ongoing research about its safety. Nonetheless, exposure to the untreated disease itself has been demonstrated to have detrimental effects on the mother, the developing fetus and the newborn, and these can persist into the latter's adulthood. Therefore, the risk of exposure to medications has to be carefully weighed against the effects of the illness. Not treating these suffering women is not an option!

For postpartum blues, simple reassurance and support is usually enough to alleviate symptoms. Mild postpartum depression responds well to psychotherapy, specifically cognitive behaviour therapy. However, for moderate to severe depressive/anxiety illness, both pharmacotherapy and psychotherapy are recommended. Other than paroxetine, antidepressants appear to be safe in pregnancy. Mothers can continue to nurse while on antidepressants, as only a very small amount of the medication is secreted through the breast milk. These medications do not affect the intelligence, cognition or development of the children negatively, in either the short or the long term.

Depending on the presenting symptoms, atypical antipsychotics, mood stabilizers, hypnotics or benzodiazepines are recommended for extreme agitation in those with acute hypo-mania/psychosis. Conventional antipsychotics such as haloperi-dol transfer across the placenta at a higher rate than some of the newer, atypical antipsychotics such as quetiapine. Nursing while taking these compounds should be decided on a case-by-case basis. The severity of the illness drives the risk–benefit analysis of medication treatment in pregnant or nursing mothers.

Depression that follows a hypomanic episode should be treated with an antidepressant medication along with a mood stabilizer. Given that the recurrence rate of this disease after the baby is born is about 90 per cent, administration of prophylac-tic mood stabilizers may prevent relapse in the majority of the women. However, some mood stabilizers, such as valproic acid and carbamazepine, are teratogens and carry the risk of major anomalies in the newborn—about 10 and 5 per cent, respect-ively. Therefore it is best to plan a pregnancy to avoid exposure in the first trimester if possible. In case conception occurs while a woman is on these drugs, triple screening and amniocentesis is recommended. The American Academy of Pediatrics states that nursing is safe on valproic acid and carbamazepine. Although lithium is considered to be relatively safe in pregnancy, a car-diac ultrasound is recommended at sixteen to twenty weeks to check for Ebstein's anomaly (a heart defect that occurs in one in a thousand exposed fetuses). Lamotrigine use in pregnancy does not appear to be associated with cleft lip and cleft palette in the fetus, according to current research. Lamotrigine and lith-ium are secreted into breast milk at a higher rate than other psychotropic medications, and the decision to nurse while taking them should only be made after an in-depth discussion with a treating physician.

Despite the mental health issues that plague women in the perinatal period, health care providers are reluctant to diagnose and institute treatment in this population. These biases cause further barriers and stigmatize women, making it challenging for them to seek help; they feel marginalized and isolated. In writing about her haunting struggle with bipolar disorder, Margaret Trudeau has spread a message of bravery, determination and resolve to fight the perils of mental illness.

Shaila Misri, MD, FRCPC
Clinical Professor
Psychiatry and OB/GYN
University of British Columbia
Medical Director
Reproductive Mental Health Program
St. Paul's Hospital and BC Women's Hospital

ACKNOWLEDGEMENTS

I would like to sincerely thank all those who helped me with my book. First of all, Caroline Moorehead and Lawrence Scanlan, for listening to my endless stories and crafting my voice into narrative. A special thanks to Ash for his devotion. To my BFF, Ann White, who separately helped me face all the trials and tribulations of this project (including some major grammatical corrections). Big thanks to my girls, who helped transcribe all my words, and to my beloved doctor, Colin Cameron, who took my hand and led me back to sanity. I am also grateful to Dr. Paul Grof and Dr. Shaila Misri for taking the time to read the manuscript and to contribute essays for the appendix.

I could not have done this book without the ever cheerful but so compassionate Iris Tupholme, my publisher, and her talented team at HarperCollins, including Neil Erickson, Rob Firing, Catherine MacGregor, Alexis Alchorn and Noelle Zitzer. My appreciation

to my Quebec publisher, Flammarion, and particularly to Louise
Loiselle and my translators, Claire Chabalier and Louise Chabalier.
And of course, thanks to Kathy Gillespie, long in my inner circle,
who brought her extensive expertise in photo reproduction and
helped me sort, choose and get permission for all the memorable
photos. Thanks to Michael Levine.

Without my family, I would have remained alone and lost
forever. My deepest gratitude is for the love and support of
my children: Justin, Sacha, Michel, Kyle and Ally—you are my
everything.

PHOTO CREDITS

INDEX